BLOOD SWEAT & STEEL

BLOOD SWEAT & STEEL

CURTIS MCGRATH

with James Phelps

The ABC 'Wave' device is a trademark of the Australian Broadcasting Corporation and is used under licence by HarperCollins*Publishers* Australia.

HarperCollins*Publishers*
Australia • Brazil • Canada • France • Germany • Holland • India
Italy • Japan • Mexico • New Zealand • Poland • Spain • Sweden
Switzerland • United Kingdom • United States of America

HarperCollins acknowledges the Traditional Custodians of the land upon which we live and work, and pays respect to Elders past and present.

First published in Australia in 2021
This edition published in 2023
by HarperCollins*Publishers* Australia Pty Limited
Gadigal Country
Level 13, 201 Elizabeth Street, Sydney NSW 2000
ABN 36 009 913 517
harpercollins.com.au

HarperCollins *Publishers*
Macken House,
39/40 Mayor Street Upper
Dublin 1, D01 C9W8, Ireland

A catalogue record for this book is available from the National Library of Australia

ISBN: 978 0 7333 4079 6 (paperback)
ISBN: 978 1 4607 1218 4 (ebook)

Cover design by HarperCollins Design Studio
Front cover image by Mac Pitcher
Back cover image by Peter Brew-Bevan
Typeset in Sabon LT Std by Kelli Lonergan
Printed and bound in Australia by McPherson's Printing Group

I dedicate this book to the men and women who have served their nations and paid the ultimate sacrifice. As well as those who came back with wounds to the body and mind. Your sacrifice is never forgotten.

CONTENTS

PROLOGUE

23 August 2012

The day began like any other in Afghanistan, with a grey dawn sky fast turning flawless blue, lit by a blazing sun. We were in the district of Khaz Uruzgan. Desert-brown mountains loomed in the distance.

I pulled on my boots, a week old and still not broken in, and laced them up. Army-issue boots weren't exactly made for comfort, and I was sure to have a few extra blisters by the end of the day. After a quick breakfast of cereal, orange juice and sunshine, I grabbed a couple of crackers with cheese and Vegemite for the road. It would be another long forty-degree summer day.

We were here to reclaim and re-establish a checkpoint that had been taken by insurgents. The enemy was nowhere to be seen. We'd already cleared the area of landmines or improvised explosive devices (IEDs), as we called them, and fortified the small buildings that would be used to both attack and defend. Now, with the Afghan soldiers in place and ready to defend the area themselves, we were almost done. There was just one nearby road to clear, currently blocked by a large boulder the size of a small car. I was already thinking about the next day, the last day, when we'd be going back to Firebase Anaconda and putting our feet up, a hard operation done.

'Kiwi!' My good mate Livo snapped me out of my daydream. Livo was the lance corporal who led our 'brick', or crew. 'We've been given the green light to blow up the boulder. Can you go ahead and check it out? We'll meet you over there soon.'

'No worries,' I said. I grabbed my gear.

With the sun behind my back, I walked down the hill over the ridge and towards the rock. It was about sixty metres away from the checkpoint. but didn't seem as big as it had yesterday. I yawned. All the hard work we'd been doing was catching up with me and I felt like taking a nap, even though it was ten o'clock in the morning. Everything was that little bit harder at 3000 metres above sea level.

If I didn't move, I'd fall asleep, so I grabbed a handful of rocks.

Thud!

The first one went crashing into the sand, not nearly as far as I would have liked.

Thud!

The next one went further, but still not far enough.

Rock throwing is a sport in the army, something we always do. Whenever there's a lull, rocks will be found and rocks will be thrown.

'What are you doing?' From nowhere, Pitch appeared. Tall and easygoing, at nineteen Pitch was the youngest in our brick. 'This isn't the boulder!'

I was about to throw another rock. 'What are you talking about?' I uncocked my arm. 'Yes it is!'

'Na, mate,' he said. 'This is the service road. You're supposed to be at the rock on the main road.' He grabbed a rock of his own and threw it.

I turned and started off without him. I wasn't searching as I walked, the trail I was on already cleared, with fresh footprints everywhere, heavily used. I was soon approaching the wall of Hesco baskets, large mesh containers filled with dirt used as a temporary blast wall.

Suddenly I was on the ground.

How?

I had no idea why. I didn't hear a bang. I didn't see a flash. But here I was on my back, looking into a shitstorm.

Everything was dark, a cloud of sand and dirt blocking the sun. I looked around. Tried to find a hint. A clue. But I could only see dirt.

'Kiwi!' someone screamed. 'Fuck! Where are you? Are you all right?'

It was Pitch. I couldn't see him. Shit. My ears were ringing so bad I could barely hear him. I dug my elbows in the dirt and raised my torso to get a better view. That's when I saw there was blood gushing out of me. Then the pain hit me like a freight train ...

[illegible] and the [illegible] was the youngest [illegible] [illegible] the [illegible]

I was about to throw another rock. 'What are you talking about?' I [illegible] my arm [illegible]

[illegible]

[illegible]

[illegible] on the ground.

[illegible]

[illegible] a [illegible] I [illegible]

[illegible] a cloud of [illegible] and after [illegible] [illegible] around [illegible]

[illegible] someone screamed [illegible] 'Where are you?' [illegible]

It was [illegible] him [illegible] so [illegible] I [illegible] my elbows [illegible] and raised my [illegible] to get a better view. That's when I saw [illegible] [illegible] like [illegible]

1

TONKA TUFF

I DON'T REMEMBER THE first house I ever lived in. It was in a little town called Alexandra in Central Otago on the South Island of New Zealand. All anyone can tell me is I had a Tonka truck that I'd push through the vegie patch, leaving a trail of destruction. Seems like I was already making my mark.

When I was two, my dad sold the fencing company he owned and he, Mum and I moved to Wanaka, a small resort town with a population of around 9000. It was on Lake Wanaka in the centre of the South Island and was surrounded by glaciers, forests and lakes.

Paul, my dad, became a tour bus driver, catering for all comers but mostly Japanese tourists. He'd be on the road, driving them across to Christchurch, down to Milford and all the way to Picton in the north of the island.

We lived in a house perched on the top of a hill above a tourist attraction called Puzzling World, a collection of mazes and optical illusions that's now famous for being 'the weirdest attraction in the world'. Our house had a bright red roof that was visible from the road and was surrounded by rolling green grass topped with sheep.

Born in 1988, I was a typical kid of that time. I preferred peanut butter sandwiches to just about anything else and my favourite shows were *Looney Tunes*, *Rugrats* and *Transformers*. But while cartoons were okay, I preferred to be outdoors riding my first set of wheels – a bright blue trike. It wasn't long before I graduated to a real bike, a BMX. Black and orange, it had pads and stickers in all the right places. It looked even tougher when I ripped the training wheels off.

During the holidays, we'd go camping, mostly to Glendhu Bay on the other side of Lake Wanaka, where Dad would race his boat.

Dad was tall, fit and adventurous. Maybe a little too adventurous. I vividly remember going to a rodeo at Wanaka and watching my dad ride a wild horse. Yep. A bucking bronco. My dad was no cowboy, but he'd grown up on a farm and apparently that qualified him to jump into an equine ejector seat. I'm not sure how he fared. I just know he made it home in one piece – at least before he had to deal with Mum!

My mum, Kim, is the emotional rock in our family. She's strong, calm and compassionate, but also straight-up and decisive. You always know where you stand with Mum, because she'll tell you!

Once, as a little kid, I was drinking milk from a glass cup.

I bit into the glass, shattering it, and a shard shot straight into my eyeball.

'I can't see!' I screamed. I was in agony.

Mum gave me a quick up and down then bundled me into the Camry and floored her way to the after-hours medical centre through pouring rain.

'We can't treat this,' I overheard one of the doctors say when we got there. 'It's bad. He needs to see an eye surgeon. He's in danger of losing his eye.'

The closest eye surgeon was in Dunedin, a three-and-a-half-hour drive away. So we got back into the Holden and Mum put her foot down. We were about forty-five minutes into the drive when I interrupted Mum.

'I need to pee,' I shouted.

She asked me if I could wait.

'No,' I said. 'I need to go now. Right now. I'm going to wet myself.'

Mum slammed on the brakes and turned towards the shoulder. Rain was pelting on the windscreen.

'Bugger,' she said as the brakes locked up. The car began to slide. She'd hit a muddy bank.

I braced but we didn't hit anything. The mud stopped us. Stopped us good.

'Arghhh!' Mum muttered in frustration as she hit the throttle and the wheels moved only mud, slosh flying everywhere. 'We're bogged.'

I didn't care. I jumped out of the car and whipped it out. It was the best piss I ever had. I was still doing my thing when the stranger stopped.

'Looks like you need a tow,' he said after he got out of his van.

We got to the hospital eventually. Must have. While I don't remember the surgery – only taking that piss – I still have my eye. Twenty-twenty vision, in fact.

***

When I was five, we moved again, to Christchurch this time, about five hours north-east of Wanaka. While it was no Sydney or Melbourne, Christchurch, with almost 400,000 residents, might as well have been New York after coming from Wanaka. The house in Christchurch was a little bigger than our last place. I thought having two storeys was great because I could grab the sleeping bag and surf the stairs. Yep. I was no angel.

Soon after I arrived, I began school at Wairakei Primary. My first memories of school are around sport, not learning. We played soccer, cricket, tag and handball in the school yard and it wasn't long before I was begging my parents to let me play sport on the weekend.

Like everyone else in NZ, the McGraths were a rugby family. I can't ever remember watching a soccer game on TV. I'm not sure it was even *on* TV. But my parents wanted me to play soccer first. They thought it would be a good way for me to develop my skills and get used to a team sport before moving on to rugby. So they took me down to a soccer club in west Christchurch called the Nomads. Turns out I liked soccer. Not because I liked the sport. I liked soccer because I was good at it.

I played two positions from the get-go. On a half field at first, then a full field as I moved up the age groups, I played both in attack and defence because I was so fast. I remember having to run my arse off. I would tackle an attacker, steal the ball and fire into the midfield. I would then sprint up the field, passing the midfielder I'd passed the ball to, and get myself into a position to receive the ball.

It was exhausting but I loved it. I would have played every position if it were possible. I was an energetic kid. Always full of beans. Sport finally gave me an outlet. I also liked the praise. They'd give out a Blockbuster voucher – remember video stores? – for best on field. Sometimes a McDonald's meal. A trophy too. I ended up watching plenty of movies while eating free cheeseburgers.

In 1992, my brother Brent was born. Five years younger than me, he was too small to play with. The few early memories I have of him involved him getting hurt. I remember him trying to climb a tree when he was a toddler and falling flat on his face. I also remember him going tits over arse off the top bunk. I don't think I pushed him, but I can't be sure. I was a bit of a tearaway and not above causing havoc if I was in the mood.

Take the old lady across the street, who was always yelling at me for one reason or another. One day I decided I'd teach her a lesson and set about stomping on her roses and pummelling her perennials, her pride and joy. This was payback. I hated her.

'You little bastard,' she yelled.

I didn't see it coming. *Whack!* She smacked me across the back of the head. She must have moved like lightning to get to me before I had a chance to react. I went down.

She stood over me and screamed, spittle coming from her mouth. I was about to piss my pants.

'Get your hands off my son,' boomed a voice from the other side of the road.

Mum. *Thank God.*

I looked up, past the old woman. Mum was running across the street towards us, her fists clenched. She looked like she was ready to kill.

'Touch him again and I'll end you,' Mum said. 'How dare you. He's just a child.'

I didn't even get in trouble for destroying her garden. Turns out Mum and Dad disliked the woman as much as I did.

***

While I didn't play rugby, it was very much my sport. I got my first Crusaders membership when I was eight. I would go to Lancaster Park with Dad to watch them play. I was in awe of guys like All Blacks legends Andrew Mehrtens and Scott Robertson. Gods. They were fast and fearless. Clad in muscle and covered in dirt. I remember the sounds their bodies made when they went into a scrum. It sounded like a car crash. We went to a game every other week.

Unfortunately, the Crusaders weren't very good during my first year as a supporter. But come 1998, they were in the mix. They had a big rivalry with the Auckland Blues. They were sworn enemies. I hated the Blues too. Mum and Dad took me to a final – Crusaders versus Blues. Oh yeah. I was pumped. I still have vivid memories of that game.

'Carlos the wanker,' I screamed, joining in with the crowd when the chant erupted. We were giving it to the Blues' best player, Carlos Spencer. I wasn't allowed to swear at home but here anything went. I smiled when Dad joined in.

I shot to my feet when Justin Marshall made a break. It was a neck-and-neck match, and a try could be enough to seal it.

'Go,' I screamed. 'Go.'

He was in the clear. Running down the sideline. Right near me. I was close enough to hear the sound his Achilles made when it snapped. *Ouch!* I thought that was it. Game over, we were going to lose. Again. But then something remarkable happened. Even though he was clearly injured and in terrible pain, Marshall kept on going. On one leg, he defied the agony and scored the try. It's something I will never forget. His courage and determination had a profound effect on me.

I remember wondering if I could ever be as brave …

2

'WE SPEAK ENGLISH HERE, NOT NEW ZEALAND'

I WAS TEN YEARS OLD when my parents told me we were moving 'across the ditch'. To Australia. To a place called Wyalkatchem in Western Australia. Dad wanted a lifestyle change. He said we were moving to Australia to become farmers. It sounded like a big adventure.

Mum and Dad had grown up in Otago, which is a big farming town, the sheep capital of NZ, and I suppose he wanted to get back to his roots. Why he chose Australia, I don't know. I had seen plenty of farms in NZ and couldn't understand why we had to move to another country to become farmers. I would later learn that it was because there were more opportunities in Australia and better money to be made.

Mum was fine with the move. By now she was a successful banker – the only female commercial manager on the South Island – but she was also looking for a change. I guess she needed a break. The fact that she was pregnant at the time may have been a factor. I don't know how she'd worked full-time while raising two children. And soon it would be three.

I didn't understand the magnitude of the move before it happened. There were no tears when I left my family and friends. No sadness. I didn't know how far away it was. How different it would be.

***

The adventure started with a stressed mother and a nearly missed flight. Dad had gone over before us. To move in and set up. Mum was screaming at us on the morning of the move. We were being tardy. Of course. She told us we were going to miss the flight.

After a few hours in the air, I was wishing we had. The flight took what felt like an eternity. Seven hours of squirming in my seat.

Dad picked us up from the airport and we spent our first night in Australia at a friend's house in Perth. I thought all the travelling had been done. But the next morning, Dad bundled us into a car, a Holden Commodore, and off we went, into the unknown.

The landscape was like nothing I'd ever seen. For starters, everything was flat. Nothing like New Zealand's South Island with its snow-capped, cloud-kissing mountains. And the colours! While everything in New Zealand was blue and green, out here the land was all brown, orange and red. I remember the nothingness. The only thing to look at is the Kalgoorlie pipeline, a steel snake following the Great Eastern Highway, which seemingly had no end.

It was almost dark by the time we rolled into Wyalkatchem, home to 4000 people and 600,000 sheep. We turned off the main highway and onto a dirt road surrounded by endless plains of golden wheat.

Our new home was on a huge property that stretched further than the eye could see. About 25,000 acres, it was also home to nine other families, who lived in different houses scattered across the farm.

Our house looked out over a salt flat and was about a kilometre and a half from the front gate and fifteen kilometres away from where the owners, the Davies, lived with their three daughters and pet kangaroos. It was newer than some of the other houses on the farm, certainly newer than the 'settler's cottage', which was at least 100 years old.

The heat was something new. I'd go outside barefoot and burn my feet on the concrete. On the really hot days, you couldn't do anything much, just find some shade and sit in it. Going from green New Zealand to dirt, dust, salt lakes, the odd tuft of grass and a gum tree – everything felt so different. But I soon found out that, as far as the locals were concerned, I was the different one.

'We're going to have to work on you,' my new teacher Mrs Bruce said in my first week at school. 'We can't understand you. You need to learn how to speak English.'

I went to Wyalkatchem District High School, which catered for kids from kindie through to Year 12. It was a 35-kilometre bus ride from the front gate. Dad built Brent and me a go-kart so we didn't have to walk the 1.5-kilometre length of the driveway each day. I loved driving that thing. Blue with an orange spoiler, the go-kart was powered by a four-stroke lawn mower engine. Brent would hitch a ride on the back to go to school. But I did the driving. Always.

The school was tiny. There were only about fifteen students in each form. And as I said, I was an oddity. Something called a Kiwi.

'You need to speak properly,' Mrs Bruce went on. 'We speak English here, not New Zealand.'

Luckily, as well as grumpy teachers who thought New Zealand was a language, the school had sport. And that's where I was introduced to a strange game called AFL. Aussie Rules is a mix between rugby and soccer and so it suited me. I ended up joining a weekend team and we'd travel to nearby towns on Saturdays to take on their best. I also got into golf – Mum and Dad both played and had joined the local golf club.

Not long after we arrived in Australia, my little sister Sophia was born. Mum was now pretty busy with us all, so whenever I wasn't at school or playing sport I helped Dad. There is no such thing as a day off on a farm. Swapping my Nike runners for a pair of steel-capped workboots, I'd do everything except operate heavy machinery – that was Dad's job. I fed animals and fixed fences. I checked on mobs of sheep and opened and closed gates. I collected lunches and took them to the farmers.

Taking pride of place in the front paddock was an old ram called Percy. He was a $60,000 stud. He was quite friendly and always up for a pat – unless it was mating season. He was way too frisky to go near when it was mating time.

Not long after I arrived, I encountered a snake. Mum and Dad had warned me about them: 'Don't lift up logs or reach into holes and watch where you step.' I was walking up the driveway after being kicked out of the car for being naughty. As the car left me in a cloud of dust, I saw something up ahead on the road. Dark. Curled up. Definitely not a stick. I moved closer. Yep. A snake. I moved even closer. A brown snake. I decided I was close enough. I jumped over the fence and walked into the paddock. There was no way I was going near the snake. Turns out it was dead. Mum had run it over. So ... I went back and poked it with a stick. As you do when you're ten.

Snakes weren't the only reptiles in the wheatbelt. We had bobtail lizards that always ate Mum's strawberries. I'd go out into the patch on most days and attack them with sticks. I wouldn't hurt them – just flick them away.

Then there were the wedge-tailed eagles. I'd watch as one would swoop down from the sky and pick up a dead lamb and fly off with the animal in its talons. With a wingspan of up to 2.5 metres, the wedge-tail is a serious predator. Death from above. They especially loved the burn-off season. They'd gather in the sky as soon the back-burn began, ready to swoop down on any animal that was forced to flee the flame.

Death was a way of life on the farm. One day I was with Dad when he put down a sheep. It was flyblown and in a world of pain, so Dad pulled out his knife and cut its throat. I also went shooting, which was common on a farm. I think the first thing I shot was a rabbit. We had to get rid of the pests and restore the natural balance. I never had my own gun and wouldn't say that I was into them. But on the farm, they had a purpose.

***

My best mate was a guy called Luke Norris. We were both very competitive, especially when it came to swimming. Both blond and athletic, we would spend most afternoons battling it out at the local pool. He was a better swimmer than me. At least at first. I was better at other sports, but he had my measure in the pool. It really gave me the shits. I was determined to beat him and eventually would.

Another guy, Ben Pladdy, became my mate when I saw him drawing a plane.

'What's that?' I asked.

'An F-16,' he replied.

'Cool,' I said.

This is where my passion for aviation began. Ben and I would try to name planes as they flew over, and we spent hours drawing them. My favourite plane was the F-16. We both wanted to be fighter pilots. I can't tell you how many times I watched the movie *Top Gun*.

It didn't take me long to find trouble. Funnily enough, it involved a girl.

Lauren Jennings had a little crush on me and would drift her hand across my shoulder every time she walked past. It really gave me the shits. I eventually had what I thought was a brilliant idea. I waited until the teacher left the room before I struck. Coast clear, I got a crayon and put it on the end of my ruler. Flick. It torpedoed right towards Lauren. Slap. Straight in the eye.

Lauren started balling. The teacher came back into the room and asked her what was wrong. Lauren didn't say anything but someone else did.

'It was Curtis,' some dibber-dobber blurted.

The teacher grabbed me by the shirt and dragged me over to Lauren. She made me look her straight in the eye. At the damage I had done. Yeah, I felt pretty bad. I then had to sit in the naughty circle at recess and lunch, which was right in the middle of the basketball court.

***

In 2001 at the age of thirteen, without fuss or fanfare, I packed my bags and made the 192-kilometre trip to Perth. While the school in Wyalkatchem went all the way to Year 12, most families in the area sent their kids to Perth for their high school education. Nearly everyone I knew was going to go to a boarding school, and Mum and Dad had decided it would be the best option for me too.

I was enrolled at Kent Street Senior High School after being awarded an aviation scholarship. I'd also been offered a golf scholarship at another school, but, much to my dismay, Mum and Dad decided that golf was a sport, not a vocation. While initially disappointed that I wouldn't be spending my school days playing golf, I was happy to be going to Kent Street. I still had a strong interest in planes, and learning about aircraft was almost as good as golf in my mind. I felt hugely privileged when I learned that more than 500 children had applied for the scholarship.

It was another adventure. No big deal. Not for a kid who'd never spent more than six years in the same place.

I moved into the Rotary Residential College in East Victoria Park on a warm summer's day. I said my goodbyes to Mum and Dad, Brent and Sophia, and strode into the boarding house, a big brick building that had long, wide corridors and catered for five different secondary schools. I reckon 150 kids lived there, juniors, seniors, boys and girls. Everyone had their own room – there was no sharing. We even had our own bathroom. I thought that was great until I found out I had to clean it myself.

There was a common room, a kitchen, a computer room and a dining hall. There were boys from Years 8, 9 and 10 in our block. Year 11 were around the corner and Year 12 had their own building. The girls were in separate buildings, unfortunately. I was very much interested in girls by this time and had played my fair share of catch and kiss back in the country.

There were strict rules about fraternisation. In fact, there were strict rules about everything. We were told when to eat, study and sleep. The little free time we had, we mostly spent playing table tennis or watching the communal TV. We were always being watched, either by the staff or by the cameras that seemed to be everywhere.

Kent Street High was no Cambridge, in fact, it was pretty run-down in parts. Most of the buildings were constructed of timber, tin and weatherboard, and my classes were often conducted in demountables, but by and large, I enjoyed them. I was a little bit disappointed that the aviation lessons were theoretical and not practical. I wanted to be flying planes, not learning about those who had: Amelia Earhart, Charles Lindbergh and Howard Hughes, to name a few.

I became quite homesick after a few weeks, but that passed as soon as I made some friends. I ended up having a bunch of great mates, and we would spend our free time hanging out at the shops or the beach. We also went to watch the West Coast Eagles at the WACA whenever we could. I even ended up buying a West Coast blanket and putting it on my bed.

I also got into some trouble.

Yes.

Again.

I was dragged into the principal's office on what had been a normal afternoon until I was summoned. He sat me down and played me a videotape.

'Is that you?' he accused more than asked as he pointed towards the hooded teenager on the video screen.

There was no denying it.

'Yes,' I confessed.

To be honest, I can't believe we'd got away with it for so long. Me and my mates had been stealing jellybeans, of all things, from the same store. We called it a 'five-finger discount', and over a few weeks we'd managed to help ourselves to hundreds of dollars' worth of confectionery. It was no laughing matter. Not now. Not after being caught. I broke down when I was forced to call my parents to confess. As punishment, we had to pay for the things we'd stolen, but the embarrassment was worse.

3

BACK IN BLACK

THE MOVE BACK TO NEW ZEALAND could not have come at a better time. While it had nothing to do with me or where I was headed, Mum and Dad decided to quit Western Australia and head home just as I was getting into strife. Mum's family owned a sizeable piece of land back in Queenstown, which Mum had been helping manage from Western Australia. The family wanted us to move back so we could take more of a hands-on role with the property, given Mum's banking background.

I didn't fight the move. I was getting into a bit of trouble at school and my marks were dropping. I needed to refocus. Still, leaving Australia was hard. I'd made some good friends and this time I most certainly had a tear in my eye when I said goodbye to my mates. They even lined up outside the college in a guard of honour to wave me off.

It was autumn 2002, when we touched down in Queenstown, my new home. The contrast between Wyalkatchem and Queenstown was stark. Black and white. Night and day. The endlessly flat vista I'd become accustomed to in Western Australia was replaced by some of the most mountainous terrain on earth. And while it was still twenty degrees plus in Perth, the average high temperature on the South Island in May was just twelve degrees. *Bruhhh!* I shouldn't have been surprised, because my Nan and Grandpa lived in Queenstown, and when we lived in Christchurch we visited them every school holidays. But stepping off the plane with a suntan and an Australian accent, well ... it was quite a shock.

I went to school almost as soon as we arrived. With the year already under way, there was no time to waste. Following an aptitude test, I was put into Year 10 at Wakatipu High School. While I had been in Year 9 in Australia, the system in New Zealand was different. My age meant that I was old for Year 9 and young for Year 10. It could have gone either way. I must have done well in the test given I was put straight into Year 10. I soon learned it was a glaring mistake.

'Letters,' I said to my math teacher on my first day. 'Why are there letters in this problem. This is maths, right?'

I thought I had stumbled into an English class.

She looked at me like I was an idiot. Like I was joking.

I wasn't.

I'd never even heard of algebra let alone been asked to do it. The teacher didn't care. I needed help but I didn't get it. As a result, I was lost. Looking back, I can pinpoint this as the moment I gave up on being academic, at least until much later in life. I went from being an A student to an F student in the space of a term.

So I turned my attentions elsewhere, firstly to sport.

'You play rugby?' asked Mike, one of the lads in my class who would become a good mate.

'Of course,' I beamed with my chest out.

'Where?' he continued. 'What team?'

'Um … No team. I was actually playing AFL in Australia.'

Cue the jokes.

'Aerial ping pong,' someone laughed. 'Are you a nerd? Why the hell would you play that stupid game?'

Only two sports existed in New Zealand: rugby and cricket. I took the West Coast Eagles blanket off my bed and reacquainted myself with the Crusaders, much to the disgust of my new Otago Highlanders–loving friends. And the All Blacks, of course.

I also signed up for the local rugby team. Training was on Tuesday and Thursday and we played on Saturday. It could be pretty rough playing in Queenstown because the grounds were covered in ice in winter. It was like playing on concrete. I lost a lot of blood playing Under 15s. I made a school representative team and got a bit of a shock when we travelled out of the area and came up against the teams that had Maori kids. They were big boys and at another level. I knew I was never going to be a professional rugby player after coming up against some very elite kids. I was sixty-two kilograms and some of the opposition players were 130 kilograms. The following year, I broke my leg and dislocated my ankle during a game, which further dented my rugby aspirations.

Wakatipu High School was in a valley and didn't get a lot of sun. The concrete yards only got a few hours of sun in winter and would freeze over. I must have been an idiot because I always wore shorts to school. Even when it was below zero. For some reason I just didn't like wearing long pants. Ice wasn't great for handball or rugby, but it was brilliant for something else – snowboarding. I'd done a bit of skiing before, but snowboarding was a new thrill. As a Year 10 student, I got to do it for sport every Wednesday with a couple of gun skiers called Michael Eyles and Tyson Lynes, who showed me the ropes. We ended up becoming good mates and still are.

I was still interested in aviation even though I was no longer learning about it. We lived right under the flight path for the local tour helicopters. My cousin was a local helicopter pilot and I ended up doing work experience for him, which helped keep my passion alive.

I was also introduced to what would one day become my obsession. A teacher called Mr McIntyre showed me how to kayak while we were on a school camp. In a part of New Zealand that looks like a scene straight out of *Lord of the Rings*, I took on the white water for the very first time and loved it right away. Mr McIntyre, who had been a national slalom kayaker, was a great guy and an even better teacher. I wonder if he had an inkling of what he inspired in me.

Dad went back to tour-coach driving and Mum worked for the family business. She also picked up another job with the company that Dad was working for. I started working in 2002 too, when the local supermarket decided to take me on. The largest grocery store in Queenstown, New World Supermarket, was about 800 metres from my house in the suburb of Franktown. I took pride in my job and completed each task I was given to the best of my ability. While the job was good, the money was better. I suddenly had cash and I spent it all on snowboarding gear.

I had my first real girlfriend around this time, a girl called Lucy Forrest. We hung out at parties and other get-togethers and made some mates for life, people like Ryan Frisby, Mike and Tyson the gun skiers, Luc VB, Harriet Mahaffie, Erin Aston and Toby Mills to name a few.

Brent, my brother, started high school just as I started my final year. We weren't all that close because of the age gap, but I certainly made it clear that no one was to mess with him. Not long after he started, he told me some kids were bullying him and throwing away his handball. I went down and watched on as some little dick from Year 9 walked into Brent's handball court, took the ball, and threw it over the fence.

I stormed across the yard and grabbed that kid. 'Don't you dare mess with my brother!' I threw the kid against the fence. Brent didn't have too many problems after that.

I'd like to say that I was never a bully myself but it isn't true. I *was* a bully. A dick. It was even highlighted on one of my school reports. I picked on my fair share of kids. In fact, I was heading down a dangerous path. Then I had a big wake-up call.

***

The night began with a bag of potatoes. I was with a group of kids I occasionally hung out with. I'm not sure where we got the potatoes from but we decided to carry them around town and hurl them at things. I grabbed a big one from the bag and chucked it through a glass shop sign. I wish I could say that was the worst thing I did that night.

Then we made our way out to the airfield.

One of the boys pushed at the chain-link gate. It was locked by way of a padlock and chain but there was a gap wide enough to fit through. So in we went.

Not satisfied with wrecking signs, we decided to attack an aircraft. One of the boys had a knife.

'Give me that,' I said.

I took it and slashed a tyre attached to an aeroplane. Someone else grabbed the knife when I was done and cut through the ropes that kept the plane tied down to the tarmac.

I knew I was in trouble when it made the local newspapers. I hadn't seen any cameras but I suspected they would work it out. I figured the smart thing to do was fess up.

Mum had just come home from work and was packing away groceries.

'I need to tell you something,' I said. 'Something bad.' I told her the whole story, and that I was the vandal who'd broken into the airport and damaged a plane.

Mum dragged me out of the house, threw me into the back of the car and took me straight to the police station. I cried the entire trip and was still sobbing when I gave the police a formal statement.

I was astounded not to be punished. Well, not officially. I volunteered for community service and did it happily but I wasn't charged with an offence. I ended up being far harder on myself. I realised I was heading down the wrong path and made a vow to change. I stopped hanging out with those kids. I decided vandalism was no fun. I learned that there was a consequence for every action.

It wasn't my finest moment, but thanks to Mum sticking to the rules and handing me in, I learned a great lesson. I wouldn't be the person I am today if it hadn't been for that night of criminality. And Mum's firm hand.

4

THE PLEDGE

'SO, WHAT DO YOU WANT TO DO?' my Year 13 teacher asked. 'What will be your career? You need a plan.'

I was seventeen and in my last year of school when I was put on the spot. I don't think I answered the question. I probably said 'I don't know' or something lame like 'become a jet pilot'. I know I just shrugged, even though I had a fair idea of what I wanted to do with my life.

I'd always had an active lifestyle. Ever since I was a toddler, I'd loved the outdoors. I liked running. I liked hiking. I liked riding bikes. I liked the wind rushing through my hair, mud flicking my heels.

The natural beauty of the country around Queenstown had drawn me into the great outdoors. I enjoyed nothing more than strapping on a pack and climbing cliffs. I didn't know much back then, but what I did know was I never wanted to work in an office. Some of my mates were planning on becoming lawyers. Others were going to study accountancy. But wearing a suit just wasn't for me.

I loved the great outdoors, but I also still had a passion for aviation. I didn't necessarily want to be a pilot, but I was interested in pursuing a career in that area. So what are the options for someone who wants to travel and explore? To climb cliffs and run? And to play with planes?

Perhaps the New Zealand Army recruiter who visited my school had the answer.

'Who likes adventure?' he asked. 'Who wants to see the world? And get paid for doing it?' He handed out flyers that were jammed full with pictures of planes, helicopters and heroes.

Sold ... I signed up to do three weeks' work experience with the New Zealand Army. It was hard but rewarding. We were allowed to choose what we did for those three weeks from a list of jobs the army offered. I chose combat engineering, infantry and cavalry. I had a fair idea what the last two were from movies. I selected combat engineering simply because it contained the word 'engineering'.

The full-time soldiers ran demonstrations in a rather flashy way in order to get us in. During the combat engineering demonstration, we got to look around the army's ammo storage, where they kept 2000-pound (900-kilogram) bombs and other interesting things. I also got to play with their bomb disposal robot and put on a bomb disposal suit. It opened my eyes. The army could give me a genuine career path.

I began to seriously consider joining. A lot of my mates were thinking about university, but I wasn't much interested in that. I was growing tired of classrooms and just wanted to get out and get amongst it.

I started looking at what I could do in the New Zealand Army. I ploughed through brochures. Looked at all the lists.

Infantry. Paratrooper. Cook. Cavalry. Combat Engineer. Mechanic ...

I couldn't find anything that started with 'air'. There was no mention of helicopters or planes. I made some enquiries and it turned out that you had to do a fixed-wing plane course with the air force before going back to the army to start again. It seemed like a lot of wasted time to me. I had New Zealand–Australian dual citizenship, so I decided to have a look at what the Australian Army was offering.

Infantry. Paratrooper. Cook. Cavalry. Combat Engineer. Mechanic ...

I kept on reading.

Air dispatch. Driver. Artillery man. Electronic Warfare Technician. Aircraft Engineer.

Bingo! Finally, something related to planes. Perfect.

I could have pursued a career in aviation away from the armed forces. And I'm not entirely sure why I didn't. I suppose my love of the outdoors and my work experience with the New Zealand Army pushed me down the military path. I was never interested in becoming a soldier, but I thought the military would offer me the best career in aviation. I thought the training would be more practical than theoretical, and that appealed as I was always much better at learning through experience. I had a passion for aviation, not for soldiering. But soldiering would offer me the most practical way to pursue my ambitions in aviation. Being a dual citizen meant that I could also serve in the Australian military.

But I'd have to leave family and friends and move to Australia. When it came to my friends, well, I knew we were all destined for different things, set to walk our own paths, and would drift apart, but also that our friendship would be able to withstand the distance over the ditch. But when it came to family, I wasn't so sure. It would be hard. I'd miss them. Maybe I couldn't make the move.

I thought about it deeply. And then came the revelation and the debate was over in a moment. It came in the form of a question. *Will you see your family more during a six-month stint in the Middle East if you're serving in the New Zealand Army?* Nor would I see them any more if I did my three-month basic training course locked away in a base in Waiouru, in the middle of the North Island.

I realised that any career I pursued in the military – in New Zealand or Australia – would separate me from my family. It was time for me to grow up, whether I was ready or not.

***

I told Mum and Dad of my plan to move to Australia.

'Really?' Mum asked. 'That's a bit strange.'

'Strange?' I replied.

'Well not *strange*,' Mum said. 'More of a coincidence, because your father and I are also thinking of moving to Australia.'

I graduated from school in 2005. I didn't complete what's called 'Year 13' but I achieved everything I needed to in order to join the Australian Army as an aircraft technician. It worked out quite well, given my parents had decided to join me. Maybe it was fate. Certainly it was convenient. I wouldn't have to find my own place. Wouldn't have to do my washing. And I wouldn't go hungry.

The day after my graduation ceremony, I flew out to the Gold Coast, where Mum and Dad had found a place to live. I left most of my friends behind, but I was okay with that. They were bound for three years of university, and then desk jobs. I was ready to move on to bigger and better things.

As soon as I arrived, I started applying for positions with the Australian Army. I had a few problems because New Zealand had only recently introduced a new curriculum and the Australian Army hadn't had time to equate it with Australian educational standards.

I needed to speak to an Australian Army officer face to face, so I applied to attend what was called a JOES Day or a recruitment day. At a JOES Day, they interview you and put you through a series of aptitude tests, first to see if you're right for the army, and then to find out what job you might be suited to.

I went along to the JOES Day in Brisbane and sat down with a recruiter. He was a corporal in the Australian Air Force who also just happened to be an aircraft technician.

We had a brief chat. I told him why I wanted to join the army and what I wanted to get out of it. The recruiter then put me through the tests that would determine my fate. I'm no genius but I found the tests quite simple. Common sense was enough to get me through.

'You've passed,' the recruiter said. 'You have all your prerequisites.' He went on to tell me that I'd scored in a high percentile band and that my marks were particularly high when it came to the parts of the exam that tested my aptitude for engineering.

Perfect!

I'd also nailed the fitness tests, so the recruiter presented me with a list of jobs he said I'd be suited to.

I thumbed my way through the document. 'Yep,' I said. 'There it is. That one. I want to be an aircraft technician.'

The recruiter shook his head. 'Sorry,' he said. 'Pick another. Unfortunately, we're not recruiting aircraft technicians at this time.'

That came as a surprise. 'When will you be recruiting them?' I asked.

'You're looking at a wait of six to twelve months,' he deadpanned. 'Why don't you keep on looking down the list. I'm sure we can find you something that you'll like just as much. Maybe more? Take a look at these.'

He showed me a list of other jobs that he said would suit me according to the results of my test. But I was so disappointed, I wasn't really listening. I had my heart set on becoming an aircraft technician. I'd moved countries, uprooted my entire life, and now they were telling me I had to wait up to a year to do what I came here to do.

I had to think about my options. I was working part-time in a garden nursery in North Brisbane, a wholesale business that grew natives to sell to other nurseries. It wasn't the easiest work – lots of shovelling and lifting and planting – and the money was pretty ordinary.

The only thing I did for fun was go running. That was my release. I didn't have a girlfriend. Hell, I didn't have any friends. All I did was work and run. I couldn't see myself continuing that life for another twelve months.

'Sorry,' I said. 'Can we go through those again?'

I'd need to pay attention this time. I grabbed his list and studied it.

Infantry. Paratrooper. Cook. Cavalry. Combat Engineer. Mechanic ...

No thanks.

Combat Engineering.

Hmm. Engineering.

'What's this one?' I asked.

The recruiter smiled.

'Do you like building stuff?' he asked.

I nodded.

'How about blowing stuff up?'

I nodded.

'Well, this one's for you,' he said.

The recruiter was a good salesman. That was his job. He wanted to hit his quota and get me over the line. He sold me on the promise that I'd get to build things and blow stuff up.

I had no idea what the job was or what I'd be doing. I'd forgotten about the work experience I'd done with the engineers in the New Zealand Army. In any case, they hadn't told us about blowing anything up.

The fact that this was an engineering role made it appealing, and I also felt a little bit special to be even *offered* an engineering role. From what I could tell, they take just about anyone for combat roles. They just want as many bodies as possible and they think they can train anyone with half a brain for a combat job. Engineering roles are a little bit more exclusive. For a start, you can't be colour blind. You also need a pretty good understanding of engineering principles.

'That sound's fun,' I said. 'Let's do it.'

The recruiter pulled out a piece of paper and I signed on the dotted line.

Next up was the medical. I wasn't at all worried about getting a once-over because I was very physically fit. I was running ten to fifteen kilometres at least three times a week. I was in top shape. Fit and firing.

'We have a bit of a problem,' said one of the medical officers. 'It says here that you recently broke and dislocated your ankle. We'll need to get that checked out before we can proceed.'

I hadn't thought for a minute that my old rugby injury would prove a problem when I filled out my medical history. I had indeed broken and dislocated my ankle two years before, but it was all fine now, fully healed and standing up to more than thirty kilometres of running a week. But I was sent away and told I had to go and see a specialist for a series of tests, and my old injury ended up delaying the recruitment process for another month.

I eventually got in to see an orthopaedic surgeon in Brisbane. I was nervous when I went in because this doctor could rule me out of the army. He could end my military career before it had even begun.

'Stand up,' the surgeon said. 'Now, jump on one foot.'

Righto. Weird. But okay ...

'Great,' he said. 'You're fine. You've passed.'

And that was it.

Mum looked at me as we were walking out.

'Well,' she said. 'That was $550 well spent.'

***

With my shaggy blond hair badly brushed and my best shirt on – a navy blue Ralph Lauren, strictly reserved for special occasions – I sat waiting for my turn. Mum and Dad were sitting either side of me. Nan was also there, in the oversized room on the eleventh floor of a Brisbane office block, as were Brent and Sophia. It was 12 June 2006 and they'd all come to watch me take the oath that would forever change my life. I was going to be a soldier.

'Curtis McGrath?' The army recruitment officers called my name.

I nodded then stood.

'Over here.'

I walked to the spot, piece of paper in hand, and took a deep breath before looking down at the words on the page. I'd been offered a choice of two oaths: to swear my allegiance to God and Australia, or swear my allegiance to the Queen and Australia. Religion isn't really my thing, so I'd chosen the second option.

Doing my best to mask my thick Kiwi accent and sound as Australian as I could – I probably should have dropped a 'mate' or two – I pledged to serve my adopted country and to fight her enemies, both domestic and abroad. It went something like this: 'I, Curtis McGrath, swear that I will well and truly serve Her Majesty Queen Elizabeth the Second, Her Heirs and Successors according to law, as a member of the Australian Army for the period of four years and that I will resist Her enemies and faithfully discharge my duty according to law. So help me God!'

And with that I was a soldier.

After finishing the oath, I looked towards my parents and Nan. They all smiled.

I had no problem pledging my allegiance to Australia. Sure, I was a Kiwi, but, to me, Australia is just an extension of New Zealand. When it comes to the big picture, I think Australia and New Zealand are very similar. We speak the same language and have a similar ideology and upbringing. We've been through a lot together and are bonded not just by our proximity but also by the challenges we've faced together. We're all ANZACs.

So while I was a Kiwi by birth, I was willing to proudly work and fight for the Australian Army. I think the only time I ever disliked Australia was when the Wallabies beat the All-Blacks – so I've always liked Australia! And yes, I was happy to pledge my allegiance to the Queen, to Australia and to the Australian Army.

I took the whole process in my stride, as did Mum, Dad, Brent and Sophia. Nan, however, got a little emotional. She'd always spoiled me as a kid and was always interested in what I got up to. I think she was crying because she was proud. I'm the eldest of her grandchildren. I was the first one not only to join the military but to go off into the big world.

I had no idea how big that world would be.

5
THIRTY-TWO PLATOON

THE CAMO-CLAD SOLDIER STORMED onto the bus. 'You will refer to me as corporal,' he shouted. 'If you have a question you will finish with "corporal". You are going to get off the bus. You will then stand next to your bag and await further instruction.'

The corporal told us in no uncertain terms that he wouldn't be taking any shit. I wanted to smile – but didn't dare. I wanted to laugh because this man who was screaming was the military man from every movie I had ever seen. He wasn't quite as full-on as Gunnery Sergeant Hartman, the fictional drill sergeant from Stanley Kubrick's *Full Metal Jacket* who was played by a real-life marine who'd served fourteen months in Vietnam, but he was cut from the same cloth. I had been waiting to meet a guy like this from the moment I signed up.

I had just arrived at Kapooka, near Wagga Wagga in NSW. Straight from the oath and the tears from Nan, I had been bussed to Brisbane airport and put on a plane to Sydney. After a short stay in a cheap motel – we had to wait for recruits from all over Australia to fly into Sydney – we were loaded onto coaches and carted another 400 kilometres south-west.

'Blamey Barracks,' the sign on the gate read. 'Home of the soldier.'

We'd arrived late at night, probably orchestrated for mood and effect. I found out pretty quickly that the army likes to get you out of your comfort zone.

I was soon off the bus and standing in the driving rain. Orange lights cut through the dark and cast a supernatural glow across the base. I grabbed my bag and the corporal barked again.

'Form a line,' he said before firing off a series of instructions. Again, he told us he was the boss and that we'd follow his rules.

'And if you don't like it you're welcome to leave,' he blasted.

No one flinched.

'Does anyone have anything they shouldn't have?' he said, pointing at our luggage. 'Contraband? Guns? Knives? Grenades? If so, declare them now and there will be no consequences. But if we find them later, and we will find them, you will be punished.'

Knives? Guns? Grenades? I thought he was joking. He wasn't.

'Yes sir,' said a recruit. 'I need to declare a weapon.' The confessor pulled out a knife.

'Corporal.' Another recruit stuck up his hand. 'I have contraband too.' This bloke pulled out a gunsight.

Another hand went up: a slingshot. And then another: a hunting knife. It was bloody huge – Crocodile Dundee specification. I couldn't believe it. There were people who'd actually come with weapons in their bags.

Next we were separated into groups of about forty-five people.

'You are 32 Platoon,' the corporal said. 'Meet your new family.'

We'd train, eat and sleep next to these people for the next three months. My platoon was inducted with 31 Platoon at the same time. I looked around at my new family, a rag-tag assortment of soon-to-be soldiers that included about twelve women. The recruits came in all shapes, sizes and ages, and were destined for different roles in the army: infantry, intelligence, logistics – you name it.

'I'm going to be an electronic warfare technician,' said one of the recruits who had introduced himself.

'Oh, what's that?' I said. 'Sounds cool.'

'I'll be listening and tracking the enemy,' he said. 'Top-secret stuff."

It was then I realised there was a heap of potential jobs I hadn't been told about. Later I met a couple of guys who were doing air dispatch – throwing equipment out of moving planes – and I thought that sounded pretty cool too. I considered changing my choice of job, but I'd been warned that the process was difficult and lengthy, so I stuck with combat engineering. It had already taken me long enough to get here and I was determined to get on with it.

***

The next morning, we were lined up in alphabetical order outside the issuing facility. Still dressed as civilians, we were there to collect our gear.

Finally, we got to the surnames beginning with 'M'.

'This is what you keep everything in.' The woman at the first station handed me a big green trunk. 'Use it like a trolley as you go through each section and collect your gear.'

So far so good. I moved to the next station.

'Size?'

I guessed.

The woman sensed my uncertainty as she handed me a 100L-size shirt. 'Would you like to try it on?'

'Yes,' I said.

I heard a groan from the person behind. I gathered he wasn't happy to wait while I made sure I got my size right. Too bad. There was no way I was going to risk getting anything that didn't fit. I suspected basic training was going to be hell. If the movies I had seen, and books I had read, were even partly true, these clothes would soon be drenched in blood, sweat and tears. And while the training might cause all that discomfort, I didn't want ill-fitting clothing to make it worse.

I later found out that most people didn't bother to try on their gear. They just grabbed whatever they thought looked right and shoved it in their bag. I was staggered that some of those people extended their 'that'll do' attitude to their boots. Amazed that they happily accepted a piece of equipment they would live in that was either too big or too small. They would pay with blisters and blood. I guess we were given so much stuff that most people just couldn't be bothered.

When I got to the station for footwear, a woman handed me a pair of green-brown boots to try on. I was particularly careful to make sure they fitted – the last thing I wanted was ill-fitting boots. I found out later that army-issue boots are not as sturdy as they look.

The trunk weighed almost fifty kilograms when it was finally full. Getting the gear was just the start of the process. It took just as long to be told what each item of clothing was for and when it would be worn. We were also told how to wear it and store it.

After getting, sorting and storing our gear, we were sent to the medical centre to be poked and prodded. Jabbed and stabbed. Seriously, I couldn't tell you how many needles I was stuck with. I think I was given every vaccine known to man.

Medically, we were prepared to go anywhere in the world at a moment's notice. But physically and training-wise, we had a long way to go. Which is where personal training (PT) came in.

PT could be any form of exercise including swimming, running and circuit. Swimming wasn't much fun because it was about two degrees in Kapooka when we arrived. I loved swimming and I had no complaints once I got in the heated water, but standing outside before sun-up, wearing just a pair of togs while waiting to be told you could go in was torture. Sometimes the corporal would just leave us standing there for shits and giggles. Or maybe to toughen us up.

Talking of tough, the hardest type of PT was battle PT, a type of training designed to get us fit for battle situations. For these training sessions we were required to wear our full battle gear, including our webbing, which is a harness-like device with a series of pouches attached to store gear in. It could weigh up to ten kilograms when fully loaded. We were also required to carry a rifle, which at the beginning was just a prop but the same size and weight of a real weapon. We were to treat our prop rifles like real weapons, as if they were fully loaded and capable of taking a life.

So, fully kitted up like a real soldier, we'd go out onto the oval, or into a paddock and sometimes the bush, and we'd be put through a series of exercises and drills designed to leave us completely spent. We would do burpees, chin-ups, sprints, rolls and sometimes get down on all fours and leopard crawl. We would also do star jumps, knee lifts, push-ups and hill climbs.

Before I went to Kapooka, I'd trained hard and I thought I was incredibly fit. But all I did was run. I was running fit. Unfortunately, we didn't do too much running, and when we did it was slow running. We did everything in groups, and we would have to wait for the slowest person. It was all about teamwork. I ended up losing fitness during my basic training because we were held back.

Generally, the PT sessions went for an hour. They could be a little shorter – or a lot longer depending on what we were doing and the mood of the corporal.

Our goal was to get fit enough for the Basic Fitness Assessment (BFA). To pass basic training you needed to pass your BFA, which involved doing a number of push-ups in two minutes, a set amount of sit-ups and a 2.4 kilometre run.

Some people really struggled with the PT. There was always a really slow person. The fit, strong people, of which I proved myself to be one, would have to go back and help the weak by carrying all their gear and pushing them along. I had no problem with going and helping others.

We could do PT first thing in the morning – or we could do it in the middle of the night. We never really knew what we were doing until just before we were doing it. That's the army way. But most days began with breakfast, PT and then it would be shit, shower and shave and off to a lesson.

While the lesson could be on any of the many topics that were covered in basic training, they were all conducted in the same way: first a theory component and then a practical. The theoretical lessons generally went for an hour to an hour and a half. I struggled to stay awake for most of them. The heaters would always be on, warm and inviting a nap, and I would be buggered, especially after PT. Most of what I remember about theory was just fighting to keep myself awake.

We spent plenty of time in the lecture theatre learning about the rules of engagement, which isn't just another movie starring Samuel L. Jackson and Tommy Lee Jones. Rules of engagement is also something that Australian soldiers live by and was probably the most important course I took.

Say you're confronted by the enemy in a hostile environment. He has a weapon but isn't pointing it at you or acting aggressively. Should you shout or shoot? Should you ask for a translator or pull the trigger? Should you take aim or extend an arm?

The rules of engagement will give you the answer. The course teaches how to know when to engage an enemy with lethal force and when not to. It's also about giving you a way to justify an action that could potentially take another human life. It can silence the nagging voice in your head that's telling you not to shoot.

Australia has very good rules of engagement, in my opinion at least, and they would later give me confidence that I was always doing the right thing. Basically, we have three different levels of rules of engagement in the Australian Army and they are represented by coloured cards, commonly referred to as 'ROE cards', which we are given in basic training and were later required to physically display on deployments. We are given a green card, a yellow card and a red card. Each has its very own set of rules and instructions.

The green card indicates that we are operating in an environment where the threat is very low. The green card is used in peacetime, and under that card, one person in every ten may carry a weapon. The weapon is only there as a deterrent and isn't intended to be used. You wouldn't be pointing that weapon at anyone unless you were attacked.

Next is the yellow card, and that means the threat is intermediate. In this situation, all the Australian soldiers will be carrying a weapon. You expect that there could be enemies around you with weapons, but you don't expect that they will use them. You are to watch the enemy and be aware of their movements. You will discharge your weapon only under threat of attack.

The red card means the threat is high. You are in the front line or very close to it. The enemy is around you and if you see an enemy combatant moving around you should engage. We are authorised to engage. You may fire without warning but only after correctly identifying the enemy.

Each deployment has its own rules of engagement. They are predetermined by very high-level lawyers and generals. And as I said, the card thing is more than a metaphor. We actually carry the cards in our army-issue notebook. I still have them to this day. The cards provide the basic rules of engagement, but obviously not everything can be expressed on a card.

The principles were drilled into us – and they had to be. You can't hesitate in the heat of battle and you have to be very aware of what you can and can't do. If you should shoot or if you shouldn't.

But first I had to learn how to shoot.

The first lesson was theoretical, of course, and was all about safety. Always point the gun at the ground. Never aim unless you intend to shoot. Never pass somebody a live weapon. How to clear a weapon and render it safe. And a whole lot more.

We also learned about the weapon we would be using; the F88 Austeyr assault rifle. We were told how it was made, its capabilities and its limitations. We were also shown how to strip and clean the weapon.

We were then told – and taught – how to do a complete strip in case the problem could not be solved with a field strip. A complete strip is where you further break down component groups into the individual components.

Our next phase of training was conducted in the Weapons Training Simulation System (WTSS), a virtual weapons range, or an Xbox on steroids. The weapons look real, feel real and act real. The only thing that isn't real is that the weapon shoots a harmless laser beam instead of a bullet. The laser is incredibly accurate, simulated to be exactly like the real thing. And you go through all of the drills you will be required to do on the live fire range in the WTSS, shooting at life-sized images on gigantic screens.

Then, finally, we headed out to the range for our first day of live weapons training. I have to admit, it was a little bit scary. There I was, standing metres away from a person I hardly knew holding a lethal assault rifle. We'd all heard the stories of recruits who'd lost it on this very range and ended up with a corporal pointing a gun at them ...

But I'd done my fair share of shooting while growing up and had a pretty good understanding of what guns were and what they were capable of. Relaxed, and in what I thought was the perfect position, I pulled the trigger. With the weapon in single-shot mode – there is also full automatic mood – I sent the bullet from the barrel and smack, bang into the middle of the target.

Or so I thought. Truth is, I was a terrible shot.

For every shoot, no matter the distance, we were required to put five shots around the target. We were judged on our grouping – which is the distance between your best shot and your worst. You need to group it as closely as possible. As tight as you can. Despite never troubling the centre of the target, I got a grouping of 190 millimetres to just pass my first shoot, which was called an LF1. That was pretty poor considering some were getting groupings of just fifty millimetres. We had some pretty accurate marksmen, but I wasn't one of them.

Shooting at targets was easy. But would I be able to shoot at a person? Aim at the centre of their mass with the intent to wound, not kill? I suppose I had already come to terms with the prospect of shooting and of being shot at. But looking back, a lot of the training was designed to get us progressively used to the prospect of both. I think self-defence is the justification used most. You're taught that if you don't kill that person, they might kill you. I didn't think about it seriously until a few years later, when it got real, deadly real.

***

Basic training finished with a five-day bush exercise, a presentation and finally a piss-up.

First to the bush. We went out in the wilderness and dug into the ground – like concrete, mind you – and carved out a fighting pit. There were twelve in our section, three in my pit with a corporal, and we had to make our position ready to repel attacks that might come at any time. We set up a camp nearby, but it got so cold one night we slept in the pit hoping it would be warmer. It wasn't.

One of us had to be awake the whole time. It was during one of my stints that I got my first taste of sleep deprivation. I was absolutely rooted. Exhausted. I reckon I'd been awake for about twenty-four hours. The body can go without sleep for that long, but your ability to perform tasks quickly erodes. So does your attention to detail, which is something the army insisted on and drummed into us. My fine motor skills vanished. It was a little like being drunk.

We were attacked by raiding enemy parties and we attacked others. It was like the best-coordinated and resourced game of cowboys and Indians ever, complete with night vision, which is green, just like you see in the movies, and cam paint, which comes in black, green and an earthy red. We are given a kit that also includes a mirror. There isn't much of a science to it. You basically slap it on. It will work as camouflage as long as you've covered all the skin on your face. There is no wrong way. For me it was always stripes. I would stick three fingers into the can and rip a stripe across my face. I would repeat the same process for the other colours. It wasn't pretty but it worked.

The five-day bush exercise had been exhausting but fun. And I'd passed my final test. Next would be presentation day, when three awards were given out: a shooting award, a fitness award and the best overall soldier.

***

I was pretty happy with how I'd gone. I thought I'd performed pretty well in most of the courses. Turns out the establishment agreed, as I ended up taking out my platoon's top award.

I was completely surprised at being singled out for the 'soldier of merit' award, which was an across-the-board award for best soldier and took in all facets of training, including shooting. Because, truth was, my shooting was terrible.

But luckily, we'd learned other stuff as well – rules of engagement, drill and all the other aspects of basic soldiering. We learned how to listen to orders and how to obey them. We were also taught to respect both tradition and rank. We'd learned about mateship, teamwork and professionalism too. But the biggest part of basic training was learning the regimental nature of the army. Getting used to routine and being critiqued.

So I was stoked and proud to get the award. I had to march out in front of everyone to the commandant of the base, who presented my award. It was cool to have Mum and Dad in the crowd. I got to hang out with them for half an hour after the parade before I was ordered to take my weapon back to the armoury. We were then allowed to go and celebrate with a few beers or, for some, a few too many.

The next morning, I set about packing all my gear. It wasn't easy because we had to fit about sixty kilograms of gear into just one trunk. With my trunk packed I was on my way. At last I felt like a real soldier.

But I shouldn't have. I still had a lot to learn.

6

JOINING THE GINGER BEERS

THERE WERE NO EMOTIONAL farewells as we prepared to leave Kapooka. No tears or hugs as we were loaded onto buses. Some of us were heading to Darwin, others to Townsville, some to Brisbane and a bunch to Sydney. That's where I was going, to the School of Military Engineering (SME) in Moorebank, to join the Ginger Beers, as the engineer corps are called. Others were going off to be Grunts (Infantry) or Cloud Punchers (Artillery).

The best thing was, I had money in my bank account. A lot of money, or at least it seemed so at the time. We'd been put on a wage as soon as we arrived at Kapooka. It was only $400 a week but back then it seemed like a fortune, especially considering everything was paid for, except haircuts and beers. Now I had $8000 in my bank account. I felt like a millionaire.

Things were looking good. Cash in the bank, on my way to a big city, and my real training about to start. I'd be a soldier in no time.

It was afternoon by the time we arrived at the School of Military Engineering. The place looked even more tired than Kapooka, but it had a golf course, which was promising. The next morning, I discovered there were another fifteen or so people at the base waiting for their Initial Employment Training course to start. That was the first sign there was going to be a wait. The next was when I was introduced to the corporal of what was called a 'holding platoon'.

'You'll be kept in holding until your course is allocated to you,' he informed us. 'Most of you won't be on a course until early next year.'

Early next year? It was only September! I had no idea I'd be in for a four-month wait to begin my course.

'While you wait, you're going down to Puckapunyal,' the corporal said. 'To Victoria, to do a driving course.'

I was being sent to the Australian Army School of Armour, School of Artillery and School of Transport to learn how to drive a truck, even though I didn't even have a licence to drive a car.

I was worried my course had been changed, that I had been taken out of engineering and put into a future career in transport. I was gutted. I'd come here to be a combat engineer. I hadn't joined the army to drive trucks. But to Puckapunyal I went, and I returned fully licensed and ready to roll.

I was still keen to learn about explosives. Itching to build a bridge. Looking forward to purifying water. Most of all I wanted to earn the right to become a full-time soldier and be done with school. I was never one for classrooms and learning by way of lecture.

'Sorry, we're putting you back into another holding troop,' the corporal said. 'Still no courses available. You'll be starting in March.'

It was only October. By now I knew what being in a holding troop involved – base maintenance and odd jobs like cleaning toilets or clearing gutters. Any menial boring job they could find to keep us occupied.

'I have my truck licence,' I said, desperate for an out. 'Anything I can do with that?'

It turned out there was. I was detached and sent to work in the transport yard on SME. The work would be boring and useless for what I wanted to do and ultimately become, but it was better than picking up leaves and scrubbing shit.

The transport yard was responsible for doing all the logistics for the base. Small as it was – only 300 guys at a time compared to some bases that operate at a capacity of 10,000 – there was always plenty to do. I drove supplies around the base. Picked up troops and transported them from A to B in a small bus, drove the base commander to Sydney airport several times. I felt like a Grade A chauffeur. And before I knew it, I was heading home for Christmas.

Contrary to popular belief, the holidays we get in the army are pretty good. Much longer than the stock-standard four weeks afforded to the rest of the world.

I went back to Brisbane and stayed with my folks. While I might have changed in the past few months, nothing else had. Mum was still working for the bank and Dad was working in mining. Not much had changed for Brent and Sophia either. It felt like I'd moved on but the world hadn't.

I didn't go crazy during the break. I thought I might have revelled in the freedom but I didn't. I pretty much just stayed at home. I wasn't much of a party person or a drinker, and I reckon the only time I left the house was to run. I wanted to make sure I kept as fit as possible.

It was good to have home food and spend time with the family. But really, I just wanted to get back and get on with it. I was frustrated with the delay and wanted to finish my training as quickly as I could. The Christmas break just seemed like another hold-up.

When I returned in January, I still had two months to kill. I spent another month in the transport troop before I was put back into the holding troop. Great. Picking up leaves and scrubbing shit.

***

Finally, the first day of the course arrived. It was the reason I'd joined the army in the first place, but it sure felt like it had been a long time coming.

By now, I had a fair idea of what I'd be learning and what the job of a combat engineer involved. A corporal at basic training who had served all over the country told me that the official role of a combat engineer was to provide mobility and deny mobility. Providing mobility can be anything from building a bridge to clearing a road. Denying mobility can be anything from blowing up a bridge to destroying a road. I learned terms like improvised explosive devices (IEDs), bridging, demolition, water purification and search. It all sounded pretty good to me.

Initially, we learned about the course and curriculum.

What was expected of us, the different phases and what we needed to achieve to pass. And then they gave us a length of rope.

'You'll take that length of rope everywhere,' the instructor said. 'It will become you best friend.'

The rope was thick and 1.5 metres long. We were to knot it and lash it. Half-hitch, figure-eight, bowline, and the reef knot – we were told to learn them all. I could see the logic in learning how to tie knots – it would be something we would use.

Then we spent a week learning about hand tools. What they were called and what they were used for. I couldn't for the life of me work out why we needed to know the name of every hand tool ever invented. If I needed to dig a hole, I'd grab a shovel. I didn't really care whether it was a round-headed or square-headed shovel. I had never questioned anything in the military to this point, but I questioned why we were learning this. It all seemed so pointless, especially because we wouldn't be requesting the tools in the field, they would just be given to us. I likened it to learning algebra in school. I would never use it.

And then came the test.

'You'll need to correctly identify thirty of the thirty-three tools to pass,' the corporal said.

Shit! I hadn't paid the slightest bit of attention.

I failed miserably.

I had to do retraining for the most basic course I'd ever taken. Had to spend the weekend naming tools. It was a bit of a wake-up call. While I'd failed plenty of tests at school, I don't think I had failed anything in my military life. It was a little embarrassing.

The second time around, I did the work and I passed. Phew! I decided that from then on I'd take everything seriously in the army. No short cuts.

***

'Run!' shouted the corporal. 'Go. Now!'

I turned and looked at the first fuse. The smoulder and smoke had almost reached the explosive.

'Run!' the corporal shouted again.

I was already running – I didn't need to be told twice. Arms pumping, legs powering through the dirt, I was about three metres away from the blast zone and nearing the exit to the trench.

Boom!

Soil fell from the sky, little chunks falling over the blast wall. I didn't stop running though. Not until I was clear of the bunker that had been purpose-built for this test.

'That was close,' the corporal said, smiling. 'Another couple of seconds and ...'

My first practical lesson with plastic explosives was literally a burning-fuse moment. All tick tock, run as fast as you can. After learning loads of theory, we were taken out to a bunker area at the back of the base, broken up into groups of four, and each given a golf-ball-sized amount of plastic explosive and a detonator.

'You're all going to set up your explosives with a fuse time of forty seconds,' the corporal said. 'You will set off the charge and move to the safe area away from the blast zone.'

Forty seconds seemed like a piece of piss.

'But there's a catch,' the corporal said. 'You will set your charges one at a time. The second person will not be able to light their fuse until the first person's fuse is lit. It should only take you about five seconds each, so you will have twenty seconds to spare after the fourth and final person lights their charge. Then you'll exit the bunker safely.'

Except we didn't.

'Hurry up,' I thought as the first guy fumbled and fidgeted. He was having trouble connecting the fuse. 'Clear,' he said, after ten seconds.

The next guy took even longer. 'Clear,' he said, after fifteen seconds.

'Go,' said the corporal looking at me. I took a deep breath, did my best to ignore the clock, and set the fuse as fast and as calmly as I could.

'Clear,' I said, completing the task in just five seconds.

Ten seconds and counting.

The final guy went in.

Tick. Tock.

He was another fumbler, hands shaking, brow dripping sweat.

The final recruit hadn't even set his charge. With just three seconds until the first charge blew, the corporal issued the order to run.

Turns out the blast was only small. There wasn't enough explosive set to do any real damage, but we didn't know that as we were setting them. Or as we were running.

The exercise really showed how people react in a high-pressure situation. Some are cool, calm and collected, others are just outright afraid. I felt I handled the situation pretty well, considering.

Like everything in the army, we'd first learned about explosives in the classroom. I was surprised to learn that plastic explosives aren't particularly explosive. You can drop them, hit them with a hammer, set them on fire and they will not explode. Called 'C4' in America, plastic explosives are very stable. They are what's called a 'secondary explosive'.

The 'primary explosive' is the detonator, and you wouldn't want to be hitting this guy with even a feather. There are two basic types. An electric detonator is a five-centimetre-long silver pin, a little like the inside of a pen, with a hollow end with wires coming out of the base. We were first taught about the other type, manual fuses, which required us to crimp the end onto a length of fuse cable.

The instructor rammed home how dangerous a detonator was by showing us a photo. Projected onto a pull-down screen, in vivid colour and crystal clear, was a picture of a man who was missing half his head.

'He didn't have a crimper or pliers,' the instructor said. 'So he thought it would be a good idea to crimp the fuse with his teeth.'

It obviously wasn't a good idea. It was a fucking terrible idea. We were told the guy in the photo managed to live.

After being taught how volatile, delicate and dangerous detonators were – rammed home with half a head – we were shown how to crimp one using a crimping tool. We were also told that we could use pliers, but we had to be careful not to cut all the way through.

After the graphic safety lesson, we marched out onto the range, a cleared-out area at the back of the base.

Is that a pig's head? A pig's head on a stake? 'Looks like we're having pork,' I said to a fellow recruit.

The corporal set up a detonator in the pig's mouth, set the fuse burning time to thirty seconds and cleared out. From about sixty metres back, we watched as the dark green rubber around the wire smoked and melted. It isn't like the movies when you get out a lighter and it burns down with a spark. It just smoulders and smokes.

Boom!

Porky was blown to smithereens. I decided the guy in the photo was lucky to live.

We were trained in a few different scenarios for using explosives. The first and most exciting are called 'assault demolitions'. Assault demolitions are used in an attacking situation. Basically, we blow up whatever is preventing the attacking force from moving forward. It could be a door, a wall or an object blocking the road. Assault demolitions are done with speed – you carry everything on you and slap it up as quickly as you can. You can just cut up a piece of plastic explosive and stick it to a wall with a bit of duct tape or a zip tie. Then you run around the corner and wait for it to blow up. The infantry or us then breaches whatever you have destroyed.

Assault demolitions are what you see in most action movies. One of the worst movies to watch for a combat engineer is *The Hurt Locker*. It won an Academy Award but it's utterly unrealistic. The main character in the movie puts himself in totally ridiculous situations and operates in a way that's extremely dangerous and unnecessary. And as for the way he handles IEDs it's a joke – except it isn't funny.

'Reserve demolitions', which are defensive-measure explosions, are meticulously planned. A great example is the Battle of the Ruhr during World War II. The Germans were attempting to blow up all the bridges and block all the roads as they made their retreat back into Germany. They wanted to block access to the forward-moving Allies. The Allies scored a major victory when they managed to prevent the Germans blowing up Ludendorff Bridge.

We also touched on land mines, but the training was pretty basic. We were shown how to find the mine and how to disarm it, but then we moved on.

The mines we trained with are called Mark V mines, big things like cake tins dating from World War II. Given it was 2006, they weren't the best things to be training with. They were massive metal structures that were easy to find due to their size and the fact that we were using modern-era metal detectors and location technology.

Finding a mine is generally the hardest part. Depending on the mine, disarming it isn't particularly difficult, just dangerous – if you can identify what type of mine it is – but you have to find it first. The metal detectors we used in training – and would use in the field – were very strong and very sensitive. The area we trained on was basically a beach volleyball court, so it was very easy to find the big World War II mines. The whole process seemed pretty unrealistic.

The only challenge came when we were taken out at night to repeat the exercise in the dark. We were told not to use our metal detectors because we were likely to step on a mine we couldn't see. Instead, we were instructed to get down on our bellies and slide forward, thirty centimetres at a time, while using a mine prodder, a chopstick-like device for prodding through the earth. You kept on moving in this manner until you prodded something with your prodder. You then used your fingers to determine if it was something man-made or just a rock. If it was man-made – mostly based on whether the object was metal or plastic – you got out your paint brush to sweep away the dirt and fully expose the object.

I was never afraid of mines or of the process involved in finding and disarming one. I felt quite comfortable dealing with them and wasn't concerned about the prospect of dealing with live mines in the field.

Back then, IEDs were not very common – you were much more likely to find surplus mines from past wars – and we heard little about them during training. Some IEDs were being used in Afghanistan, but they weren't particularly complicated or difficult to find. The IEDs that were being used were big, full of metal and easy to detect. They hadn't started using radio-controlled or infrared IEDs. They hadn't yet invented non-metal IEDs or the self-activating type that are triggered by complicated chemical combinations. Those came later ...

We were told to be aware of IEDs and informed that combat engineers could be required to search for them in deployments to Afghanistan. But we were also told they were very uncommon and that we were more likely to encounter a mine.

It was cool to know how to make explosives and how to blow things up, but I knew I'd never use these skills away from the military. I had no dreams of becoming an international CIA operative afterwards. I preferred building things to blowing them up.

Luckily, there's a part of combat engineering called 'bridging'. Bridging, as the name suggests, is all about bridges. Building them and moving them. Being able to cross a mass of water can be of vital importance in a combat situation, and bridging is the task of building a temporary bridge to make that possible.

I loved bridging from the get-go because it was like playing with gigantic pieces of Lego. A team of four men would lift and connect panels weighing about 240 kilograms each. Starting with one piece, we would soon have a bridge that spanned thirty metres or more. Called an MGB (Medium Girder Bridge), it would be strong enough for trucks to drive across. Other bridges float and, once constructed, can be moved around the water feature.

One of my favourite days of training was when we constructed a bridge in the Georges River near Moorebank and then towed it all the way to Coogee. Once the bridge was connected and functional, we drove a truck into the middle of it before using two high-powered boats to pull the whole thing thirty kilometres or so upriver and then out into the ocean.

We were also taught about 'watermanship', which is a big part of combat engineering. Aside from building bridges, part of our job was to maintain, build or destroy any structure that could be found or used in water. We learned all about boats and I ended up getting a boat licence – not bad for a kid who couldn't even drive a car a few months back. We also got to muck around with plenty of power tools at SME, and my favourite was a device called a HydraPak. The HydraPak is a portable hydraulic pump that you push around like a wheelbarrow. It weighs about 200 kilograms. It could power nearly all our tools. You simply plugged it into your chainsaw or your jackhammer, whatever you wanted to use, and away it went. No need for wired electricity. You could even use the HydraPak underwater.

We spent a lot of time learning how to use and maintain tools. Looking after a tool – and being able to fix it – was just as important as being able to use it, given we would be responsible for equipment in the field.

All the lessons were structured like basic training: theory first and practical next. The practicals could be quite physical – imagine lifting 240-kilogram bridge sections all day – and I often came home completely spent. We always seemed to be lifting, digging and dragging. Carrying and carting.

We covered a heap of topics, but we didn't spend a lot of time on any one subject and were only given a general knowledge of each. Looking back now, it wasn't a great system. They were almost setting us up to fail. You're briefly and basically taught something, but not enough to make a difference in a real situation.

The course culminated in another five-day bush exercise where we dug holes, built bridges and hallucinated.

'WHAT the fuck?' I shouted. 'Look at that.'

'At what?' came the reply.

'That,' I said as I pointed. 'That big spring.'

'What spring?' came the reply.

'That one,' I said pointing again. 'That giant spring bouncing across through the bush.'

'You really need some sleep, mate,' my fellow trainee said after shaking his head. 'There's nothing there.'

After going three nights and three days without sleep I was hallucinating. First, I saw a field full of mushrooms. Big and juicy, sprouting from the ground, they hadn't been there earlier that day.

I walked over to take a closer look. They vanished as quick as they appeared. Next had come the spring. It was the size of a car suspension spring, going end over end, making its way across the field. Boing. Boing ...

The bush exercise was similar to the one we'd done to finish basic training. It was a culmination of all we'd learned but put into a real-life test. But, unlike basic training, this one had an engineering focus. We would dig holes, build bridges, blow things up and do it all without a wink of sleep.

We were given back-to-back tasks for the first four days. We'd go from one task to the next, no matter the time, for ninety-six hours. There was no opportunity to sleep during that time. At least, not officially.

'Wake up,' a trainee shouted. 'What are you doing? Don't you dare drop that thing.'

It took me a moment to come to. Another moment to work out where I was and what I was doing.

'Shit,' I said. 'Sorry.' There I was, one of four trainees holding a 240-kilogram bridge section, and I'd fallen asleep. I don't know how or when. I just know it was bloody dangerous.

I wasn't the only one who struggled. My good mate Shane Gibbs, a bloke from Papua New Guinea we called Gibbo, spent three days straight on a sawmill, milling timber for a road we had to construct. Sawing is not something you want to do without sleep, and I reckon he was lucky to keep his arms.

7

'FUN' IN THE JUNGLE

SHOUTING ORDERS WHILE SUNNING himself in a wheelbarrow, the first senior digger I met was a dick. 'Na, that's shit,' he yelled. 'Keep on going. That axe is as dull as you lot.'

Now posted to the Robertson Barracks in Darwin as part of the 1st Combat Engineer Regiment, I was finally a 'sapper', the engineering equivalent of a private. As the lowest-ranking soldier in the army, I didn't get a pay rise or a stripe on my sleeve. But I did finally get my own room.

'Nup,' yelled the senior digger, still in the wheelbarrow and now playing with his mobile phone. 'Still not sharp. Put some bloody effort in, you fucking lids.'

I hadn't met a senior digger until I got to Darwin. They weren't quite corporals, but they'd been around the traps and knew there was a hierarchy. 'LIDs' – the nickname given to junior diggers like me and short for 'live-in digger', because we lived on the barracks – were the lowest: axe filers, tool oilers, shitkickers.

'Get into it,' he shouted again from his wheelbarrow. He had a smug look plastered across his face. These senior diggers were nothing like the famous ANZAC diggers we'd learned about at school. I would later learn that it was all a rite of passage. And copping a bit of shit from above was all part of the show.

The posting orders had come through a week before we left SME. I didn't really care where I went, so I'd put down Darwin as my first choice. And that's what I got.

Technically I could have been deployed. Could have been sent straight to Afghanistan. While it's quite rare to go straight into a conflict from training, it does happen. And it may have done had the world been at war. But in 2006 things were pretty quiet, even in the Middle East.

Not a lot was happening in Iraq. Seized in 2003 after a 21-day fight, Saddam Hussein had been dragged from his hidey-hole and was on trial. Only a minor American force remained in Iraq to keep the new-found peace.

Having kicked off in 2001 after the bombing of the World Trade Center, the conflict in Afghanistan was now confined to minor skirmishes after the coalition forces killed off a Taliban resurgence in 2005.

Or so they thought.

Part of a coalition of forty nations, Australia had a single regiment operating in Afghanistan in 2006 as NATO replaced US forces to lead 'Operation Mountain Thrust' – a series of targeted attacks on Taliban insurgents in southern Afghanistan.

Had I graduated a year earlier, I might have been sent straight to South-East Asia. As I arrived in Darwin,

Australian forces were withdrawing from an eighteen-month clean-up and reconstruction mission in Indonesia and Thailand following the 2004 earthquake and tsunami that had killed more than 230,000 people. Measuring 9.1 on the Richter scale, the earthquake ruptured a 900-mile stretch of fault lines off the west coast of Indonesia's island of Sumatra and sent thirty-metre-high waves to the shore. Banda Aceh on Sumatra was hardest hit, with 100,000 killed. Another 130,000 died as tsunamis hit Thailand, India and Sri Lanka. Australian forces were deployed to first clean up and then help rebuild the places worst hit. Apparently, it was a horrible assignment: bodies everywhere, pulling the dead from holes, gutters and rubble.

I had begun to take note of world events not long after I joined the army – well, at least the events that could affect me. I was well aware of what was going on in the Middle East because I knew that's where I could be sent. In terms of a conflict deployment, it was number one on the list. I always expected to be sent to a conflict; in fact, I hoped I would. That's why I'd joined the army – not to sit on a base in Australia and train.

Dangerous? Sure. But to me, travelling across the globe to the most dangerous parts of the world, places most people would never see, seemed like an exciting adventure.

I also wanted to put my skills into action. What was the point of having learned all this stuff and not being able to actually help anyone? I wanted to contribute positively to the world. I didn't want to go overseas to kill people or cause more problems. I wanted to do some good. Contribute to peace. I had the ability to help and that's what I wanted to do.

***

Daily life in Darwin was all training, exercises and drills. My regiment was off-line when I arrived, which meant we were in a train-and-refit phase. One of the other two combat engineering units was on-line, and they would be the unit mobilised in the event of conflict. Online meant you were at a heightened state of readiness and ready to be deployed without notice. One of the three units was always on-line – my regiment had just come off-line.

I gravitated towards the guys in my troop who I knew from SME: Shane 'Gibbo' Gibbs, Brenton 'Neilly' Neill, John 'Longy' Longrigg and Tim 'Youngie' Young. I was on my best behaviour and did my best not to piss anyone off. Destined to be with this group of guys for at least a few years – they were going to be my unit for the foreseeable future – I had to get on with them all.

No one was cast from the same mould. The soldiers came in every shape and size, aged from eighteen to forty-five. There were a couple of guys I thought I might have to avoid, but for the most part everyone seemed okay. Except for the senior digger with the wheelbarrow. In the troop of about thirty, there were three corporals, one sergeant and one lieutenant. The rest of us were sappers at the bottom of the pile.

***

After five months of tool sharpening and hole digging at Darwin, we found out we were heading for the jungle. Our troop had been selected to go to South-East Asia to do an Infantry Minor Tactics training exercise to teach soldiers about fighting and surviving in the jungle. We'd be going to Malaysia and Brunei with an infantry company called the 5th Royal Australian Regiment for three and a half months. Everyone I spoke to said it was a great trip and that the work was hard but rewarding.

The pre-deployment planning information we were given before we left warned of tigers, panthers and orangutans. I may have taken that warning seriously had it not been for the plants. The Malaysian jungle was all skulls and crossbones. Death at every turn. Poisonous barbs, vines covered in spines and people-trapping plants with flesh-piercing hooks – even the vegetation was deadly.

We were also warned to watch out for scorpions and centipedes, the little killers creeping and crawling all over the jungle floor. There were also giant ants – an inch and a half from tip to tail and with pincers the size of pinkies.

And the apes? Well, sometimes they attacked in packs. All teeth and terror, far from cute, 75-kilogram orangutans were known to drop from trees at night in ninja-like assaults. Then there were the deadly diseases – dengue fever and typhoid. Trench foot too.

But I didn't care. After five months of sharpening axe heads and being shouted at by a bludger in a wheelbarrow, I was absolutely stoked to be going on this training deployment.

Finally, I was getting my adventure.

We were loaded into the back of an elephantine C-130 Hercules and flown to Royal Malaysian Air Force Base Butterworth near Penang. The trip would have taken less than four hours in a commercial jet like a Boeing 777, but in the Hercules, with a top speed of only 593 kilometres per hour, the flight took eight and a half hours.

It was February, the hottest and wettest month of the year. I wasn't looking forward to working in the sauna-like heat. And work we did.

The commanding officer of the company made it immediately clear he didn't like engineers, and we started our stint in South-East Asia digging holes and doing dirty work. A specialist unit set to provide expert engineer support, we should have been utilised for engineer-specific roles. We weren't. I thought the pain was over when we were sent off to the jungle for a 'survival course'.

Turns out I was wrong.

I wasn't really worried about the tigers. Less so about the plants. I was, however, a little concerned about being left in the middle of the jungle with no food.

Our Malaysian Army instructors, the undisputed experts on the jungle, had prepared us as best they could. They'd shown us how to make fish traps out of bamboo. How to make animal traps from gathered fallen wood. They had also shown us what plants we could eat – and warned us about the ones that could kill.

They then left us with nothing more than a litre of water and an instruction not to travel more than two kilometres in any direction. That was it. Our only job was to survive.

It started to rain as soon as we arrived. Not normal rain. Tropical rain. Drops the size of marbles. We were hammered from above. Flash floods and soaked in seconds. And it was relentless. Wouldn't stop for days.

We needed shelter, fast. But what would we build it with? Everything was drenched.

'What about the bark on those trees,' said a sapper. 'Looks pretty dry. Let's rip it off.'

It worked a treat. One by one, we stripped towering trees, thirty metres high and obviously ancient, of their bark and constructed crude huts.

We had shelter, but we couldn't start a fire. Nothing we could find would light. Too wet. Eventually, someone had an idea. 'Bandages,' he said. 'In our first aid kits.'

Wrapped in plastic, the bandages were dry and flammable. Soon we had both shelter and fire. Still hammering rain, we didn't have to worry about water. But we didn't have food.

I was hungry on the first day. Ravenous on the second. And almost starving on the third. So was everyone else. Fish traps empty, we decided to go and look for the edible plants. We couldn't find any. I had never gone that long without food. Never been that hungry. It started on the first day and got worse on the second. It came on in waves. You would forget about it for a while, especially when you were busy with a task, and then, out of the blue, it would hit you.

But then you remembered the warnings.

'Many of the plants are poisonous,' the instructor said. 'Some are good to eat. Most not so good. Some will make you sick. Some will make you dead.'

Some decided it was worth the risk. It wasn't. They all ended up sick, spewing all night. I can only imagine what came out the other end. Eventually the instructors saved us. They came back and led us to a cage full of chickens.

'Dinner,' the instructor said.

Another instructor pulled a freshly killed and skinned monkey off the back of a truck and threw it onto the ground in front of us. 'Also, dinner,' he said.

We were told we would have to kill the chickens ourselves. Thankfully, we didn't have to kill the monkey.

'A monkey tastes like shit,' he said. 'But it will stop you from starving.'

One of the senior diggers on the trip was actually looking forward to eating the monkey. He'd tasted monkey on a previous trip and liked it.

We were handed a live chicken. Flapping and clucking, one for each group of ten. Some weren't too keen on the killing, but I had no qualms at all. I'd grown up on a farm, so I knew how food got to my plate. I was also starving.

We killed, bled, plucked and finally cooked the chicken on a fire started with bandages. Now they were looking more like KFC than feathered friends, but some refused to eat them.

Sweet. More for me. But I only ended up with a mouthful, and with the taste of meat in my mouth, the hunger was suddenly unbearable.

Cue the monkey.

'No way,' said one of the soldiers who'd had no qualms about eating the chicken. 'I'm not going there.' He wasn't on his own. Skinned, fur gone and meat pink, the monkey looked a little too much like a little human for most.

I was too hungry to care. 'Throw some over here,' I said after the monkey had been cooked.

It was a bit like pork. Really shitty pork.

***

The instructors returned on the fourth and final day. We were all high-fiving and happy. We'd made it. Survived.

'What did you do?' an instructor yelled, his face turning white. He pointed at a tree, then a shelter. 'Did you take the bark from the tree?'

Tree? Try trees. We'd stripped the bark from every tree within 100 metres of our camp.

Totally bemused, wondering what was going on, we nodded and shrugged.

'You've killed them,' he said. 'They'll all die.'

None of us knew what 'ring-barking' was. That stripping the bark from an entire circular section of the tree was a death sentence for the towering timber.

We felt pretty bad. We'd been taught to respect the environment and it wasn't our intention to kill trees. We just didn't know what we were doing.

***

Bellies finally full after a proper feed, we thought the worst was behind us. Digging done, jungle survived, we were hoping for some sightseeing and sitting in the sun. But instead of beer and beaches we'd be going to Brunei. Back to the jungle for a bush phase they said would be brutal. I wasn't too concerned. Didn't think it would be any tougher than surviving the jungle in Malaysia. A jungle was a jungle.

I had no idea that I was going into the world's oldest jungle. Possibly the deepest and darkest too. Estimated to be 140 million years old, the rainforests on Borneo cover 430,000 square kilometres. The island is basically a gigantic jungle.

After being flown onto the island, we were transferred to trucks, which took us as far as they could go. We then boarded a barge for a two-hour ride up the river, taking us into the belly of the beast.

'Time to march,' came the order.

We were instructed to go on an 'admin' march, which is not a tactical march. With no set speed or enemy to evade, an admin march is strictly about getting from point A to point B. My packed weighed a staggering fifty-five kilograms: five days' worth of rations, eleven litres of water, an arsenal of ammunition, sleeping gear and night-fighting equipment. I was also wearing fully loaded webbing and carrying a rifle. A three-kilometre march usually takes forty-five minutes, maybe an hour in difficult terrain. This march took eight hours.

Up a mountain, down a mountain, up another mountain and then back down, it was like traversing hell. At best, we were walking through thick mud; at worst, we were sinking in bog. Roots, trees and vines covered the path. We had to fight for every inch, cutting our way through. Our troop commander fell over and broke his hand. We lost another two to heatstroke. It became a walk of attrition.

I thought about the soldiers who came through here during World War II, after the Japanese occupied British Borneo in 1941. Australian commandoes, a force of 74,000, had been deployed to the island in 1945 to take Borneo back. More than 2100 of them were killed.

Even without bullets and bombs, the jungle was proving too tough for some.

'Can you carry this?' I was asked about halfway through the march. 'We've lost another one to heatstroke.'

The soldier asking the question was holding a 'light' machine gun, badly named given it weighed eight kilograms. I nodded and took on the extra weight.

I struggled my way through to the clearing littered with huts. Completely exhausted, I walked into one of the huts ready to collapse. I needed a bed.

I'd spend the night tossing and turning on a piece of plywood.

***

'Prickly heat' struck on day one. We were sent into the jungle for a three-day exercise, but the first rash – red raw and insanely itchy – appeared after only a few hours. Prickly heat is a skin condition that occurs when extreme heat and humidity blocks skin pores and traps sweat, and some soldiers were covered in it. I only got it on my back. It felt as though someone had thrown fibreglass down my shirt.

Some didn't even get through the first day. Exhausted and covered in the red rash, they bowed out and went back to the huts as heatstroke set in. I was itchy and tired, but not about to quit. I made it to the end of the day. Even deeper into the jungle.

We were warned about the darkness. That it would be pitch-black. The Bruneian jungle has a level-five canopy. Jungles are classified on a rating system of one to five, where one is the thinnest and five the thickest. The jungle here was at the top of the scale. Only a little light made it through the canopy and to the jungle floor during the day. None at night.

We were told that even our night-vision googles would be useless. Even with an infrared torch, we would be basically blind. We set up a series of sleeping stations and tied a rope from one to the next around the perimeter of the camp. We were told not to move anywhere in the dark without holding the rope. It would be our only guide.

Darkness descended and all was quiet. Not a sound. Then a monkey shattered the silence with a booming call.

Whooop! Whooop! Whoop!

The jungle responded with a tsunami of sound. Rolling in like thunder, a deafening roar, an army of animals screeching, gibbering and growling. Chirping, whistling and yowling. Shrieking, humming and buzzing.

I'd never heard anything like it. Soon the silence returned. Animals all screamed-out, the jungle went back to sleep. But not for long. The animals started and stopped all night, going from deathly quiet to a rainforest ruckus. There was no way I was getting any sleep.

A monsoon-like lashing of rain had also soaked me and my bedding through, beginning at 3 pm and finishing at 7 pm. A flash flood had filled my sleeping hole and drenched me to the core.

It was more of the same for the next two days. Sleep deprived and physically exhausted, we slaved away in the heat and humidity, in the mud and the rain.

I almost collapsed during an uphill contact drill – a fire fight where we shot blank rounds at rival troops. Sprinting from one firing position to the next, dragging myself through mud while carrying the eight-kilogram 'light' machine gun, only sheer will – and throwing away my excess ammunition to lighten my load – got me through. It was the hardest thing I had ever done in my life. While I remained standing, many fell. There were broken wrists and ankles. Heatstroke and physical failures. We would repeat the drill eight times.

We slept the final two nights in the hut before marching our way back through the jungle. Of the thirty who went in, only eight made it out still functioning. The other twenty-two were either carried, stretchered or airlifted back after being beaten by the jungle.

***

We did a host of other drills and exercises during our three-and-a-half-month stint. Mostly digging, riveting and hard labour, we also had the odd good day. A highlight for me was going to a range with the mortar section. Chilled-out guys, really good dudes, they had a live firing drill and they let us do what's called 'an all arms call for fire'. That is, they allowed us to call in an artillery fire strike. We just needed to learn their language so we could pick up the radio and tell them where to send the strike.

We could actually see both the weapons being fired and the targets being hit. Mostly you see neither, war by remote control, so it was strangely satisfying to be able to see both.

Using compasses, calculations and precise orders issued in the language learned, we directed fire to riverbanks, berms and trees, which we were this time encouraged to kill. Go figure. I guess, the main lesson was having respect for the jungle, because the enemy is not really the biggest problem there.

Being an infantryman for three months definitely wasn't for me, and although the commanding officer hated us we made some good mates from the infantry and we appreciated the fact they were the ones that would have to fight this way if we ever had to deploy to a war zone that was in a jungle.

***

We were given twelve days off when the final exercise was over. I decided to fly over to Vietnam to check out some of the history. After spending time in the jungle, I had a new appreciation for all of those who fought in the Vietnam War. It was hard enough surviving the jungle in a time of peace. I went to the site of the famous Battle of Long Tan, and to the former Australian base at Nui Dat.

After my history lesson in Vietnam I headed to Thailand for a bit of rest and recreation. After surviving tigers and deadly plants, typhoid and trench foot, I figured scuba diving would be pretty safe.

The army did not agree.

I ended up receiving my first infringement for ignoring a directive to not partake in any dangerous activities. In an incident elsewhere, one of the infantry lads got drunk and jumped on a scooter. He was hit by a car and permanently paralysed.

The army launched an investigation following the accident. We were specifically warned before we were given time off not to hire scooters or partake in any other dangerous or extreme activity. So I decided it would be better to tell them about the scuba diving. About thirty of the eighty soldiers ended up being infringed for a travel offence.

It wasn't a charge but a permanent mark on my record. It was also a reminder that we were bound by two sets of law – civil law and military law. We could not disobey orders, go AWOL, drive a vehicle or operate machinery without authorisation, or operate outside our rules of engagement, to name a few.

Anyway, it was time to go home. Back to Darwin. To axe heads and grindstones.

8

TIMOR TIME

WHEN I RETURNED FROM MALAYSIA, I got the welcome news that I'd been given a three-week break from tool sharpening in Darwin. After heading back to Brisbane for a few days I flew to New Zealand to hang out with two of my best mates, Mike and Tyson. They were both going to university in Dunedin and I'd been meaning to go over and see them. It was also university orientation week, yep, party time, so this proved the perfect opportunity.

I arrived at their flat with a bag full of duty-free alcohol.

'Shit, bro,' one of them said when they saw the oversized bottles of hard liquor. 'We'll be getting into that.'

They thought I was rolling in money because I had a few bottles of spirits. Both full-time students, they had to scrape all their money together just to buy a six-pack of beer. Food was just an afterthought. It seemed strange to me that people my age didn't have enough money to eat properly. Being in the army had its perks. Watching them eat noodles and stale bread sandwiches all week even made me appreciate military food.

I asked where I could sleep and one of them pointed to an old futon in a corridor.

'Sweet.' I walked over and started to unpack, rolling out my sleeping bag. A soldier takes his bedding everywhere.

A door leading onto the corridor opened and an attractive stranger appeared.

When she saw me she froze. Then she spun on her heel and left as quickly as she'd arrived. No hello and no goodbye. Nothing.

That was the first time I laid eyes on the woman who would become my wife. I'd like to tell you that it was love at first sight. That my heart fluttered, and with one look I knew she was the one. But to be honest, my first impression was 'That was a bit weird ...'

We weren't introduced properly until the next day. Her name was Rachel and I found out she was going out with one of the uni students who lived in the house. I didn't give Rachel too much thought. Not then. I thought she was pretty, but it was also obvious she was seeing someone else. I've never been one to go after a girl who is spoken for.

I didn't have much more to do with Rachel on that trip. She did tell me she was studying microbiology and eventually wanted to get into medical school. But I was there to hang with the boys.

It was a week and a half of partying. You have to see a university town at the beginning of semester to believe it. Every second house had a keg. I'd never seen so much alcohol, let alone drunk it. And it was a load of fun. If it wasn't for seeing how broke they were – searching under the lounge for spare change to come up with enough money for a pizza – I might have been jealous of their lifestyle. I guess I was a little envious of their lives – all carefree to do whatever, whenever. It made me realise I'd been forced to grow up quickly. The military had fast-tracked me to manhood.

I got to relive my youth and turn back the clock during a fancy-dress night at the Captain Cook Hotel. Wearing nothing but the adult diaper and a bib I'd bought at the grocery store, I rocked up to the pub dressed as a giant baby. I'm *pretty* sure I didn't take advantage of wearing the nappy …

***

The three weeks went fast and I was back on base sharpening tools and digging ditches before I knew it. After the excitement of Malaysia and then the fun of New Zealand, I struggled with my return to the Top End. It was all routine for routine's sake. We weren't actually doing anything. More treading water than training. The thing that kept me going was that I knew I could be sent on a trip at any time. There were rumours floating around about some upcoming trips. Apparently, there were going to be deployments to Afghanistan, Iraq and East Timor.

I was pretty keen on Iraq at this point because Afghanistan was still pretty quiet. Iraq was a little bit more interesting because Australia had been involved in Security Detachment Operations (SECDET), in charge of escorting international officials and dignitaries around Iraq, and a serious contingent of combat soldiers was needed.

I didn't know a lot about East Timor, but that sounded pretty good to me. Anywhere but here. Anything but fishing, hunting and drinking.

The unfounded rumours became founded when they began officially announcing deployments. And I didn't have to wait long with my squadron to be told we were first in line. We didn't know where we were going, but we knew we were going somewhere, which was good enough for me.

Eventually we found out that our troop was being deployed to East Timor. None of the guys in my troop had ever been there, so we didn't really know what we were in for. All we knew was that it was a humanitarian assignment. An adventure.

Pre-deployment training started pretty much straight away. We did a variety of practical exercises, one of which was to build a shed. That might sound mundane, but it was preparing us for what was ahead. We weren't going over to East Timor to fight people, but to help them. To build, not blow up.

We were scheduled to deploy on 18 October and were given three weeks leave at the end of September. I'd had such a good time in Dunedin during my last break I decided to go back. It was more of the same: drinking, partying and having fun with the boys. I also saw Rachel again, but we were nothing more than friends.

Towards the end of the trip, one of the boys asked me if I wanted to play a game of rugby. A social game. Nothing serious. Just students – would-be doctors playing would-be lawyers.

'I don't have boots,' I said.

One of them offered to lend me a pair.

I went down to a chemist and bought myself a mouthguard and was good to go. What could go wrong?

I was going great, playing number eight and holding my own. I made another break. I was in the clear. On top of the world. And then someone tackled me. I hit the ground hard. Right on my shoulder. The bodies piled on: one, two and finally three. I actually heard and felt the ligaments in my shoulder snap. Three little *pings*. Like rubber bands breaking.

It didn't really hurt but I knew I'd sustained some serious damage. I stayed on the ground and held the ball. The referee blew the whistle and asked me if there was a problem after he penalised me for not releasing.

'Yep,' I said. 'My shoulder's fucked.'

I couldn't move my arm at all.

I hobbled off the field. 'My shoulder's fucked,' I said to Mike.

He had a look. 'Yep, it's fucked,' he confirmed.

My acromioclavicular (AC) joint was almost sticking through my skin. I suddenly thought of East Timor. My first deployment. The trip I was supposed to be going on in just four weeks. It wasn't just the prospect of being ruled medically unfit to go. It was also the threat of copping an infringement. One of the rules of the army is that you can't play any team sport without seeking prior approval from the commanding officer. I didn't have that approval. I was going to get into some serious shit.

In the car on the way to hospital, I was thinking the worst. I'd have to spend the next year on base, sharpening tools and shovelling dirt. I felt no better when the scans came back, confirming I had grade-two ligament damage.

The doctor said that the only way to fix my shoulder was to have surgery. I'd need to have tissue taken from somewhere else in my body and put into my shoulder. I told him about East Timor and that I had to be right in four weeks.

He took another look at the scans. 'Well maybe,' he said. 'But only if you don't want to have the surgery and are prepared to live with the pain and restricted movement.'

I could live with the pain. Given hope that I could be physically fit for the deployment, I now had to come up with an excuse for the injury. I looked down at the medical certificate I'd been given.

'... injured playing rugby.'

It was there in black and white. An infringement in waiting.

Back at Mike and Tyson's, a bunch of lads turned up to watch the All Blacks play.

'Hey,' I said to a guy called Jonesy, who I didn't know very well. 'You're studying graphic design, right?' I handed him my medical certificate. 'Reckon you can fix this?'

Jonesy nodded.

I had a perfectly passable forgery the next day. Scanned, altered and printed, it now said I'd injured my shoulder when I slipped on a riverbank.

I'm not too proud of resorting to forgery, but in my defence, I did it to get into something, whereas most people do it to get out of something.

It looked perfect, but I was still nervous when I handed it to the army doctor in Darwin. He didn't suspect a thing.

He told me to go on light duties and that my deployment should not be affected by the injury. I thought I was in the clear. I wasn't. My troop commander informed me that I'd have to pass the final BFA before being cleared. He said I wouldn't have to do the test until three days before were flew out, but he also said I wouldn't be going if I didn't pass. A bunch of guys were waiting in reserve.

I did everything I could to pass that test. I went to physio and did all my rehabilitation exercises. Finally, the day of the test came around. I was nervous as hell. I didn't need to be. All I had to do to pass the test was push-ups, sit-ups and a run. The sits-ups and the run were easy; the push-ups were painful, but I managed to do the forty I needed to pass. While I got through the fitness test, I almost didn't get through the farewell parade ...

***

The first padre started his spiel.

'I am proud of you,' he said. 'I am proud of each and every one of you. And it's not just me who's proud. Australia is proud. The world is proud. God is proud. Most people board planes and ships for themselves. They leave their own countries looking to escape something or find something. But it is all about them. You, all of you, standing proudly before me today, you are all leaving this country for others. To help. To make lives better ...'

A battle group parade is held before each deployment. It's a big affair, conducted on the parade ground with all the brass attending. The padre's job was to inspire us with some choice words. A padre is a chaplain. They come from all walks of life and don't have to belong to any particular religion, although most in the Australian Army are Christian. They are as much a counsellor as a religious adviser. They're the first point of contact for a soldier having trouble. They always have a mobile phone and are connected to the outside world, so they're your go-to when you need to contact your family in an emergency.

On this day the padres had the pedestal. It was their time to shine.

The army pastor talked on and on and on. He must have spoken for fifteen minutes. That would have been fine if he was the only speaker. But there were two more padres waiting their turn – one from each of the three battle groups – and they were ready to say basically the same thing.

Trouble is, it was forty-two degrees, and we were standing at attention in the blistering sun on the melting asphalt of the parade ground. It took just ten minutes for the first person to faint, a guy not far away from me. I saw it out of the corner of my eye. The padre kept on going, not missing a word, and everyone except the medic ignored him. The heat-stricken soldier was pulled out and the parade continued.

The second guy dropped a minute after the first. Right next to me. I went to help but he was scooped up and dragged off before I had the chance. We'd all been instructed to only help if one of the assigned medics was not available.

I was wearing full battle cams and was soaked in sweat. Droplets of sweat were running down my arms and off my hands, making puddles at my feet. By the time the second padre began, I was struggling but I stayed upright. Many didn't. They were dropping left, right and centre. As the third padre droned on, I started getting dizzy.

But I made it till the end. Seventy-eight soldiers didn't. The hospital had to send for extra staff to treat all the men and women who'd been struck down by the heat. That was as close as I've ever been to fainting.

***

It only took forty-five minutes to get to East Timor, one of Australia's closest neighbours, with only 600 kilometres between the two countries' closest points.

When I got my first look at the place from the air, I was stunned by its natural beauty. Sheltered by a mountain range and buried firmly in the tropics, its capital, Dili, stops the green from rolling off the mountains and melting into the sparkling blue sea.

At the airport, which was almost derelict, we were ushered across the runway towards a truck. There we were given our battle gear and an intelligence briefing. As we expected, the threat was classified as minimal.

As I said, I didn't know a lot about East Timor before we arrived. During our pre-deployment training, we'd been given only a vague rundown of its history. I knew that East Timor had been occupied by Indonesia and that it gained its independence in 1999. I also knew that the East Timorese had been treated badly during the occupation and the nation had been stripped of nearly all its natural resources. As far as Australia went, we'd been part of the rebuilding effort and we'd been involved in a United Nations–led operation to install a stable government. We were told the East Timorese were a lovely people, but that if there was a political situation, they were likely to participate in protests and could become aggressive. As Australians, we were told they would be quite vocal if we did something wrong.

I remember another briefing about the local fauna and flora. We were told the climate and vegetation were quite similar to Darwin. We were also told that there were no dangerous animals in East Timor. They clearly forgot about the crocodiles, of which it turned out there were plenty. They swam all the way over from Darwin.

I was pretty keen to get straight into whatever it was we'd be doing. It was my first deployment, and I was determined to give it my all. I was there to make a difference. To do as much good as we could.

Our base was just down the road from the airport. Called Forward Operating Base Chauvel, our home for the next eight months was on the western outskirts of the city. It was quite a large base and I was pretty impressed: it had fully hardwired internet, a running track, a volleyball court, a big screen television and even a swimming pool.

Fully airconditioned, our rooms were pretty good too. We slept on bunks, three in each room. Due to the damn mozzies and the threat of malaria, mosquito nets were a must.

There was plenty of building material around the base and we were told we could use it to make anything we needed. It was like having a big DIY Ikea store, and we would later make our own beds and other bits and pieces to make it as comfortable as we could.

We had a couple of chippies in our troop and two plant operators who could work heavy equipment. I could tell from the make-up of the troop we were going to be involved in building and maintenance. We were in the back corner of the base, nice and close to the chill-out area. Some guys in a previous rotation had made an officers' quarters. And the swimming pool I previously mentioned was built by another previous rotation. They got a gigantic water tank and added a filtration system to make a fully functional and very popular pool. They even built a sundeck.

My first role was to be the driver for the Australian liaison to the UN. I got the gig because I had my licence and was in the right spot at the right time. It turned out to be a good role, because the liaison was a mid-ranked engineering officer named Andrew Oxlade. He had a wealth of knowledge about both engineering and the army, and I learned a lot from him during the three-week posting. Turns out he was a good man to know because he later became our troop commander.

Our first job was to build a water tank for a village outside Dili. We took all the material with us and constructed a 60,000-litre tank from a kit. I didn't know until we got there but it was for an orphanage. That was pretty cool, to be involved in such a rewarding project first up. It was almost Christmas when we were there so we all decided we wanted to give all the kids a little gift. We chipped in twenty dollars each and used the money to buy toys. We ended filling a truck. It was priceless to see the looks on their little faces when we handed them all out. But to be honest, I think we got more out of it then they did.

All the locals were welcoming. The kids were always following us around asking us for *aqua*, their word for water. That's all they wanted. The kids at the orphanage were a little different from the rest. They were under the strict discipline of nuns and would never ask for a thing, which made it especially rewarding when we gave them those Christmas presents.

I quickly settled into a routine and enjoyed the work. Basically, we were there to build and maintain. We spent a lot of time at other army bases, building and maintaining facilities. We built everything from awnings to garages. The most common job we did was roofing. There was always a roof that needed to be repaired.

Most of the jobs were good. But some were shit – literally. We were working on a roof one day and a red-hot screw fell into a pile of dead leaves. We didn't notice until it was too late. What had started as a smoulder had fast turned into a fire. We put it out pretty quickly and got back on with our work. We thought nothing more of it until the corporal ran over screaming.

'What have you done?' he yelled. 'Look at all this shit.'

The fire had melted a semi-submerged sewage tank that was under the leaves. We didn't even know it was there. But we did now, as shit was visible for all to see and smell.

We were ordered to stop building and start cleaning. We had to use a 44-gallon drum to scoop all the sewage out of the tank. After pulling it out, we then had to burn it. Eventually, all we could smell was the diesel we were drenching the shit in before setting it alight.

Workdays started at 6 am and finished at 4 pm, and we spent most afternoons at the beach. We'd drive down and go for a swim. A couple of guys would stay with the vehicles and the weapons. The water was crystal clear and there were fish everywhere.

I was maturing, both as a person and as a soldier. It was while I was in Timor that I was promoted to third-in-command of my section. As a 3IC, I was given extra responsibilities and was put in a leadership role. I wasn't really keen on becoming a leader as I enjoyed being one of the boys. I didn't want to order anyone around. Thankfully, there wasn't much of that, as the job was more of an administrative role, looking after stores and acquisitions.

Then, when our sergeant had to return home for personal reasons, I was temporarily promoted to 2IC.

I was now beginning to get a good understanding of the job of an army combat engineer, and it wasn't what I'd expected or signed up for. I felt like we were glorified labourers rather than engineers. All the jobs we were doing didn't require too many specialised skills and didn't have an engineering focus. But I was learning skills that could be used elsewhere, which isn't always the case in the army. Being able to shoot an assault rifle isn't something too many employers are looking for on a résumé.

But I wasn't thinking about the future back then. I was just into the work. It was hard and I don't think I got an opportunity to think too much about anything else. One of the only times I dreamed of doing something else was when I saw a couple of Black Hawk helicopters come flying in. I still wanted to work on aircraft.

A memorable job we did was in a place called Uaimori, a remote community in the mountains of East Timor. It was an eight-hour journey through treacherous terrain – rugged, mountainous and inaccessible. We went up there to build a medical centre and a footbridge to access it. The significance of Uaimori was it was the headquarters for the resistance during the Indonesian occupation. It was a place famous for its freedom fighters, so it was an honour to go up there and build something significant. It was a big operation to get all the equipment into such a remote area. We had to use helicopters to get some of the material in. I am hoping that the bridge I helped build is still there and hasn't been washed away. I hope I did a little bit to help improve some lives.

Living on top of each other for so long can be testing and occasionally tempers flared. I almost came to blows with my roommate on a job. We were building a shelter at the time and I was 2IC. It was a really hot day and every time I turned around, he was sitting on the bonnet of a vehicle, bludging. We were all working, holding beams, sweating our tits off, and I was really pissed off that he wasn't pulling his weight.

I started chirping at him, just little remarks at first. 'Fancy joining the rest of us?'

Eventually I was more direct. 'How about you get off your arse and do some work,' I said.

He came at me, fists up and ready to go. I didn't back down, but one of the boys got in between us and stopped it before it started.

While I was in East Timor I did a junior leadership course so I'd be eligible to become a lance corporal. It's a standard course, but in our case it was a bit special for being the first to be conducted outside of Australia since the Vietnam War. They did it as a pilot to see if they could offer more of them during overseas deployments. Because it was the first of its kind, we didn't have the infrastructure they had back home, but all the instructors were flown over specially for the course, and a major even came to check it out.

Each of the candidates was given the opportunity to lead a group for a 24-hour period and graded on their command ability.

I had my twenty-first birthday during this training. We didn't have live weapons on the course, so we decided it was safe enough to sneak some grog in. One of the interpreters bought some beers and a bottle of rum from the service station in town.

I wasn't too concerned that I'd missed out on a traditional twenty-first. I'd become good friends with all the guys on that course and I was happy to have a quiet celebration with them. I guess celebrating a twenty-first is about becoming an independent adult, but by joining the army when I was eighteen I'd crossed that bridge a few years before. You don't really get a choice about how and where you celebrate your personal milestones in the military. You could be anywhere, doing anything.

At the end of the course we had a parade. I was with some very good soldiers, so it was a big honour to be named the student of merit. Some of the guys in that course went on to become special forces. I guess I went on to other things ...

***

I really enjoyed my first deployment because I felt like I made a difference. I was able to provide people with things we take for granted, like drinking water. More than that, I was able to make some people happy. Nothing was more rewarding then seeing those kids smile when we gave them Christmas presents.

I also loved the country. It is an amazing place, a real untouched gem just a stone's throw away. Everything was unspoilt and beautiful. I was starting to become aware of the rest of the world, learning about different cultures and ways of life, which gave me an appreciation of how good my life was. Timor was right on our doorstep and yet its people didn't have easy access to something as basic as clean water. I became very big on wanting everyone in the world to have a fair chance. And I learned that my job was to leave a place better than it was when I got there.

9

THE FOUR-YEAR ITCH

AFTER A SHORT BREAK, it was back to sharpening and shovelling at the base. Then, on 30 September 2009, the island of Sumatra, off the coast off Indonesia, was rocked by an earthquake with a magnitude of 7.6, leaving almost 1500 dead and another 3000 injured. It also left a mess – homes levelled, buildings ruined and infrastructure wiped out.

Australia immediately put up its hand to help. And so did I. I wasn't on one of the teams selected for the initial deployment, but having recently returned from East Timor, I was packed, immunised and ready to go. So I approached a sergeant.

'I'm good to go, Sarge,' I said. 'Can you slot me in? You can put me anywhere and with anyone. I am willing to do whatever it takes.'

He didn't have to think too hard. The government had already recognised that the Indonesians needed more troops on the ground and, given I was an engineer, my skill set was in high demand for what was essentially a reconstruction mission. I was immediately slotted into a section. To my surprise I was the most senior person there, with two more years' experience than the corporal, who hadn't yet served overseas. So, I was off again, heading to a disaster zone.

***

HMAS *Kanimbla II* took us from Darwin to Padang. On the way over, we began hearing some nasty stories about what we were heading into. Apparently, the work was horrible. Everyone was digging through rubble looking for bodies and dragging out the dead. A tale about a unit having to dig up a school was particularly disturbing. I shuddered at the thought of all the dead kids.

We soon arrived off the coast of Padang and began what was a huge landing exercise. Due to a stroke of luck, we engineers were assigned to a new group and set to work at a water-purification point, where we set up and maintained a high-tech desalination machine that turns sea water into potable drinking water. It was definitely a better job than digging through rubble for bodies.

As we drove through the city of Padang, the destruction from the earthquake was evident. The city was in ruins, with buildings and roads destroyed and mountains of rubble everywhere. The locals were trying to go about their lives like nothing had happened. Going to work in half-destroyed building, apparently not fazed by the real prospect of a total collapse.

Our waterpoint was set up on a rock wall at the end of the beach. The machine was soon sucking in thousands of litres of ocean water and turning it into drinking water as good as any bottled water.

We would fill up council trucks, which would then return to villages and towns. I was proud of the work, knowing we were making a big difference.

There were three water points in Padang. We worked on all of them. We ended up making just shy of a million litres of clean drinking water. That was a pretty cool effort. The machines were brand new to the army, and we were the first to put a big amount of water through them. Once we were told we'd produced enough water we were no longer needed, so we packed up the machines and got ready to go home.

On our last night, in a heart-warming show of generosity, the locals pulled together the little food that they had, cooked it and delivered it to our door. It was a huge offering considering they had so little and were giving us all the food they had. It made us all feel very special, and gave me further appreciation of how lucky we are to be Australian. Having experiences like this took away my sense of entitlement. Seeing how happy these people were despite the daily difficulties they faced, gave me a new perspective, especially when it came to material things. They didn't need fast cars, computers or wi-fi to be happy. They just needed each other. They were always smiling.

The trip ended on a high when we were transferred to Jakarta for a stopover. In a totally unexpected but welcome surprise, the Australian government had organised a night in the Shangri-La for our little waterpoint team. It was my first time in a five-star hotel and it was a big shock to the system after sleeping in a tent on the beach for three weeks. I lapped up the room service, had a spa and spent the evening in the nightclub with the guys.

We flew back to Darwin the next day. I had an almighty laugh when I found out the unit I was supposed to be in, the one that had left me on the beach, would not be home for another four weeks. They were stuck in Padang, working and waiting to be ferried back on the crappy ship. I was given another short break when I returned. And, you guessed it, I went back to New Zealand.

***

I got my chance to leave Darwin soon after I returned. I applied for a posting in Brisbane at the Enoggera Barracks, widely regarded as the best base in Australia. It was right on the edge of the city and I'd be closer to my family. It made sense to relocate there, no matter the job.

A posting order for me to move to the 21 Construction Squadron in Brisbane came through in just two weeks. I was stunned, because posting orders usually take six months, and postings to Brisbane are especially rare. I didn't know much about the 21 Construction Squadron when I applied. I didn't know any more when I arrived, in January 2010, turning up for my first day at my new job not having a clue as to what I'd be doing.

I soon found out that 21 Construction Squadron was an advanced engineering unit specialising in large-scale construction. Mostly engaged in humanitarian work, it was often involved in big Army Aboriginal Community Assistance Program projects.

I was put into a transport troop as soon as I arrived and sent on my first trip with my new troop out to the centre of Australia.

After landing in Alice Springs, we jumped in a four-wheel drive and drove for what seemed an eternity, seeing nothing but red dirt and the odd road train. Eventually we arrived at our destination: Pukatja, South Australia.

In the eastern Musgrave Ranges and thirty kilometres from the Northern Territory border, Pukatja, a former Presbyterian mission, is an Indigenous community with a population of just over 400 people belonging to six different cultural communities.

The main task of our unit was to build houses and fix roads. We stayed at a base about twenty kilometres out of town, and sadly didn't really interact with the community much. We were just in and out, all work, no talk. I had a little bit of interaction with the kids and they were great. I would have loved to have had more involvement with the elders to learn something of them and their culture and to find out whether we were improving things for their community.

It was while we were at Pukatja that we heard the news. Two Australian soldiers had been killed in Afghanistan. It was June 2010 and things were hotting up over there. It turned out to be the deadliest month for NATO soldiers since the war began nine years earlier.

We all froze, stopped whatever we were doing and looked at the TV.

I took in enough to know that the two soldiers were both engineers and they both died in an IED blast. My stomach dropped. I felt numb.

The newsreader provided few specifics. No names. No regiment. We tried to get further information from the army higher-ups, but they didn't know or wouldn't tell us. We soon found out that the two diggers were from the 2nd Combat Engineering Regiment in Brisbane. I racked my brain, trying to think if I knew anyone in that regiment. I didn't think I did. But I was wrong.

The names of the soldiers were released the next day. Sappers Darren Smith, aged twenty-five, and Jacob Moreland, twenty-one, had been killed by an IED in the Mirabad Valley, southern Afghanistan, on 7 June 2010.

While I didn't know Jacob, I knew Darren. I'd been his driver in Sydney while he was doing his explosive-detection dog handling course. I'd done a bit of personal training and hung out with him. He was a champion. A great bloke.

I was stunned. While I was fully aware of the risks we all faced, I never expected any of my friends to get killed. I always thought it would be someone else. Suddenly it all became real.

We later learned that Darren had stepped on an IED while on a patrol with his dog. Jacob was standing next to him when the IED exploded. The dog also died in the blast.

As a group we talked about it casually, but there was never any sort of official briefing and we only found out the details through the news. Counselling wasn't offered, although the padre was there if we wanted to talk. I didn't really deal with it. As shocking as it was, the whole situation seemed so distant from where we were and what we were doing.

But it was the first real indication that things were escalating in Afghanistan. And the first time I thought seriously about being sent there, and that if I was, I could be injured. Or worse.

Later in 2010 I was sent on a Combat First Aid Course. It was one of the best things I ever did in the army. Run by a sergeant medic, it was an interactive four-week course that was both involved and interesting. I learned about IV fluids, how to inject morphine and how to counteract an overdose of morphine. I also learned how to treat a sucking chest wound, which occurs when an injury caused by gunshot, say, creates an open hole in the chest; and how to treat an amputation and apply a tourniquet. It was interesting, but I never imagined I'd need to use it.

***

I was starting to have serious doubts about my future in the army. It was not long after I received my Australian Defence Medal, better known as 'the Coca-Cola Badge' because of its red and white ribbon. It's given to a soldier after four years of service and is a milestone. It's also an out. After four years, you've met all your service obligations and paid the army back for its investment in courses and training. You can now leave if and when you like.

I was in two minds about continuing. Sometimes I felt like a glorified labourer, that the engineering component of the job was minimal and that the role wasn't what I'd signed up for. I wasn't sure I wanted to continue but I also had no idea what I'd do if I quit the army.

I can't say if the deaths of Darren and Jacob had influenced the way I was feeling. If anything, I think I wanted to go to Afghanistan even more. Part of the reason I was having second thoughts about the army was that I *hadn't* been sent to Afghanistan. I'd trained for conflict, signed up for it, but hadn't seen it. I also had a sense of obligation that I needed to go to a conflict zone to do my bit, pay my dues. I had mates there and I wanted to join them. I wanted to do my part.

Should I stay or should I go? It was a big decision to make.

I decided to apply for four months' unpaid leave. I had plenty of money because I'd been earning and not spending, so cash wouldn't be a problem. My leave was accepted but would not begin until the following year. I would have to wait and work another six months or so before taking off, which was fine. More time to think.

It started raining in Queensland before Christmas 2010 and just didn't stop. Cleaning up the devastated homes in sweltering forty-degree heat was some of the worst work I've ever done. We were sent in to clean flood-damaged houses: pulling, ripping and banging out anything that was water-affected. Mostly it was plasterboard, but there was also a load of carpet, saturated and stinking. A lot of the structures were okay, so we just physically gutted the houses, leaving only the bricks and structural timbers. The most disturbing thing we had to remove from homes was the photographs. Box-loads of them. I had a bit of a moment when I threw a box into a skip bin and it broke, ruined memories spilling out everywhere. It felt like I was throwing away a family. It was a terrible time for everyone involved, especially for those who lost their homes. In the end, I had to leave the clean-up early for an ankle reconstruction, due to torn ligaments. The operation went well and I went home to my parents' place in Brisbane to recover.

***

'Hey Curtis. Can I come stay with you?' Rachel, the pretty girl I'd met at Mike and Tyson's in Dunedin, had lost her Australian summer job on Fraser Island when the floods shut down the tourism industry in south-east Queensland. She didn't have any plans or any money, so she called me.

Now a single woman, she'd been living in Canberra, where she was studying at the Australian National University, and we'd stayed in touch.

'Yeah, of course,' I said. 'Come on down.'

So Rachel came to stay. I had nothing on or planned, given I was on paid recovery leave, so I was able to spend all my time with her. We ended up going on a road trip to Sydney, and it was during that one-on-one time that I really got to know her.

I think it was a case of opposites attract, because we were quite different. Rachel was intellectual and extremely focused. She was academically driven. I wasn't. In fact, she was way too smart for me. I'm a dead-set dummy next to her. But that didn't matter. We just clicked.

And she happened to be beautiful, the type of person who becomes better looking with every glance. Above all she was fun, always the centre of the party and always making sure that she, and those around her, were having a good time.

The fact that we liked each other looked certain to become an issue, given I was in the army and she was set to return to New Zealand. I think we both wanted a relationship, but we didn't really talk about it because we didn't think it was possible. I certainly didn't want to push for it because I knew she wanted to return home to complete her medical degree.

She'd started studying medicine but had deferred to come to Australia. I didn't want to be the one who stopped her from going back. I didn't want to pressure her into staying in Australia, or be the one to ruin her dream.

In addition, I'd just committed to taking a four-month break and was planning to travel around the world, so the timing wasn't great for starting a relationship.

We decided it was best to part ways – for now. I went back to work, and she went back to New Zealand to resume her degree. I'm glad she did, because I think she'd have ended up resenting me if she'd stayed in Australia for me.

But it wasn't long until we were together again. Given a short break a couple of months later, I headed over to New Zealand. Unlike all the other trips, when I had gone to party with my mates (although I still did a bit of that), my prime motivation was to see Rachel.

***

I began my big break with a Contiki Tour. Tyson bravely agreed to join me. The 28-day tour began in London before taking us all over Europe, to places that included France, Italy and Greece. We were on a bus full of Aussies and Kiwis, and it was strange to go all the way to the other side of the world to hang with your own. We'd see all the sights, do the walks and tours, but mostly, it turned out, we would drink. I wasn't a big drinker so sometimes it was a struggle. There were some nuclear hangovers.

I spent the next part of my big break in New Zealand. The Rugby World Cup was being held in Auckland that year, 2011, so the boys and I decided to have a rugby holiday.

My mate was living in a flat across the road from Eden Park, and that became party central for the next month. It was a great time to be in Auckland and to be a Kiwi. The All Blacks hadn't won a World Cup since 1987, so there was a lot of expectation and excitement, given our team was ranked number one in the world and were playing at home.

I'll never forget the two old fellas we sat next to at the final. They would have been in their seventies and they were silent the entire game. Not a word. But you should have seen them when the final whistle blew. When we won. They went fucking nuts, screaming, yelling and even crying. One of them spilt a full beer on me before giving me a huge hug. It was cool to be a part of both the historic win and the party afterwards.

And in the blink of an eye my big break was over. Now I had a huge decision to make.

10
SLIDING DOORS

I WAS IN THE ROBINA SHOPPING CENTRE on the Gold Coast, looking through a rack of shirts, when my mobile phone buzzed. I fished it out of my pocket, backed my way out of the store and answered the call.

'So are you coming back or what?' It was Sergeant Saxby, the 21 Construction Squadron Resource Troop sergeant.

'Mmm,' I said. 'Well ... About that.'

Sergeant Saxby already knew I was considering leaving the army. That I was having doubts at the very least. I'd spoken to him before I went on leave. Had a bit of a heart-to-heart. Told him where I was at.

'Well, I have some news that might help you make up your mind,' he said. 'You want to go to Afghanistan, right?'

He knew I did.

'Well, our unit is on the next rotation,' the sergeant continued. 'Do you want me to put your name forward?'

He knew the answer. That I'd joined the army to go on that very deployment.

And with that I was a soldier again.

Looking back, it was a sliding-doors moment. A phone call that would change my life. A decision that would define it.

The unit had been doing sweet fuck all for six months. Nothing had changed except the mood. Everyone was upbeat, buzzing, knowing they were going to be deployed. Everyone wanted to go to Afghanistan. It was the trip we all wanted to be on. Still, a lot of water had to pass under the bridge before we shipped out. A lot of training and preparation. Box-ticking and paperwork.

The preparations began immediately. Almost as soon as I got back, we were sent out to central Australia, a place called Woomera, for high-risk search training. Infamous for its secret nuclear programs and rocket testing, Woomera is an out-the-back-of-nowhere town in the far north of South Australia that's home to a series of army and air force bases.

It was the most similar environment we could get to Afghanistan in Australia, and we were there to learn more about IEDs and further our skills. We were also there to be certified. We'd be ruled out of the trip unless we passed the course, so it was something we all took very seriously.

Put into a group for the training exercises, I was immediately drawn to a soldier who reminded me a little of myself. We were about the same age – even though he looked a lot older thanks to his diet of cigarettes and Red Bull – and almost as soon as we met, Daniel Livesay and I became mates. He was about the same height as me, so we would probably have had the same build had his diet actually included some food.

I also got on with a couple of younger guys, Wertsy and Pitch. Ryan Werts, a strawberry blond with freckles all over his face, displayed a confidence that suggested he was yet to be put in his place by a higher rank. But I liked him all the same. Smart, witty and lots of fun, he had the makings of a good soldier, even though he did his best to avoid work.

Mac Pitcher was a bit like Wertsy when it came to attitude. Tall and lanky, he pretended he was staunch, one of those guys who walked like he was always carrying shopping bags. I liked him right away.

My new-found mates and I learned all about the types of mines and IEDs that were being used in Afghanistan – how they were made and by whom, and where they were being deployed.

At the time, most IEDs in Afghanistan were housed in either pressure cookers or oil containers made from plastic. The oil containers were called YPOCs because of the type of container that was most commonly used – yellow palm oil containers. They came in various sizes, the smallest being the five-litre container and the largest the twenty-litre container. The largest metal component of an IED was often the battery pack.

Most of the IEDs were made from everyday household items. The explosives could be a range of things, from military-grade products to ammonium nitrate mixed with fuel – usually farming fertiliser mixed with diesel.

There was also a newer type of explosive made from potassium chloride that was far more powerful but harder to make. The precursors were also controlled and only available to those with a permit. Ammonium nitrate was just one of the tightly controlled substances in Afghanistan. But you can put a bomb in just about anything if you have it: a vest, a car, a donkey. If you name it, they had probably done it.

Insurgents were looking to place the IEDs at what were called vulnerable points. They were areas likely to be used by the enemy, where they could target large groups and/or vehicles. Examples of vulnerable points included intersections, tree lines, footpaths and alleyways.

We spent the first couple of weeks learning all about IEDs and vulnerable points. Specialists from the explosive ordnance disposal squad – the highly trained army unit that disarms bombs – were brought in to teach and instruct. It was our job to find the IEDs and their job to disarm them. I reckon we got the pointy end of the stick, because IEDs aren't particularly dangerous once they've been found. Especially when you have robots and bomb suits. But don't get me wrong, they will still kill you if you're not careful or you don't treat them with respect.

This course was very specific to current IEDs in Afghanistan. Recently, they'd begun making more sophisticated IEDs, using chemicals that required no metal and were therefore harder to detect.

Finding an IED is simple in theory – you swing a metal detector around until you get a hit. It's a lot more complicated in practice. We were taught to use our metal detectors in a very systematic and strategic way. Working in pairs, with about ten metres between you and your partner, you wave the detector in a staggered pattern. All the ground between you and your partner should be covered. For example, if you're looking for an IED on a road, one guy stands on the left edge of the road and the other on the right. Making sure you don't step on the wheel ruts – which is where the pressure plate is put so the vehicle triggers it with its wheel – you wave your metal detector as far as you can to your left and to your right. You have to make sure that, between you and your partner, you 'paint' the entire surface of the road. At the same time, you're looking up and around for anything that's out of place and could be used as a marker, or even anything on the ground that could indicate that an IED has been buried there.

If you get a hit, you get down on your belly and poke. Yep, literally. Lying on your stomach, you explore the area of the metal-signature hit with your fingers – carefully, of course. Sometimes the ground is too hard to use your hands and you'll have to use a knife, although we'd never do this in front of an instructor. Officially you're supposed to use a tool called a mine prodder, but it's useless. Made of plastic, the mine prodder is blunt and bendy – only good for searching in sand. So when the ground is tough – and it is mostly rock-hard baked clay in Afghanistan – you use a knife. You hold the knife at an angle and stab the ground. Yep. Stab. Stab. Stab. You chip away at the ground, removing the dirt bit by bit, until you find whatever it is that has been buried. You then sweep the dirt away with a paint brush, mark the object out. Then you step away. Finally, after checking the surrounding area for further metal signatures, you go back to your hard point and call it in.

***

The course exposed me to the real danger that existed in Afghanistan. Looking at all those devices and the destruction they caused made it clear that there were people over there looking to hurt us. Kill us. It does put you on edge. You start to worry about what could happen. But it didn't change my opinion about going. I wasn't worried. I was going over with a team I trusted and had worked with. This is what I had been waiting for.

Another two combat engineers had been killed since Darren Smith and Jacob Moreland. In two separate incidents, although both were serving in the same regiment – my old regiment, 1CER – Richard Atkinson, aged twenty-two, had been killed in an IED blast, and Jamie Larcombe, aged twenty-one, had been killed in a fire fight. They were killed in February 2011, Jamie gunned down just seventeen days after his regiment lost Richard. I knew them both.

Part of the course was to look at those cases and examine what they did right and what they did wrong. We didn't really know what had happened until that course, having only heard bits and pieces, nothing official.

Some of the guys I was doing the course with had actually been over in Afghanistan with Darren Smith and Jacob Moreland when they were killed. They'd been on the ground with them, in the same rotation, and yet they were almost flippant about the training, which I found strange. Perhaps they thought the training was nothing like a real combat situation. In some ways, they were probably right.

I quickly learned that everyone outside the military had an opinion on Afghanistan. Whether we should be there or not. Whether they had any knowledge about the conflict or not. Mostly they didn't know a lot. But they were quick to voice an opinion, which I found interesting. It became a common topic of conversation with acquaintances when they learned of my looming deployment. Most people were against the war and had no hesitation telling me so. Why we shouldn't be there. That it had nothing to do with us. That it was a waste of time and money. A waste of life. Some people saw the military as a peacekeeping force. As a humanitarian organisation out to do good. Others thought the military was just a bunch of guys with guns. The negative comments often came from the second group of people, the group that saw us as mostly conquerors and occupiers, and only sometimes defenders.

Whether or not we should have been in Afghanistan is still a divisive topic today. I get asked about it all the time. Whether I'd go back if I knew the price I would pay. I'll get to that later, but back then, before I was deployed, I certainly knew that Afghanistan was dangerous. I now had three mates who had died in the conflict, all combat engineers who were performing the role I was going to perform when they were killed. So yes, I was very aware that I could be injured or killed. Deep down, I was a little concerned, but I did my best to ignore whatever worries I had. I certainly never showed it. All that was locked away, buried deep in the back of my mind.

***

Once I'd received my certificate, I returned to Brisbane to continue the pre-deployment training and certification process. I was attached to the 2nd Combat Engineering Regiment on a six-month rotation. We were going to serve alongside the 3rd Royal Australian Regiment, an infantry unit based in Townsville. It would be our role to support the larger battle group, providing and denying mobility and using our specialist skills.

Soon after we got back to Brisbane, our ten-man section was divided into two groups of five – called 'bricks'. I was happy to have Livo, Werts and Pitch in my brick but not the bloke who was going to lead us. He was the most senior soldier in my brick, but he was incompetent. More than incompetent, he was dangerous. I had no confidence in him at all. I didn't want to put my life in his hands. Thankfully, the other guys in my brick were of the same opinion. I was the next most senior soldier in my brick of five, which would be culled to four before deployment. I'd been in the army for about a year longer than my mate Livo. But while I'd been in the army longer than Livo, he'd done the engineer-specific promotion corporal course, which I hadn't. I'd done the leadership-specific course, which he hadn't. Together we made a great team.

We got together and decided we couldn't work under the corporal who'd been put in charge of our brick. So we went to the squadron sergeant major and stated our case. We said we didn't think the corporal was competent and we didn't think we would even get to Afghanistan with him as our leader, because we'd fail all the certification requirements under his command.

Warrant Officer Class 2 Allan Waugh was the squadron sergeant major, and he was very approachable and reasonable, a really good guy, a proud Scottish man. He listened and took it all on board. And, thankfully, he ended up agreeing with us and made the decision to replace the senior corporal. 'I want both of you to put your names forward,' he said.

I didn't end up throwing my hat in the ring because both Livo and I agreed that he was best suited to leading the brick. He'd lead with his engineering-specific knowledge and I'd be the 2IC, backing him up with my expertise in soldiering and my experience. Having the senior soldier removed came with the added bonus of having Pitch promoted from reserve to part of the proper four-man brick that would be deployed.

Our brick became a solid unit after the corporal was removed, and we developed well. None of us had been to Afghanistan but it didn't matter. The dynamic was right, and we were all on the same page.

***

'What happens if you lose your legs?' Rachel asked.

The question came out of the blue. A week away from me getting on a plane and going to Afghanistan, I was back in Brisbane for a short break with Rach before heading off.

'Then I'll go to the Paralympics,' I replied.

We'd been given two weeks' leave when we got through all our pre-deployment training. I really wanted to see Rachel one more time before I went away for six months deployment, so she flew over from New Zealand. One of the first things we did when she arrived was take some photos. I decided I wanted to make some memories and take them to Afghanistan with me. Back then, mobile phone cameras were rubbish, so we didn't take a lot of photos. In fact, Rachel and I had never been photographed together, not properly. But now I wanted to take a piece of her to Afghanistan with me, even if it was only a memory. So I grabbed a camera, employed my sister as a photographer, and took Rachel down to South Bank in Brisbane to get some pictures.

I knew it could be the last time I had my picture taken, but I didn't think about that, and it wasn't my motivation.

I suppose Rachel also knew it could be the last time we saw each other.

I got the photos printed up the next day, picked out the ones I wanted to take with me and gave the rest to Rach. It was later that day that she asked me about my legs. I was packing my bag, checking all my kit, and she started playing with my body armour. I suppose she looked at it all and realised that while my chest would be protected, there'd be nothing protecting my legs.

I dropped Rachel at the airport the following day. There were no waterworks. It wasn't the big emotional send-off you might expect. I just gave her a big hug and a kiss. 'I'll see ya later,' I said casually.

But while I showed no emotion, it was only because I was holding it all back. For a moment there I had the horrible thought that I'd never see Rachel again. I didn't want to let her go. But I steeled myself and dismissed the thought. I couldn't think about something that hadn't happened and might not happen. You can't afford to have those negative thoughts. You need to keep a positive outlook and be happy with the decisions you've made. I was in this position because of the steps I'd taken, and it was all by choice if not design.

I spent my final couple of days with my family. They didn't completely understand what my role was to be overseas and I didn't explain it to them. I didn't want them to know how dangerous it would be. They were oblivious to it. They didn't know that my job would put me directly in harm's way. I downplayed it and assured them it would all be okay. I didn't want them to worry.

I thought I was ready when it was finally time to leave. I'd done all the training, passed all the tests, and said all my goodbyes. The only thing that I felt I lacked was an understanding of the place I was going to, the people I'd be helping, and the people who would being trying to hurt me.

We learned little about Afghanistan in terms of history and culture during our pre-deployment training. I knew nothing of their language – or languages, as I'd soon learn – or their religions. I knew nothing about their government, their police or their military. I felt I should have had some understanding of the people I was going to help – or fight – before I got on the plane. I knew nothing of their motives or how they operated. Had no context for the behaviours I'd soon see. But aside from that I was ready and willing, even excited, to finally be going to Afghanistan.

Going to war.

11

THE FIGHTING SEASON

I FINALLY FOUND THE courage to open my laptop. I hit 'new' and 'document'. I needed to write a letter. A death letter.

Dear Mum and Dad,

If you are reading this then ...

I deleted it all and started again.

Dear Mum and Dad,

Just wanted to let you know how grateful I am for everything you have done and that I love you.

I deleted it all and started once more. And on it went.

It was my first day in Afghanistan. I was sitting on what would be my bed for the next six months, writing letters to my loved ones on my laptop. Called 'death letters', they're notes written by soldiers that are to be given to family and friends in the case of death. I hadn't even thought about writing letters like these until a mate, Shane 'Gibbo'

Gibbs, mentioned it. Gibbo had already done a full stint in Afghanistan the year before, serving with the 1st Combat Engineer Regiment in 2010.

'You written your death letters?' he'd asked shortly before I was deployed.

'No,' I said. 'Do I have to?'

He told me I didn't have to but that he had. He'd written his before he was deployed in 2010, and now had them saved on his computer for future deployments.

Until the second round of deployments in Afghanistan, it probably wasn't common for Australian engineers to write death letters. Then Darren and Jacob were killed on the rotation that was called Mentoring Task Force 1 (MTF1) in 2010. Apparently, a lot of guys who went on MTF2 – including Gibbo – wrote death letters, and even more who went on MTF3 after Richard Atkinson was killed.

Anyway, Gibbo suggested it'd be a good idea to get them done. Just in case. So I decided to write them on the day I arrived. I can't tell you exactly what I wrote because I got rid of them when I left the army. I wrote one to Mum and Dad, another to my brother, Brent, one to my sister, Sophia, and one to Rachel. I also wrote a generic letter that was to be given to my mates.

I'd been dreading writing the letters, but once I got to work I found it pretty easy. It wasn't a lot of fun though. Basically, I just thanked everyone for being part of my life, for raising me or looking out for me, for being there for me. I told them I loved them and would miss them.

I saved all the letters in a folder on my desktop, so they could easily be found if anything happened to me. I named the folder 'Family Letters'.

I think I was the only one in my group who wrote the death letters. I suppose I did it partly because of Gibbo and partly because I now knew five guys who'd been killed in Afghanistan. I didn't want those I loved to be left with nothing. I guess the danger had become very real.

***

My 'death photo' had been taken back in Townsville on our second-last day on base. We'd all lined up, our best combat uniforms completely clean and immaculately pressed, and waited for our turn to have our picture taken in front of the Australian flag. It was surreal, knowing that this photo would be the one distributed if I was killed. I'd seen plenty of images just like it over the last couple of years. Now it was me standing in front of the flag, trying to find a reason to smile.

Another morbid task I'd had to think about before flying out was whether to take out life insurance. We'd been advised that a company called Body Parts – seriously, that was their name – was willing to insure soldiers. Obviously, we were considered high risk, given that we were going to a combat zone, and not too many companies would issue life insurance to a soldier going to Afghanistan. I opted against taking out insurance: I didn't have any dependants and also had no debt. But for the guys with young families, it was much more of an issue.

We flew out from Brisbane airport on an Airbus A340, a chartered civilian plane. All white with no markings to identify it, the plane had no entertainment, average food and terrible seats. It made economy look like first class. I spent a long time in that tight and uncomfortable seat, the plane going from Brisbane to Sydney, from Sydney to Darwin, and finally from Darwin to Dubai. I didn't know it, but it was the last time I'd have to worry about leg room.

We landed on a military base called Al Minhad Air Base about twenty hours after we left Brisbane. Located on the outskirts of Dubai, Al Minhad was home to the Emirati Special Forces and Presidential Guard. It was also used by Australia as a logistical base for all operations in Afghanistan and the Middle East. From this fairly small base at night, you could just see the light at the top of the Burj Khalifa, the 161-floor super-building in the centre of the city.

I was used to all the worst kinds of hot after living in Darwin and touring South-East Asia, but the heat in Dubai was something else. It hit me as soon as I put my feet on the tarmac at 2 am, and did not relent for the entirety of my five-day stay. There were a series of digital thermometers around the base, all kept in the shade, but I can't tell you how hot it got because they maxed out at 50 degrees Celsius, and they were always maxed out. The airconditioning was great, all the buildings cooled, but they just made the blistering heat even hotter when you went back outside. It was like walking out of a fridge and into an oven.

We'd been sent to the UAE on the way to Afghanistan to acclimatise and prepare. There we received our fighting kit, zeroed our weapons and did some final training. We also got current updates and situational reports from in theatre intelligence. At the time, Afghanistan was fairly quiet after a long, cold winter. With temperatures in the Afghan mountains dipping below minus twenty-five degrees Celsius in winter, the insurgents mostly went into hibernation until late spring. There'd been no IED strikes or big contacts for some time. Fighting season didn't start until the weather got warm. It would soon start.

We were never given a history of the conflict. Most of what we knew came through intelligence briefings and threat reports. We all knew that the enemy was the Taliban, the group that was trying to prevent us from doing our work. We were only told things about them that were specific to our role. For example, I knew, in detail, how they constructed IEDs and why they left them. But I was never told where they left them. You had to work out the big picture stuff for yourself.

This is what I did know. Afghanistan, a landlocked country in Asia, bordering several countries including Iran, Pakistan and China, became a modern conflict zone during the Cold War, when it was caught up in the hostilities between the Soviet Union and the US. Looking to obtain access to oil in the Middle East, the Soviets gained control of Afghanistan by backing a power-seizing coup. When Afghanistan became a Soviet client state in 1978, the US and its allies secretly backed and armed a rebel group called the Mujahideen. And that's how it all started.

Armed with American weapons and cash, the Mujahideen waged war against their Soviet-backed state until the Soviet Union withdrew from Afghanistan in 1991. The country has basically been in conflict ever since, the Mujahideen and its numerous political offshoots fighting against local rivals, including the Taliban and the People's Democratic Party of Afghanistan (PDPA) – and also against itself – for control of the country.

The political instability and constant conflict turned Afghanistan into a breeding ground for terrorists. And that's why we were there. As part of the international war on terror,

US-led forces removed the Al Qaeda–linked Taliban from power in 2001 and installed a democratic government.

The International Security Assistance Force (ISAF), which included Australia, then began an operation to ensure the success of the new government, rid the country of extremists, and ensure Afghanistan was no longer a breeding ground for terrorists.

By 2012, when I was deployed, they'd made a lot of progress but still hadn't accomplished their mission. Osama Bin Laden was dead, Al Qaeda all but defunct, but the country was not secure. The Taliban was still active and hindering the efforts of the ISAF troops.

We spent five days in Dubai before heading to Afghanistan in a Boeing C-17 Globemaster. The Royal Australian Air Force had eight C-17s at the time. With a 52-metre wingspan and a maximum payload of 77,500 kilograms, the $300 million plane is the biggest in Australian service. It can carry planes and tanks, has jet engines, and is far superior to the louder and slower Lockheed C-130 Hercules.

The flight from Dubai to southern Afghanistan took three hours. We wore full body armour and held out weapons for the descent, which was something else. Due to the threat of being shot down, military planes in Afghanistan cannot land like a commercial craft. They have to spend the least amount of time possible flying at low altitude, which is in firing range, so they basically drop out of the sky. The descent was like the drop of a roller-coaster ride – steep, fast and fun. It felt like we were vertical for a while, nose pointed towards the ground, tail towards the sky. But it didn't last long. We were soon on the ground, in Tarin Kowt, Uruzgan province, Afghanistan.

***

It wasn't anywhere near as hot as Dubai. There was a lot of dust and I couldn't see much except for helicopters – Blackhawks and Apaches – which were everywhere. Formerly called Camp Holland and renamed Multinational Base Tarin Kowt (MNBTK) when the Netherlands withdrew from Afghanistan in 2010, the base, which we called TK, was located in the central province of Afghanistan called Uruzgan. All grey and beige concrete and barbed wire, it was home to 1200 soldiers, mostly Australians and Americans, but also some Slovenians and Singaporeans. There were also 4000 Afghans in a different section of the base.

TK was set against the backdrop of the Uruzgan Mountains near the town of Tarin Kowt, the capital of Uruzgan. Our sleeping quarters were housed in a huge square concrete bunker that was one of the newest buildings on the base. With no windows, and walls made from reinforced concrete up to two metres thick, the building was blast-proof, so we'd be protected from a rocket if it got past the automatically operated American defensive weapon system that was programmed to shoot down any incoming threats – and the odd bird if it flew too close.

As soon as we arrived, we were given the protocols and an introduction to routines and daily life, things like where the mess hall, hospital, store and gym were located. We were also given a variety of scenarios that could occur on the base and how we should react. They instructed us to carry our weapons at all times, which was a good indication of where we were and the threat we faced.

Our building was near the back of the base and could house as many as 180 Australians. There were about eight rooms on each level of the two-storey building, and it was ten to a room. We had great airconditioning and crappy Wi-Fi. I'd been assigned a bottom bunk, which was a win because I could hang up some blankets and towels and create a cave. As soon as I arrived, I'd pulled out my favourite photo of Rach and stuck it up on my shelf, and put another one in my field diary, which I would take on operations. She would now be with me always. It was on this bunk that I wrote my 'death letters' to my friends and family. Things were getting real.

It was so dark and quiet inside you could never tell what time it was without looking at a clock. You could walk out thinking it was the morning and find it was still the middle of the night. The thick walls blocked out every bit of light and sound, even helicopter noise.

Early on, I met a few Americans who were serving on the base. My first impressions were good. They were all friendly and professional. They had a lot of respect for us Australians, as both soldiers and people. It was also good to have them around because they had the best shop and access to all the good shit – the best coffee for starters.

Five days after we arrived, I went out on my first patrol, called an 'observation patrol'. I was part of a large convoy of around forty vehicles travelling to a neighbouring base to deliver supplies and personnel. We were going out to Forward Operating Point (FOB) Hadrian, which was the biggest base other than TK in the province.

We were travelling in a Bushmaster, a seriously good vehicle. Australian-designed and -built, it's basically a tank on wheels. Some have a remote-controlled weapons system, and they fit up to eight people in the back and two in the front. With its monocoque hull designed to deflect IED blasts, small-arms-fire protective armour and bullet-proof glass, the Bushmaster has saved a lot of lives.

I was in the rear gunner position for the trip to Hadrian, which allowed me to look out of the hatch and take in the view. I was immediately struck by the size of the mountains, which seemed to roll to infinity. The ground was barren, Mars-like, hard-packed and baked light brown. It was littered with rocks, some the size of pebbles, others as big as boulders. They made perfect cover for mines and IEDs.

The towns we drove through were all very similar. Nearly all the houses were surrounded by high mud walls, sometimes a metre thick – for privacy or protection, I wasn't sure.

Along the way, we were waved through a series of police and army checkpoints. They weren't there to stop us. There was no real threat and we didn't expect one. It was a large convoy of tanks with 25-millimetre chain guns, armour-piercing shells, and attack helicopters overhead. The insurgents didn't have the numbers, the coordination or the arms to mount an attack on such a force. They were much sneakier, using suicide bombers and IEDs, and attacking by ambush.

The only real action we saw was when a bunch of kids came out and threw rocks. Apparently it was a common occurrence. The kids knew the vehicles were armour-plated, and thought they were having a bit of harmless fun. Given my head was sticking out of the hatch, I didn't think it was a lot of fun. I was later told that a soldier had once been hit in the face by a large rock. The kids scattered fast when the convoy stopped and armed soldiers swarmed the village to politely report their bad behaviour to the village elder. No doubt the kids got a hiding later.

The trip to Hadrian took six hours. It was only sixty kilometres away, but a military convoy is all creep and crawl. We arrived close to nightfall so we stayed over and returned to TK the next day. You don't travel at night in Afghanistan unless you absolutely have to. Because of the reduced visibility and increased risk, every trip takes at least four times as long as it would in daylight.

What lay ahead I didn't really know, but I figured we'd be busy. IEDs were a key part of the insurgents' strategy, and it was working: almost half of civilian and military casualties were the result of IEDs. Clearing them was part of my role, and I was here to do a job. I was ready.

12

THE ROCKET CLUB

I WAVED MY METAL detector from right to left.

Nothing.

Then from left to right.

Still nothing.

My heart was racing and I was drenched in sweat. Conducting my first clearance patrol, I was as excited as I was nervous. I was standing in a lush green field, finally away from the road, thinking about where to look next.

Maybe beside the shed. Maybe the poppy field. Maybe the path.

I knew a bullet could whiz past at any moment. Or hit me. Maybe I wouldn't even feel it: one straight to the head. We were working in an area called a green belt, a non-desert area that could be populated. Green belts are generally close to rivers or a water source and have a topography suitable for growing crops and sustaining life. Unlike the desert, these areas can be very green indeed.

But you have to be careful while moving about them. In the desert – or the *dasht* as it's called – you can generally get about quite freely. In such a vast area without paths or tracks, it's difficult for the enemy to predict your route. There aren't a lot of vulnerable points (VPs).

In the green belt movement is more predictable. Every path, corner, bridge and row of trees is a VP. We mostly moved in a big line to provide a gate-like sweeping of the area. Our job as engineers was to make sure that whatever path we took was safe.

There was always the threat of a fire fight while working inside the green zone. It's where the life of Afghanistan thrives, a populated place with locals roaming about their daily lives. The farmers looked the same as the fighters, impossible to tell apart. The infantry was there to protect us – eyes raised and on high alert – but there were no guarantees. There were no armour-plated Bushmasters either, no vehicles at all. This patrol was on foot.

I decided to search the tree line. But it was just a guessing game. They could be hidden anywhere. Or nowhere: nothing to find.

I waved my metal detector from right to left.

Nothing.

Then from left to right.

Something.

I did it again, slower this time.

Whoop …

A hit.

Yes!

Excited by the metal detector indicating a hit, I quickly marked it out then got down on all fours and dug. I soon saw the metal and could identify what it was.

Damn! It was a ring-pull from a soft-drink can. Picking up my markers before moving on, I pressed a little closer to the tree and waved my metal detector.

Whooop …

A louder noise this time. Something bigger. Better. I got down on my knees and dug.

It was a soft-drink can missing a ring-pull. I picked up my markers again and moved on once more, even closer this time, all the way to the base of the tree. I waved the detector, from right to left.

Whooop!

And then from left to right, just to make sure.

Whooop!

Louder. Bigger. Better. I started digging, frantically, then checked myself. I had to work carefully.

'Boys, I got something,' I yelled. 'Over here.'

They all stopped and helped form a security perimeter. The men that weren't facing outwards, ready to stop an intruder, watched as I continued to dig.

'Looks like a sack,' I said looking at the material, possibly plastic hessian.

I had no idea what it contained but I was guessing it wasn't good. Someone was trying to hide something. Maybe it was arms or ammo. Maybe it was a bomb. Then again, maybe it was a dead cat.

We got the hook and the line kit. Trained to treat every find as if it was booby trapped, we delicately hooked the not-yet-revealed, could-be-anything item after attaching the line and throwing it over a sturdy branch. We were about seventy metres away when we decided it was safe enough to reel the line in. I winced as I pulled, half expecting a blast.

No bang. No trip wire or pressure plate. No explosion. Nothing.

The item popped out of the ground, whatever it was giving me no resistance. Pulled again on the cable and made sure the bag was bashed around a bit to ensure there was no booby trap. We moved back towards the tree, the mystery prize now sitting on top of the bank under the tree ... It was a plastic hessian bag.

'Open it up,' Livo said.

I grabbed my knife and cut carefully.

'Rounds,' I said. 'A shitload.'

I'd just found a bag full of bullets. A cache of 7.76-millimetre AK-47 rounds. It was my very first find and the start of what would turn into an almighty first-up haul.

***

The last month or so had been busy – a steady stream of patrols, mostly logistical supply and mail runs. We were always out and about, little time spent back on the base. We'd been involved in at least a few operations each week since we'd arrived, providing mobility and safe passage for whatever operation we'd been sent on. Nearby bases were always in need of commodities like diesel to power their generators, and food and water to sustain the soldiers stationed there.

We'd always get a message from the guys we knew out at the patrol bases to bring out smokes and some of the luxuries we had in TK. We always obliged – sometimes we were their only connection to TK.

Our first operation took forever. Tasked with providing mobility support to a supply team, we were at the front of the convoy, leading the way. It was our job to make sure the path was clear. No roadblocks. No bombs. We were guilty of being over cautious and the trip took twice as long as it should have. We were warned that a section of road we were going to travel on had been dangerous in the past, so we were particularity thorough – which means particularly slow – through that area, getting out of the vehicles and leading the convoy on foot. We searched every inch of the road for IEDs.

We were finally sent out for a clearance patrol after about five weeks. This is the best kind of search. A patrol where you look for hidden weapons and anything that could be used to make war, it's a very productive way of fighting without contact. And much safer. Without their weapons and bombs, the locals who were about to fight will go back to whatever it was they were doing before. Return to farming or teaching. Maybe go back to fixing cars.

For an engineer, this type of patrol is also generally safe. Or safer than other patrols, at least. Looking for components as opposed to ready-made, functioning and deployed IEDs, there was less risk of being hurt by something that goes bang. The cached weapons were not generally booby trapped, but we always treated every find – whether it be weapons, components or ordnance – like it was.

We were attached to a combat team based in the Chora Valley for this clearance search, which was scheduled to last five days. There were forty-five of us in the patrol: fifteen infantry, one interpreter, twenty-five Afghan soldiers, and my brick of four engineers. It was my first on-the-ground mission where I was part of a combat team. On foot and without vehicles, it was also my first time working away from the road, which meant we were closer to the locals. I'd get to see more of the country. The real Afghanistan.

The finds kept on coming after I dug up the bag of bullets.

'I got something,' yelled one of the boys while we were searching an area we intended to use as an overnight camp, or defensive harbour.

He'd found ammunition and IED componentry, both hidden in a mound of hay. We intensified and widened our search after the find, because generally one hit will lead to another. That certainly proved to be the case on this occasion, and we found weapons and ordnance hidden all over the place, including a pimped-out and fully operational AK-47. Covered in red glitter and wrapped in red tinsel, the unique weapon was a popular find. Wertsy found the AK-47 and he wanted to render the gun inoperable and ship it back to Australia. He didn't though, the prospect of paperwork and army rigmarole a hurdle he'd never attempt to jump.

A detailed report of each object is radioed in after each find: what it is, where it was found, how it was found and who found it. The item is then bagged, tagged and sent on to a forensic team for fingerprinting. They have a fair chance of finding a match given we fingerprint every fighting-age male we come across. Each combat team commander carries a biometric scanner, which is used to take both fingerprints and iris scans from everyone we pull up.

The search continued and the hits kept on coming, find after find, so much so that our patrol commander eventually stopped the search as it was getting dark and pulled us back to the night harbour. We'd been at it all day, afternoon and now into the night. We needed sleep – not that we'd get much. The green belt is considered a dangerous place to sleep. There was no real cover in the paddock where we were set up for the night. We picked the most strategic spot we could find, but there was still a space where insurgents could slip through. We set up a claymore mine in the security gap. A directional fragmentation mine that shoots ball bearings, the claymore is a serious weapon. It was a reassuring addition to our camp.

Still, we didn't get much sleep.

We hadn't taken any sleeping gear for this operation because we had so much other equipment to carry. On foot and without a transport vehicle, we'd have been overloaded had we taken swags and blankets or other creature comforts, or so we thought. We figured there would be little need for bedding given it was forty-five degrees during the day. However, we were wrong. At night it got down to ten degrees. It was freezing; I ended up rolling over and snuggling up with Wertsy, which was rather interesting. Thankfully he was happy to be the little spoon.

We continued our search the next morning.

Soon Wertsy had found something. 'Have a look at this,' he shouted.

It was an RPG round. An RPG is a rocket-propelled grenade. An anti-tank weapon. RPG rounds have what's called a shape charge, a device that creates an explosion on contact before spitting out an armour-piercing projectile. An RPG round is also quite dangerous, even to handle. They are equipped with a piezoelectric fuse that ignites when crystals are crushed and create an electric charge, so a knock to the tip can set the explosive off, especially when the round is old. And the round Wertsy found was ancient: a Soviet relic, rusted, dented and covered in dirt. But despite its appearance, throw it into a launcher and it would work like new.

After Wertsy's find we formed a team we called the 'Rocket Club' and widened the search. It remained a guessing game. We would walk over to areas that looked interesting, wave our metal detectors around and hope for a hit. Bigger items, such as a bag of bullets with a lot of metal, would give you a louder, longer sound. But that didn't mean you could dismiss the short, soft sounds, because a lot of important IED components contained minimal amounts of metal. It didn't take long for the Rocket Club to land a hit, with another RPG round found nearby.

Given their volatility, this ammunition was too dangerous to be sent on to the forensic team for fingerprinting. It had to be destroyed. So we took the rounds out of the green zone, away from people, and into the desert. Once in the *dasht*, it didn't take us long to find a suitable area to destroy the ordnance, a little cliff face providing adequate cover. We placed an explosive charge over the rockets and took cover under the cliff face before setting it off.

Booooom!

It was decent explosion. A big noise. But blasts are not as spectacular as you'd think. You're in a safe area, away from the explosion, and you don't see too much. Just smoke rising and dirt falling. Only satisfying for the briefest moment, it's really a non-event.

***

He waved and yelled. A local, an Afghani. He looked like a farmer, but over here, farmers were also fighters. I had no idea whether he was friend or foe.

'He's inviting you all over to his house for tea,' our interpreter said, quickly making the man's dubious intentions clear. 'He wants to thank you for helping his country.'

We were three days into the patrol when we stopped to break bread with this Afghani farmer. With leather-like sun-beaten skin and a smile, he yelled through a mouthful of crooked teeth and waved with a hand that had been worked to the bone.

'He says he has good tea,' the interpreter said. 'Best in village.'

The Afghan soldiers didn't need a second invitation, rushing towards the farmer, ready to take anything and everything he was willing to give. We also accepted, but with a little more grace perhaps. We instructed the interpreter to tell the farmer we'd be honoured to share tea with him, but only if he had enough to give. We said we didn't want to be an imposition or deprive him of anything he could not afford to spare.

'Plenty enough, he says,' the interpreter replied. 'Best tea. You come have. Plenty friend.'

We obliged. Sat down under a makeshift pergola, right outside his mud-brick house, while he served up his special blend. He poured this 'best in village' tea into as many cups as he had; tasted a little like chai. Green tea with cinnamon, if I was forced to guess. It was pretty good, maybe even best in village. Heaps better than his flatbread.

I took a piece to be polite. It tasted like cardboard. It was cold, dry and hard. But not wanting to be an ingrate, I ate every last pebble-like crumb.

I then sat back, put my elbow into the soft dirt and looked out at the brilliant landscape. For a moment I forgot I was in a war zone. There were no IEDs. No insurgents. Just green grass, sunshine and a smiling farmer with 'best in village' tea and ordinary bread.

***

I sat down to do some reports later that night. I had to compile a complete and thorough list of all our finds and then call them in.

'Oh,' I said as I grabbed my guts.

I suddenly felt a little off. Queasy.

'Ah,' I said, a little louder as I hunched.

My stomach started to churn.

Just wind. Bit of gas.

I lifted my leg and pushed. Tried to let it all out.

Oh no ...

Yep. I shat myself. No fart, all shart. And it only got worse. I had full-blown gastro the next day. Every bit of fluid I put in my mouth was shot out my arse. And I wasn't alone. We were all sick in some way. Shitting and spewing.

Turns out the farmer's tea was worse than his bread. I don't think the farmer intentionally made us sick, though it would have been a great tactic to disrupt our operation. Maybe it had been some dodgy creek water. I'll give him the benefit of the doubt. Regardless, it wasn't much fun.

I almost passed out the next day. I had to prop myself up against a wall. I felt dizzy, everything going blurry and then grey, verging on black. I started to fall but managed to stop myself from hitting the floor. I told the boys what had happened and how I felt. As a result, we decided to suspend the search and call it a day. We set off to our next night harbour. We were soon walking through a field. Full of plants about six foot high and green. They had a large leaf, star-like, pointy and very familiar. They also had a furry flower.

We all smiled at once, not needing to say anything. We all knew it was marijuana. We were surrounded by it, slapping through leaves that were destined to be smoked and pushing past buds that would end up in a bong. We were cutting through *Beavis and Butt-Head's Field of Dreams*. It was nothing unusual in Afghanistan. Back home, completely illegal and worth millions of dollars, a crop like this would have been guarded by shotguns and bikies had it not already been cut down and burned by the police. Here, where marijuana was as popular as tobacco, it was just another crop. Still, even with the runs, I couldn't stop smiling as we moved through the weed field. I considered grabbing a bud and putting it in my pocket, but the thought of being caught outweighed the thought of having a laugh followed by the munchies.

I also joined the 'Rocket Club' on this patrol, when I dug up a plastic bag that contained four RPGs and a recoilless rifle round.

We ended up with quite the haul – ordnance not marijuana – when the five-day operation was finished. We didn't really know how big until we met up with another team that had also just come back. Apparently, there was a bit of a competition when it came to clearance patrols. Unofficial scores were kept, and each team was ranked on a mental leader board. Anyway, the other team, which had been searching an area just on the other side of our patrol, came back with nothing. Not a thing. Not a find. Maybe they'd have felt better if we told them we all came back without underpants. But, unlike our arses, our lips were sealed.

As part of a blocking force a few weeks later, a couple of guys from my brick came across some fighting-age males during an operation in the Tangi Valley. Something about them didn't look right. Maybe it was the little wooden box about the size of a shoebox that one of them had under his arm. Or maybe it was that they were walking towards the valley we were blocking, almost as if they were trying to sneak past. Or maybe it was nothing.

The guys went in to find out. It turned out there was a white rose in the box. Again, maybe that was nothing, but it was most likely something, because the white rose is the symbol of the Taliban and the flower they use to secretly communicate belonging. Out came the biometric scanner and in went the fingertips.

The device beeped. A match. The young man with the rose was registered in the system as a Taliban fighter.

We were a little surprised to get a hit, as Taliban fighters are rarely found. The Afghan soldiers were more than surprised. They were livid. Just metres away from their sworn enemy, unarmed, outnumbered and helpless. They wanted to have their violent way with the Taliban fighter. The Afghan soldiers were much less reserved than us when it came to punishment, and if we let the Afghan soldiers have them, they'd never have been heard of again.

We had to be quite firm with Afghan soldiers. It was our job to apprehend the fighter, not to judge, let alone punish.

Protocol dictated that we get him to a jail within twenty-four hours. Once there, he'd be interrogated. We don't torture prisoners or subject them to spy-movie-like interrogation tactics. We don't hook their balls up to a battery or waterboard them. We don't even subject them to loud heavy metal. That's my understanding, anyway. I've never heard or seen anything that would suggest otherwise.

We were only halfway into our operation when we apprehended the Taliban fighter and that posed a problem. We'd have to remove our blocking position in order to take him to prison, a move that would have put fellow Australians at risk. The obvious solution was to get the Afghan soldiers to escort him to prison, but given their recent behaviour, we didn't know what they'd do with him. The other option was to ignore detainment law and keep him with us for the remainder of the patrol.

We decided it was too dangerous to split up our patrol, too risky to put his life in the hands of the Afghanis, and that we weren't prepared to break military detainment law. Our only choice was to let him go.

I suppose I'm telling you this story to show you how complicated the conflict in Afghanistan can be. How something that seems outrageous, like letting a known criminal, a terrorist, go free, is the best choice. The unintended result of bureaucracy.

But such is life.

13

THE KILL ZONE

A SOLDIER KNOWS HOW TO WHINGE – and I ended up doing a bit of it myself. About two months into our deployment things started to change for the worse. Some decisions were being made that were putting us at risk.

It all began when they told us we were set to become the last MTF. MTFs were going to be downgraded to become Observational Task Forces (OTF). Being an MTF meant our role was to train and advise the local Afghan forces. The aim was to make them fully operational and self-sufficient, so they'd eventually be capable of performing all the functions and duties of the international force.

Becoming an OTF meant our role would be limited to just observing. A consequence of that decision meant all the bases would be wound back, as fewer ISAF troops would be needed on the ground. The OTF would mainly consist of officers, who would 'observe' from bases. That meant all the resources had to be pulled out and shipped out.

Our confidence in this change was very low. The Afghan forces were great support troops during large missions the ISAF forces would lead, but as soon as we let the Afghan forces lead anything, the quality, safety and security of the patrol would go out the window. Almost as if they'd forgotten everything we taught them. They paid a high price for their negligence. You only had to look at the numbers of Afghani casualties compared to the ISAF forces to see something was very wrong.

The holy month of Ramadan, a month of fasting, prayer, study of the Quran and worship, was an interesting time. In Islam it's expected all people of the faith observe the month, and this put a strain on our cultural differences. The Afghan soldiers were quite reluctant to work during the day as they were unable to drink even water in sunlight hours – obviously a health risk in 45-degree heat. The fasting had the biggest effect on our combat capacities; the Afghanis didn't want to do any patrols in the hours they were fasting, but patrols still had to be conducted, so we had to adjust our schedule a lot. A patrol would leave the base before the sun came up, and would be a rushed affair. The Afghanis did the patrol at a slow jog, which is considered extremely dangerous, because no one can search at a jog. A lot of the time we'd lose them within the first five minutes of the patrol due to our slower and much safer pace.

After that announcement to withdraw resources, we were immediately tasked with a series of operations. We were ordered to conduct eight trips to Camp Hadrian in just fifteen days. Because Camp Hadrian was the first base scheduled to be dismantled, we were to go out in massive sixty-vehicle convoys and bring all the retrievable resources back to TK. We had no problem with the assignment, just the timeline. Conducting eight trips from TK to Hadrian in fifteen days was dangerous. Potentially deadly.

Hadrian is a difficult base to get to because you need to go through the Kandahar province. Only a 62-kilometre drive from TK, it can take a day because of the threat of IEDs and ambushes. We were always taught not to make patterns with our movements. We had to avoid being predictable, making ourselves a hard target. That meant changing our routines – taking different routes and travelling at different times. The enemy couldn't attack us if they didn't know where we were going to be and when. But eight trips to Camp Hadrian in fifteen days meant we would be on the same road almost every day and at the same time. An easy target.

If the insurgents saw us travelling out to a base, they knew we were going to have to come back. They would attempt to predict the return route and plant IEDs along the way.

One of the things we did to protect ourselves was send out a second search party that would follow behind our outward trip some hours later. They'd make sure the road was searched as we made our way back to TK, either that day or the following. Another tactic was to send a combat team from the base we were approaching. This sped up our convoy and helped mitigate the threat.

There are some tricks to finding an IED. Technically the trigger is the most dangerous part. It sets the device off, so avoiding that is always the safest option. The pressure plate, the type of trigger used in most common road-based IEDs, has to be placed on an area of road that will be contacted by a wheel. But they don't want the explosion to be under the wheel and at the front of the vehicle, so the main charge is offset from the trigger. Looking to do maximum damage, they want the explosive to go off in the centre of the vehicle. To achieve this objective, they place the explosive charge about two metres behind the trigger and also further towards the centre of the road.

When searching for IEDs, most of the time it's safer to approach them from the opposite direction to the expected way of travel. You want to approach the explosive or battery pack first and pressure plate or trigger last. While this means you avoid setting it off by reaching the explosive before the trigger, the battery pack is also the easiest part to find because it puts out a rather large metal signature for our detectors. Another thing we looked for was ground sign; any area that had been dug up generally had certain characteristics an experienced eye could spot.

Given such a limited window to make eight trips, we wouldn't have the time to take alternative roads or send out effective forward search parties. In short, they were putting our lives at risk to meet a deadline. This wasn't a normal workplace where making employees work harder and longer was just stressful. It was deadly.

We voiced our concerns. We had to go up the chain of command, from our troop commander to the engineer OC. From there it was sent on to the battle group commander. Usually it would start with a discussion rather than putting anything in writing. You only want to question an order in the army if your concern is serious and genuine. You also can't refuse an order unless you're prepared to be charged with insubordination. Although in recent times the military has become more open to group thinking and decision making, when it comes to the battle group commander making decisions that affect the soldier on the ground, it's hard to have your concerns heard.

Soldiers are subject to not only civilian law but also military law. The range of punishments for breaking military law is severe and includes prison. A military prison is not a place you ever want to be. There is a guard for every prisoner, one-on-one supervision twenty-four hours a day. They watch you eat, sleep and even shit. They also watch you clean the toilet when you're done – and it must be spotless.

The ADF prison is on the Holsworthy Barracks in Sydney's south-west. It's hidden behind a bunch of trees and you wouldn't know it was there unless you went looking for it. For a severe offence you could be locked away for a maximum of forty days before being given a dishonourable discharge. You may then be required to face civilian charges and further punishment under common law. Either way, you'll have a record and it will follow you everywhere.

We had a very good relationship with our engineering commanders. As sappers we had the ability to walk into the OC's office and relay our concerns directly. But it's still quite a process and smothered in bureaucracy, and in this instance our pleas fell on deaf ears. We were ordered to complete the eight missions in fifteen days as instructed. And we weren't happy.

But we did as we were told, even though the deadline meant we had to do each trip from TK to Hadrian and then back again in just one day. That was crazy. We called them rocket runs. Unable to survey the route properly, we just put our foot to the floor and went as quickly as we could. We were largely forced to ignore the movements of the enemy, and we conducted limited searches. It was like closing your eyes and running the gauntlet. I can't stress how dangerous this was. Ordering us to do eight missions in fifteen days was completely reckless. Almost criminal. They knew it was impossible to meet the deadline without ignoring search protocols and procedures. It was a minor miracle that we made it through unscathed, no blasts or fire fights. It was thanks to luck, not good planning, good practice or good procedure.

***

Another thing that got us wound up was a crack-down on dress. There is a thing in the military called army standard of dress (ASOD). It's a list of direct orders that dictate what clothing and footwear you're allowed to wear and how you are to wear it. The ASOD had not been strictly enforced during the pre-deployment training. In fact, it was common and not frowned upon to wear an item of footwear that wasn't on the list, as long it was practical and didn't look out of place. I'd been wearing a boot type that wasn't on that list for a year because the six different official boots were terrible. Like clogs. More than uncomfortable and unpractical, they could also damage your feet.

I had side-zip boots made by the 5.11 company. They were like wearing Nike Free sneakers: breathable, light and comfortable, and also fast-drying. Exactly the type of boot we needed in Afghanistan, given we were walking through aqueducts and rivers. The leather on the official boots didn't dry very well. Walk through a creek and you'd be forced to walk around in heavy wet boots for the rest of the day. And I'd never had a problem with my boots. Until now ...

The regimental sergeant major (RSM), the head soldier on base and the man in charge of discipline, suddenly went on an ASOD blitz. He started checking boots and issuing infringements if they weren't on the official list. We described it as his 'War on ASODs'. The RSM then went further, trying to ping as many people as he could – not only for ASODs but any type of infringement.

They even started using a surveillance blimp to check on us. This is a balloon with an ultra-powerful camera, a defensive tool that was supposed to be looking for the enemy. Instead, it was looking for soldiers sunbaking or involved in some other behaviour that was considered a breach. In our opinion it was illegal to use a very expensive piece of equipment to catch people breaking bullshit rules that had never been enforced. All because he had time up his sleeve. The blimp should have been looking for insurgents laying IEDs on roads. The morale of the entire base was affected. Everyone had a simmering resentment towards this type of authority.

The special forces soldiers had a humorous response: Housed in their own area that's off limits to all non-special forces, they hung a big sign up on their roof.

'Fuck off,' it read.

***

While on our way back from a patrol, we got word that an Australian drone had gone down a couple of kilometres past the heavy weapons range. Being outside the wire, we were all packed and ready to go, so we got the nod to accompany the retrieval team that had already been formed up and was waiting for an engineer brick to lead the way.

'Fuck,' I exclaimed. 'Is it hot in here or what? Is it just me?'

It wasn't.

The guys in the front said the Bushmaster aircon was not working. With no windows and 15,000 kilograms of armour, the Bushmaster soon became a furnace. We were already buggered after a full day's work, then turned around as we were arriving home, so the heat zapped whatever energy we had left. We were all exhausted by the time we arrived at the crash site. I jumped out of the Bushmaster as quick as I could, covered in sweat and gasping for air. It was the first time the stinking-hot desert, probably forty-five degrees at that time, provided relief.

An American team had already reached the site. They'd found the downed drone – it was like a very big remote-controlled plane – and secured it. Operated remotely by a skilled pilot back on base, the drone was used for surveillance. While the drone itself wasn't particularly important or valuable, the camera it carried was. It was worth about $500,000. And thankfully it was still intact. The emergency protection measure built into the drone to protect the camera had worked. The parachute had deployed and spun the drone into a position that had spared the camera from the worst of the impact. We recovered the camera and went about dismantling the drone, detaching the wings before loading it onto a truck. It wasn't a dangerous or even eventful mission, but I thought it was pretty cool. I doubt too many people have ever recovered a military drone. We took a little souvenir too, cutting off a parachute component before pocketing it, making sure that we weren't seen, of course.

***

I was fairly used to daily life in Afghanistan by this point, having now been there for a few months. I was fully acclimatised and now wearing new approved boots, or should I say clogs? I started recognising landmarks, houses and the like. I knew where I was and what was coming up. The landscape, the people and the job I was involved in were no longer strange.

We spent most of our time conducting patrols. It was rare to be back in base for more than a day or two. We worked long hours in very tough conditions. It was exhausting. I never had any trouble getting to sleep. When we did have a day off, I'd just sit on my bed, watching movies. Chilling out. It was a luxury to be able to sleep in a bed. The biggest break we had while I was there was a four-day stretch. That was a one-off; the longest before that was just a couple of days. The base was a very comfortable place and it was always good to be back after a patrol. I'd made my quarters as homely as possible. I also loved the coffee back on base – the MOAC (the Mother of All Coffees) was a sight to behold. It was served up in a one-litre Coke cup. The Americans like to make things big, and the coffee was no exception.

I didn't really get homesick. I guess being so busy helped, and it was only during the downtime, back on base, that I thought about family and friends. I spoke to both my family and Rachel about once a week. I wasn't into Skype or any other internet-based chat software, so I used the landline to make my calls. I found those calls a little difficult because operational security meant we weren't allowed to discuss any of the particulars of what we were doing. It became a pretty one-way conversation.

I had a difficult discussion with my parents about six weeks into my deployment. There had been an IED strike, which had been reported back home, and when I next called them they were obviously worried. I wasn't allowed to tell them anything, so I couldn't really allay their concerns. It was an awkward situation but just part of the job.

Being in Afghanistan was a little bit strange because people treated me differently from other trips. I was getting special attention: care packages, letters, emails and concerned calls. For me this was just another deployment, like all the others. I wasn't getting more or less homesick than I had while in East Timor. But for my family and friends, I was in a war zone, and the prospect of getting hurt or killed makes them more emotional. We didn't get that way. It was just another base. Another place.

As far as the work itself went, some days were better than others. I always looked forward to the clearance patrols. I felt like a kid on an Easter egg hunt while out searching for caches. Being an engineer spared me from the boredom faced by other soldiers. We were always doing something in our role, be it searching, assessing or just thinking. Some soldiers stand around for hours doing nothing. Infantry soldiers get particularly bored while in convoys. Although we have a role at the front determining the route and ensuring safety, they just sit in the back of a Bushmaster sucking aircon and sipping Gatorade. I bet many books were read on those supply trips.

But I guess there are worse things than boredom ...

***

We were on our way to FOB Anaconda, almost a full day out of Camp Wali, and only four kilometres from our night camp.

We'd travelled to, then spent four weeks at, Camp Wali without incident. In the infamously dangerous Mirabad Valley, the place Darren Smith and Jacob Moreland were killed, we'd conducted several presence patrols without incident. We'd been sent in to replace a combat team after their brick commander was injured, but encountered nothing in a region known for contact and conflict. Quiet. Nothing at all going on.

Conditions were primitive on Wali. The sleeping arrangements were particularly tight, just a piece of plywood separating you from the next guy. But even though the base was uncomfortable and low-tech, it was still blast proof, which was reassuring. The base consisted of a mortar team, a helicopter landing pad and a satellite station. Not much more. It had a good vantage point, up and down the entire Mirabad Valley.

I spoke to Rachel the night before we left Wali to tell her I was going on a patrol for about three weeks and wouldn't have access to a phone or the internet for most of that time. We'd just been told we were going to be part of a big clearance operation in another notorious part of Uruzgan called the Khas Uruzgan Valley. I told her not to panic if she didn't hear from me.

Khas Uruzgan is in the far eastern corner of Uruzgan province. It was an area well known for hostile activity. The FOB that operated up there was called Anaconda, and it was occupied by American special forces. It's generally a pretty good indication that the region is dangerous if the American special forces are there.

The drive to FOB Anaconda was about 150 kilometres. Although it's not that far on a bitumen highway without

IEDs, it's a bloody long way on a mountainous dirt track with bombs. It ended up being a two-day drive across treacherous terrain. There were three engineer Bushmasters, two alternating the lead and one in the middle of the pack. We were up the front, part of the alternating spear.

We were about four kilometres away from our sleeping location on the first day when one of the Afghan Humvees that was travelling in the convoy got a flat tyre. We stopped on a very precarious piece of road, exposed and on a cliff face. We were on our rest phase, in the second vehicle back, stopped and sitting there waiting. The engineer brick at the front were out of the vehicle and searching, as it was high threat terrain – what we'd call a VP. There were between fifty and 100 metres between each vehicle. We were a very long caterpillar and we were coming up to a big right-hand hairpin turn. I was sitting in the back having a chat to the crew commander, who was sitting on the step, looking back at us.

WHOOSH!

Then.

Bang!

Sitting in the back of the Bushmaster, I couldn't see a thing. Suddenly Livo dropped from the hatch.

'Fuck me,' he said.

Livo almost fell on the crew commander, who was sitting in the back chatting to us.

'Out of the way,' the crew commander said, pushing past Livo and into the cockpit.

He went straight for the roof-mounted weapon on our Bushmaster. I edged forward and looked out the windscreen. Towards the *Bang!* That's when I saw the dust cloud kicked up by the rocket.

An RPG.

It had only just missed us. About twenty metres to the left and we'd have been hit. We waited for the call to come, for the convoy commander to tell us to go. But instead, he told us to hold. To sit still.

Livo was white. Head out the hatch and having a cigarette while the entire convey was stopped and waiting for an Afghan vehicle crew to change a tyre, he'd heard and seen it all. The *Whoosh!* and the *Bang!*

'RPG,' he confirmed. 'Came from the top of the hill. Just missed us.'

We should have been moving. Foot to the floor, we should have been going for broke. But for some inexplicable reason, despite an RPG coming from nowhere in an ambush attack, the convoy commander had ordered us to stay still.

The soldier in control of our Bushmaster wasn't sitting still though. He jumped on the weapons system and aimed our MAG58 7.62-millimetre light machine gun up the hill. Straight at the area where the RPG had been launched. I heard the gun move. Up and to the right.

Taaat! Taaat! Taaat! Taaat! Taaat!

The crewie had been onto the weapon system in an instant and lit up the hill.

Nothing came back. But we were sitting ducks. A stationary 1.5-kilometre convoy, on a cliff face and completely exposed. It all happened so fast. I felt very helpless in the back, unable to do anything other than sit there and hope we weren't hit.

We were very lucky the RPG was not in the hands of an expert. It's a very accurate weapon. The insurgent who fired it was either very far away or a poor shot. Maybe both.

It was a hairy moment. The Afghans replaced their tyre fast after the shot, but we shouldn't have been in the 'kill zone' waiting for them after the RPG was fired. The commander of the battle group should have ordered us out, which is ambush protocol. Plenty were pissed off with his decision to make us hold, sitting ducks in the kill zone.

14

A STRANGE FEELING

PANTS SLIGHTLY SOILED BUT UNHARMED, we reached our overnight position at sundown. Formerly occupied by US forces and now patrolled by Afghans, Patrol Base Chukajoy felt like a safe place to stay for the night. While it was safe it was not comfortable: no internet or phones, just the bare necessities.

We got back on the road the next day and made a lot of ground. We didn't do that much searching because the ground was pretty open and flat. Safe. By the afternoon, we got into Khas Uruzgan, a small assortment of crumbled buildings and bustling market stands. The locals smiled and waved us in. We felt welcome.

We rolled through and into FOB Anaconda a short time later. It felt very similar to Hadrian, the base we'd just taken apart. It had a large helicopter pad, so all its supplies could be flown in, and a big mortar team to provide indirect fire for the US special forces team. There was also a large contingent of Afghan soldiers on the base, who I believe were their special forces.

We got a pretty good welcome from the American Green Berets, which was cool. Some of the first soldiers sent into Afghanistan in 2001, the Green Berets are featured in the Hollywood movie *12 Strong*, starring Chris Hemsworth. They're pretty gnarly dudes, known to love a fire fight.

The Islamic fasting period of Ramadan was coming to an end. It hadn't been an easy month from our point of view, but we respected the Afghanis' devotion and made concessions as best as we could. Anyway, the Americans at Anaconda put on a pretty big party to help them celebrate the end of Ramadan, shooting a load of illumination rounds into the sky – military-style fireworks.

But shortly after we arrived on the base, a spate of green-on-blue incidents happened across Afghanistan, forcing the Americans to suspend all operations for five days. A green-on-blue is an incident between an Afghan soldier or soldiers and ISAF forces. We assign a colour to each of the three forces operating in Afghanistan. Green refers to the Afghan forces, blue to the ISAF forces and red to the enemy.

There'd been four or five green-on-blues within a couple of days. Afghan soldiers, either converted by insurgents while they were serving, or insurgents that had infiltrated the Afghan Army, had turned their weapons on ISAF forces and gone on a killing spree. The threat was always very real, and was the reason we carried our weapons at all times while in Afghanistan, even when on base. It's hell, because you never know if the Afghan soldier you're working next to is an undercover insurgent or not. We were constantly on edge. I was always careful about how I spoke to Afghan soldiers. I didn't want to be rude or insulting in a way that might give them reason to be sympathetic to the other side.

All the Americans who were on patrol in our area came back to base and we spent some time with them. It was a great opportunity to speak to them and to learn from them. They gave us a sobering threat picture. One of the American soldiers pointed to a hill in the distance, about eight kilometres away.

'If you go past that hill you're going to get shot at,' he said. 'That's a fact. I'm not trying to scare you. I'm just telling you what will happen.'

We started to worry because he was pointing towards an area where we were likely to be sent.

There was now a real risk that we were going to be shot at and that we'd have to shoot back. It was one thing wearing your weapon on your back all day, but another thing to have to swing it around and kill someone.

The Americans also told us they didn't have an engineer contingent with them. Instead, they used a local Afghan route-clearance team, known to us as 'stick pokers'. We called them stick pokers because they didn't use metal detectors, just their eyes and sticks, which they constantly poked into the ground. They had an exceptional knowledge of the terrain and were highly regarded by the Americans. They were very good. Maybe too good. The Americans had an arrangement where they paid a significant sum for each IED found. And apparently, they were cashing in by planting their own IEDs and then finding them. The locals saw an opportunity to make some coin and they took it. We were hoping to be able to use them in our upcoming patrols because we had no intelligence on this area. The stick pokers were the only group that had conducted searches here. They didn't keep data or make reports, so we'd be going in blind. We felt we needed their expertise to ensure our safety.

Our worst fears were realised when we were told we'd be embarking on a five-day clearance patrol during the American shutdown, without the stick pokers. And that we'd be going to the area the American had warned us was unsafe. Our mission was to reclaim a checkpoint that had been abandoned by Afghan local police two months earlier amid an insurgent push. We were to regain and fortify it and re-establish it with a controlling force of thirty Afghan soldiers.

The checkpoint was on an elevated position that overlooked three valleys. Two of the valleys ran into separate provinces, so it was deemed to be of high strategic value.

We had many concerns about the mission. The region was dangerous and would be even more dangerous during the shutdown. We wanted to use the local expertise, given we had zero intelligence. We'd been told there were IEDs out there, but no one could tell us where or what type.

Thirdly, we didn't have a search dog. The one assigned to us had been sent home to Australia after being diagnosed with cancer. This poor dog got sick a couple of days before we left TK and went home before we had a chance to work with him. He was sorely missed. A search dog is so much better at finding ordnance and IEDs than a human. Its nose is a thousand times better than the best metal detector, so it was a massive loss of capability.

***

'I'm scared of this one, Mum. We're going out on a patrol tomorrow and I don't have a good feeling. There are just so many factors making this one more dangerous.' It was the night before we were due to depart, and I'd taken the satellite phone from the sergeant and walked away from the group. Clutching the oversized handpiece, I went far enough away so that no one heard what I was about to say. 'I haven't had this feeling before,' I continued.

I'm not sure how Mum reacted. I'm sure she did her best to reassure me and tell me it would be okay. It was a strange call because I couldn't go into specifics. I couldn't tell her what the operation was or why I was worried. I could only tell her that I was worried, that it would be a hard patrol, and I'd be in danger.

I didn't want to upset Mum but I felt I needed to let it out. I'd never expressed my fears to anyone, so I'm sure it would have been a shock.

After the call, I spoke to Livo and was relieved to learn that he shared my concerns and was willing to do something about it. He raised our concerns with our engineer liaison officer, and asked for a search dog. The request was denied. So he asked for the mission to be delayed. Again, the request was denied. Then he asked to use a local route-clearance team. The requested was denied.

We were told we had to proceed as planned.

***

The day began with a brilliant sunrise. A hot, clear day looming, our team of thirty-five headed away from Anaconda and into the unknown. Our plan was to search the road today, to search the checkpoint tomorrow, and then use the final three days of our operation to reinforce and then defend the checkpoint.

We had twenty-five combat soldiers, a signal man, an officer, four drivers and us four engineers. We were also accompanied by thirty Afghan infantry soldiers.

We headed out on the same road we came in on, before hooking a left. Into the *dasht*. East. Towards the area we'd been warned about.

We were bouncing along in our Bushmasters, about forty-five minutes into the trip, on high alert. Like always, we were out front, leading the way. Our Bushmaster came to a sudden stop, brakes jammed, something wrong.

'Righto, boys,' shouted Livo, who was sitting in the front of the Bushmaster. 'Looks like we have some work to do.'

Gear in hand, out of the vehicle, I saw Toyota HiLux utes, all twisted and torn metal. I saw the blast craters next. Deep and wide, they were everywhere. It was a scene of utter destruction. It was also a textbook VP. A picture-perfect place for IEDs. I looked towards the car carcasses and knew that whoever had been in those vehicles was now dead. Most likely the Afghan police from the checkpoint, given they often drove HiLux utes. I shuddered as I imagined the event that caused this.

'All right,' Livo said. 'Shake out and let's get to it.'

The four of us had to find a safe way through what could be a minefield. We decided to search the area with the craters first. While the cratered area may seem like an obvious place for IEDs, we figured that the insurgents were more likely to plant IEDs on the road, which was inviting and looked safe. We figured the blast area, where no untrained soldier would go, would be the least likely place to find IEDs. The safest path. We weren't trying to find IEDs. We were trying to avoid them. Looking for a way through.

We got through the cratered area fairly quickly. Even though there were bits of blown-up cars and steel shrapnel everywhere, we didn't hit too much metal. And we were right. There were no IEDs.

We got about 100 metres past the blast craters and decided to go into an unconventional formation: two at the front, one in the middle and one at the back. The guy at the back, Pitch, was in a roaming role. He went out to the side of the track and just ahead of Wertsy and me, who were on the track.

'Hey, I got something,' Pitch yelled.

We stopped, took a knee and let him go to work.

Pitch got down on his guts and had a feel with his hands.

'Yep,' he said. 'Something here.'

He then pulled out his paintbrush.

'A battery pack,' he said.

He then stood up and marked out the area, his bright orange plastic pegs forming a 'T', the bottom of the letter pointing towards the danger. He then began to search the surrounding area with his metal detector. He went down on his stomach after finding another metal signature. Again, he used his hands, the ground sandy and soft.

'Got the rest of it,' he said, not needing the paint brush or a knife to find the other half of the IED.

He'd found the charge, a white speaker cable linking the second find back to the first, which was the explosive.

He marked out the trigger, took pictures, and then we all combined to mark out a safe passage back to the convoy. We discussed two options: blow it up or call in the experts. Given that it was the first IED we'd found, we decided to call in the Explosive Ordnance Disposal (EOD) team, the guys with the bomb suits and robots.

Ready and waiting back at FOB Anaconda, the EOD was part of what was called a Quick Response Force or QRF. They got to us in about forty-five minutes. They had the choice to blow it up; pull it out with a robot or rope and then disarm it; or put on a bomb suit, remove it by hand and then disarm it. Generally, you want to disarm it, study the device and log the intelligence. But given the other dangers in this region, the EOD tech on duty decided on the safest option, to blow in place (BIP).

We watched on as the EODs used a robot to place the explosive. Quite compact and easy to transport, the robot looks nothing like C-3PO or Rosie from the *Jetsons*. It does, however, look a little like WALL-E. Similar to the Pixar character because it runs on tracks and is a comparable size, the bomb-disposal robot is a mini tank-like machine with two metal arms. I was like the kid who didn't get the remote-controlled car for Christmas as the operator sent it off carrying an explosive in one arm and a shotgun, used as an alternative means of detonation, in the other. When it reached the IED, the robot stopped, placed the explosive device next to the IED and came back with a cable. We all took cover in the Bushmaster as the countdown began.

Ten, nine, eight ... and, finally, one!

Boom!

Dust rained down. I felt the blast go through the Bushmaster and my body. It was a big explosion, which meant it was a big bomb, definitely meant for a vehicle. The Toyotas never stood a chance. The EOD tech got out, did a search, and gave the all-clear. They left as fast as they arrived.

We returned to our search formation and got back to work, as you never know what else is out there.

***

We moved slowly when we resumed. Always out of the vehicle and always searching. We were obviously in a dangerous area, so we looked hard and took our time.

The worst fear for a combat engineer is to miss something. To leave an IED behind. For another soldier to be injured – or worse – because you hadn't done your job properly. So we made sure the road was searched and safe before allowing the convoy to crawl on.

Searching only the width of a road, an area just big enough for the convoy, we got through the blast zone without encountering another IED. The terrain soon improved – no blast craters and flat – but still we slowly searched, always out front of the vehicle, every inch of the road checked. Eventually we could see the checkpoint in the distance, high up on the top of a hill and partly obscured by rocks. The road that we'd have to take was long, narrow and wound its way up to the top of the hill.

We reached the bottom of the hill at 4 pm.

'Hold up,' Wertsy yelled.

He'd seen a section of disturbed earth ahead, a 'ground sign'. We all took a knee as he got on his belly and poked.

It turned out to be another IED. Again, we called the EOD but this time they told us they didn't have enough time to come out. That it would soon be dark. Too dangerous. They informed us they'd come out in the morning, first thing. So we called it a day and set up for the night.

We decided to set up a defensive sleeping area – a night harbour – given all the activity in the environs. We searched and marked out a spot, deemed it safe and dug a foot into the ground before erecting a rock wall along the perimeter. This is called a shelf-scrape. Despite the threat of insurgents, I felt pretty safe. And that wasn't because of the rock wall but because of all the guns. With cannons on top of trucks and assault rifles in the hands of soldiers, our weaponry was our best defence.

We were excluded from night-guard duty because of the work we'd done that day – a small but very appreciated gesture from the patrol commander. I rolled out my swag and was out like a light. In the morning, with swags rolled back up and on the top of the 'Bushy', we were told about the twenty van-loads of insurgents.

We thought it had been an uneventful night, but a large force of fighting-age males – believed to be insurgents – were seen using the cover of night to move. The infantry spotters had watched on, but they appeared to be retreating, heading away from FOB Anaconda and away from us.

Phew!

While it was a shock to learn so many suspected insurgents were in the area, it was also a relief to find out they'd been scared away. The size of our force had spooked them, apparently. Still, we didn't know if there were another twenty van-loads of fighting-age males hiding in the hills, lying in wait.

We soon got a call to say the EOD had been delayed. They'd found another IED while making their way out to us. They needed to dispose of it before resuming the trip. So while we waited, we continued to search. Got out our metal detectors and got to it.

BOOM!

Holy shit. What was that?

I'd have never guessed that it was a donkey. Yep. That's right. A donkey. The blast that sent a shock wave throughout the entire valley had been caused by a donkey stepping on an IED. Not far in front of where the QRF had found the IED that had caused their delay, a wandering donkey had stepped on a pressure plate. The nature of the incident caused some to think it was a 'donkey-borne IED' – in other words the bomb had been strapped to the donkey and set off via remote control. But that wasn't the case. The poor animal just wandered into the wrong place at the wrong time.

Still, there was no debate about the danger we faced. We'd now come across four IEDS in thirty-two hours. That was a staggering figure given we hadn't come across a single IED in our first three months. The EOD decided the threat we faced was significant enough for them to join us full-time. Instead of going back to FOB Anaconda, they'd remain with us. It was a safe bet that they'd soon be needed again.

***

Wertsy's find was destroyed by the EOD once they arrived, and we began our push up the hill. We were soon stopped, not by a bomb, but this time a boulder. The behemoth rock was covering half the trail, which was only just wide enough for the larger vehicles in the convoy without the obstacle.

We ordered the convoy to stop so we could examine both the rock and the surrounding area. On foot and accompanied by a small infantry team in case of a fire fight, we slowly made our way towards the boulder. And when I say slowly, I mean really, *really* slowly. Only the width of a car and very tight, the trail leading up to the obstruction was a crater-covered textbook VP. It was also teeming with metal. We got a metal signature hit with almost every sweep of the detector. Treating every one of those hits as if it was an IED, we got on our bellies and went through the entire process, only to find a buried bottle top or a ripped-up Coke can. Shards and scraps, bits and pieces, there was metal everywhere. It was obviously a tactic. They'd thrown wire, shell casings and metal scraps all over the ground to slow us down. There was also a risk that they'd covered the ground in harmless metal to disguise an IED that they'd placed underneath, so we had to search each section twice. We removed the metal that had given the signature, put it in our pocket, and searched again.

Inch by inch, we eventually got to the boulder.

It was huge, the size of small car. There would be no pushing or pulling, no amount of manpower enough to move it an inch. We'd have to blow it up. But with the day almost done, we didn't have time to remove the rock, so we decided to go back and look for another path. Another way up into the checkpoint.

We soon found a suitable alternative and pushed ahead. After two hours of slow going, we came across another established path. It led all the way to the checkpoint entrance, which we could now see. But with night looming, the commander called it a day. We went about setting up our harbour for the night.

***

'Stop,' came the cry. 'Hands up.'

Camp almost set and secure, a man was spotted walking across the hill towards us. Our interpreter repeated the command in Pashto.

The man complied, stopping in his tracks and not moving again until he was searched and given the all-clear. Turns out he'd just wandered over for a chat. He wanted to see what we were doing here. He turned out to be a great source of information, giving us the best intelligence we had. Speaking with the interpreter, he revealed the Afghan police had left about two months earlier. After being attacked every other day, they'd sustained a number of casualties and given up. He also said the insurgents had left IEDs everywhere. He was even able to give us a rough indication of where they were.

Happy that we were in the area and hopeful we could bring peace to his village, the man took a huge risk by talking to us. The Taliban penalty for talking to the enemy was execution.

***

That night, I lay on my back and looked at the stars. What should have been a peaceful and uninterrupted nightscape – stars shining and the moon burning bright – was interrupted by a steady stream of man-made machines. The sky was never quiet – planes, jets and helicopters cut through the dark. And while I couldn't see the drones, I could hear them. They made a distinct and reassuring sound. The busy night sky made me feel safe, the noise reminding me that we were being both watched and protected from above. The same sights and sounds had the opposite effect on insurgents. They were absolutely terrified of our airpower.

Our objective for day three was to search to, and then into, the checkpoint. It was going to be a long slow day of searching after receiving the information the brave local risked his life to give. We searched along the new track, which we'd called the service road, and made pretty good going for a while. Then we got hit after hit. There was rubbish all over the road leading into the checkpoint too. We were getting metal signatures with every sweep. Fatigue soon became an issue. In forty-five degrees and carrying a shitload of gear, I felt like I was struggling to maintain the mental intensity needed for such a dangerous and important job.

Here we go. What's that?

We came across a big coil of barbed wire near the entrance to the checkpoint. A huge length of metal cable had been spread across the road. We suspected the worst. So it was back on our bellies. Prodding and pushing. Dirt swept away with our brushes. We were all relieved to discover the wire was just wire. It wasn't connected to anything or being used to mask another metal object underneath.

Inch by inch – again – we continued, pulling bits of metal and rubbish from the ground with every step. Pockets soon full, we had to pile the metal pieces that we'd pulled from the ground on the side of the road.

We noticed a horseshoe-shaped defensive structure made out of Hesco baskets when we finally reached the entrance to

As a kid, I was always training for a life in the great outdoors. Here I am practising my water skiing. Dad loved racing his boat on Lake Wanaka.

I was 18 when I enlisted in the Australian Army on 12 June 2006. Here I am with the family, my enlistment certificate in my hand. From left: Dad, me, Sophia, Mum and Brent.

2007, and now I'm a qualified combat engineer. I'm on a training exercise in the NT but already hoping to be deployed overseas.

It was an honour to build this bridge for the people of Uaimori, a remote community in the mountains of East Timor that is famous for its freedom fighters. My good mate Shane 'Gibbo' Gibbs is top right.

Our 'brick' in Afghanistan in July 2012. From left: Solomon Hanks, Daniel Livesay, me, Lachlan Patterson, Ryan Werts and Mac Pitcher.

Scanning a road in Afghanistan for Improvised Explosive Devices. IEDs caused almost half of military and civilian deaths during the war in Afghanistan.

Talon bomb-disposal robot training at Tarin Kowt base. Harder than it looks and you work up a thirst.

Taken from a helmet camera by one of the guys not long after I stepped on an IED. I'm on the stretcher, being evacuated from the blast site to a helicopter. It was then I said to my mates that I'd go to the Paralympics one day.

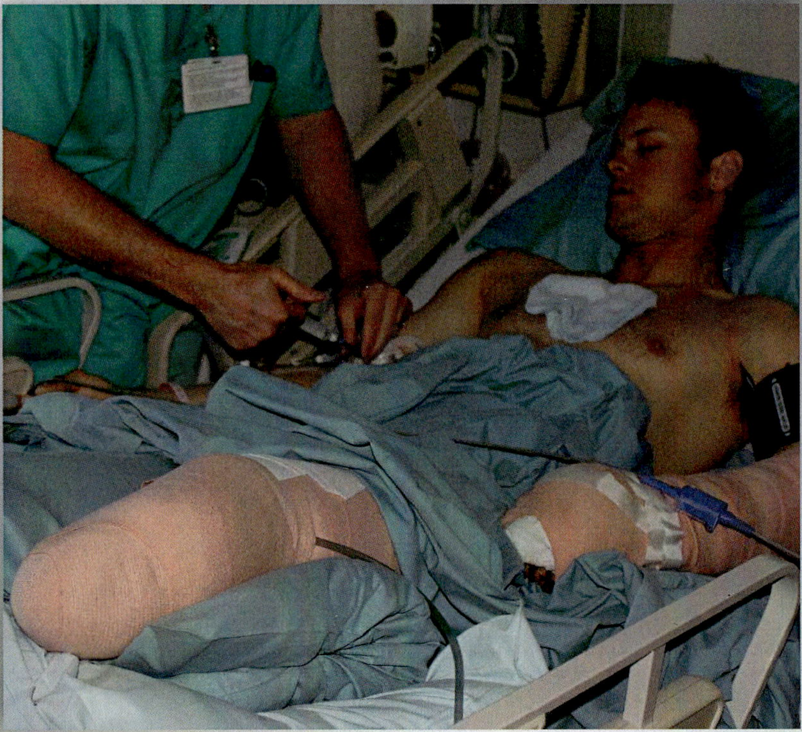

In hospital at Ramstein Airbase, Germany, about two days after I was injured.

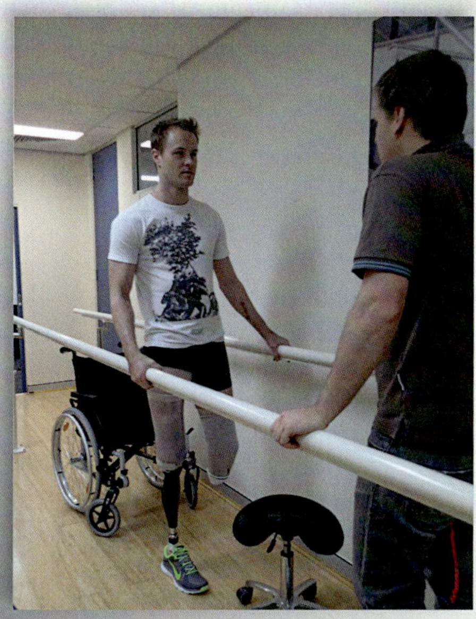

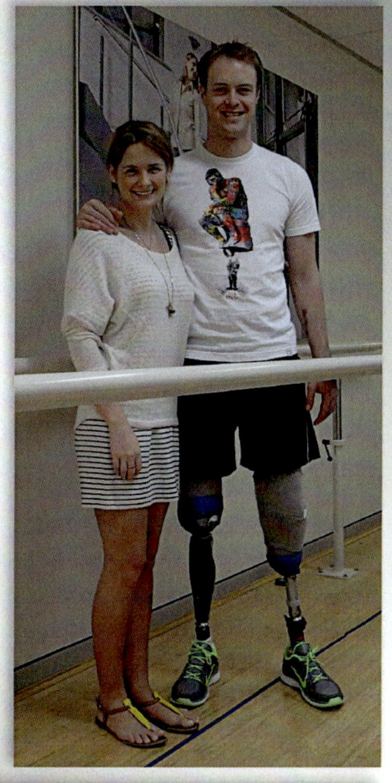

In November 2012 I visited Ottobock in Sydney to be fitted with prosthetic legs. ABOVE: With head Ottobock prosthetist Jens Baufeldt. RIGHT: Standing for the first time since my injury, with Rachel.

Walking at our official welcome-home parade at Enoggera Barracks with Daniel Livesay (left) and Mac Pitcher. The Army had provided a wheelchair but there was no way I was going in that!

Somewhere off the coast of eastern Australia in March 2013, kayaking from Sydney to Brisbane with Dad and 21 other veterans and family as part of a Mates4Mates initiative.

I took up canoeing in 2014. Later that year I represented Australia at the World Championships in Moscow and on the second anniversary of the worst day of my life, I won my first gold medal. Things were looking up. *TASS/Alamy*

On the dais after winning gold at the Rio Paralympics 2016 with Markus Swoboda of Austria (left), and Nick Beighton of Great Britain (right). 'This sport wouldn't be here today if it wasn't for you,' I told Markus. 'You're a true legend.' And he is. I still look up to him. *Al Matthew Stockman/Getty*

In 2016 I was honoured to be made an ambassador for the Invictus Games. Here I am speaking at the announcement that the 2018 Games would be held in Sydney.
Ogilvy PR/AAP

One of the highlights of my life was giving the Anzac Day national address at the Australian War Memorial in 2017. Nearly 40,000 people were there, it was raining, and yep, I was nervous. But it went off without a hitch and I will never forget that morning.
Kym Smith/Newspix

The biggest and best day of my life was 8 June 2019, when I married Rachel Martin. Rach has been my rock and best friend through thick and thin. *Cassandra Ladru*

I've never been one to celebrate. When I won my first gold medal at Tokyo, I was simply relieved. But when I won my second gold medal for the outrigger canoe, I was absolutely ecstatic. The journey to Tokyo had its fair share of hurdles, thanks to COVID. Then, days before the games began, Afghanistan fell after 20 years of war, bringing back some memories. But we got there in the end. If I had my time over, I wouldn't change a thing. *Dean Mouhtaropoulos/Getty*

the checkpoint. We were searching towards them when Livo told us to stop.

'Not now,' he said. It was almost midday. He decided we didn't have enough time to search the baskets, an exhaustive and dangerous process due to the amount of metal and debris around them. We'd section them off, continue with the rest of the search, and come back to them tomorrow. He then told us to take a break. It was welcome news, given we were completely buggered. We sat down in the area next to the Hesco baskets, but inside the line of markers that showed what was safe and what was not.

15

ONE FALSE STEP

THERE I WAS, NEAR the Hesco baskets the next morning, throwing rocks with Pitch in an area that was supposed to be safe and clear. I walked away from him, down the trail, mind fixed on the boulder we had to blow up, and the searches we had to do on what was to be our last day out there. I couldn't wait to get back to the safety and comfort of Anaconda.

And that's when it happened. I stepped on an IED that I'd missed the day before.

BOOM. I was surrounded by sand and blood. The ground was covered red. And then the pain hit me.

'Fuck,' I screamed. 'Fuuuuuccck!'

Some people say that they can't feel any pain after major trauma, but I was in absolute agony. I was in every kind of pain. It shot and it crept. It was sharp and it was dull. It ached and it burnt.

'Argghh!'

My eyelids, my earlobes, my tongue – I was riddled with pain, like I'd been cut by a thousand razors from head to toe, hit by a truck and set on fire.

The blood. Too much blood.

It was then I realised how bad it was. That blood was pouring from my wounds. From where my knees used to be.

Phweert! Phweert!

Geysers gushing, each beat of my heart sending two streams of blood onto the sand.

Stop it. Stop the flow. Stop it or you will die.

But how? I had two spurting wounds and only one pair of hands. It looked as though I was losing more blood from the left.

Or you will die ...

Running out of time, and without a better option, I reached down and put my hands around what I thought was the worst wound. Around the shredded muscle and exposed femur bone.

And then I squeezed.

'Argghh!'

Agony.

The pressure, as much as I could muster, stemmed a little of the flow in the left leg. The right continued the same.

Phwert! Phweert!

I shook my head.

Too much blood.

I'd be dead in a minute. I had to stop the blood.

I let go of my leg and went for a tourniquet: it was my only chance. I reefed the seat belt like strap – that's designed to cut off circulation – from the front of my body armour.

All I had to do was put the loop over my leg – or what was left of it – and pull it tight. I'd then turn a heavy-duty plastic lever to make it as mechanically tight as possible. Then I could move on to the next leg, another tourniquet waiting in a pouch on my arm.

With the lifesaving device in my hand, waiting to be looped, tightened and turned, I reach forward and went for my leg.

What?

My back thudded into the dirt. Lifting my torso by placing my elbows into the ground, I leant forward again.

'Fuck!'

Without my legs, an anchor for the weight of my torso, I could not lean down far enough to reach my wounds. I could not hold myself up long enough to lean over. I was fucked.

Dead.

'Help,' I screamed.

'Kiwi!' came the reply. 'I'm here.'

A saviour.

'Pitch,' I screamed. 'Quick. Get my tourniquets on. PITCH! Get my fucking tourniquets on.'

He was at my side a moment later. 'I got ya, mate,' he said. 'You'll be sweet.' He grabbed the tourniquet that was in my hand. The one that I couldn't get on.

'Watch my nuts,' I screamed. 'Make sure you don't get my nuts.' Yep. With all this going on I was thinking about my testicles. I might have lost my legs but I was going to make sure I kept my balls. I think Pitch might have even laughed.

'Sweet, mate,' he said. 'I won't get ya nuts.' He looped the tourniquet over my thigh and ripped it tight.

'Argggggh! Fuck!' Don't let anyone ever tell you that tightening a tourniquet doesn't hurt. It was excruciating. I looked down at the leg that was screaming with pain.

I howled again as Pitch pulled the plastic lever and tightened it beyond what he could do with his pulling power alone.

I took a deep breath. I looked down at my leg.

Stopped. No blood.

Well at least from that leg.

'Get another tourniquet.'

Pitch ripped a tourniquet from the pouch on his chest.

'Argh! Fuuuuckkk!'

I closed my eyes and swallowed the pain. But it didn't work. The pain stayed. I was about to scream again when I opened my eyes. The soldiers stopped my screams. I saw them come around the bend: Wertsy, Livo and Ash Murtagh. The cavalry was coming. I pushed myself up onto my elbows and watched them charge across the sand. They came fast. I could soon see their faces, all white, shocked and filled with fear.

'I'm sweet,' I said when they got close enough. 'I'll be fine.'

They were all looking at me thinking, *No, he's fucked!* So, I gave them a fake assurance. For a moment I was more worried about them. And then I started going into shock.

My breathing had become speedy and shallow. Too quick. I knew I was going into shock but I didn't know how to stop it. I figured a distraction might work, so I took charge.

'You need to get the IV kit out,' I said. 'You need to prime the line and make sure there's no air in it.'

Wertsy pulled the cord on the front of my vest that releases the body armour. He needed to get my gear off to check my torso for wounds.

'It's stuck,' he said after giving it a reef.

'Let me do it,' I said, angrily grabbing the cord. I heaved the cord and released the armour. In this motion I punched Wertsy right in the chest.

'Sorry,' I said as he fell on his arse.

I turned my attention back to the IV. 'Find a vein,' I said. 'Strap it and ... '

I stopped mid-sentence as the first-aid kit exploded. The soldier attempting to open it had ripped it and the contents had gone everywhere. He fumbled and searched for the IV.

Another soldier arrived. He was Lance Corporal Court, or 'Courty'. A senior soldier and like me a combat first-aider. A lifesaver, in fact.

'I'll do that,' Courty said, grabbing the IV. 'Move out of the way.'

'What do we do now?' Livo asked Courty.

I interrupted. 'Some morphine would be good, eh?' I suggested.

'How do we do that?' Livo asked.

Shit! I was the only combat first-aider in my squad.

'Snap the vial,' I said. 'Grab a blunt drawing needle and draw exactly 2.5 milligrams. Now change the needle to a sharp-giving needle.'

'Where do you want it?' Livo asked.

'I don't care,' I replied. 'Just fucking stab me.'

So he did, although I don't know where. I waited for the relief.

There was none.

Courty was still attempting to insert the IV. Another two soldiers were working on my legs. I pushed myself onto my elbows to see what they were doing.

'Make sure they're tight,' I said after seeing they were applying bandages over what was left of my legs.

'Sit back,' Courty said. 'Relax.'

I slumped back into the sand. And that's when it hit me. This wasn't good. *I* wasn't good. This was bad.

I started to sob. Not because I thought I was going to die, but because I knew I was going to live.

I've lost my fucking legs!

I knew I'd never be able to live a normal life again. I knew I was fucked. That my life was over. Then I thought of Rachel. *She's going to kill me*, I thought. *I'm going to have to cancel our holiday. She's going to be filthy.*

I have no idea why I thought that, but that's what was going through my mind while I was bleeding out on the ground. Yep. I thought of how my girlfriend would react to a cancelled holiday. Go figure.

'What's your pain scale out of ten?' Courty asked.

It's a standard question to determine if more morphine is needed and how much.

'A thousand,' I said. 'It's a fucking thousand.'

I was jabbed again.

Ahhhh. Finally.

The second shot of morphine worked. He dosed me up good. Real good. The pain slowly subsided, from a thousand to ten and then finally to four. To tolerable. Everything started to blur. A sweet fuzz.

***

'My pendant,' I shouted. 'Where's my pendant?'

I was about to be transferred to a stretcher when I noticed I'd lost my pendant. An image of St Christopher pressed into silver, Tyson and Mike, my friends from school, had given it to me before I left. The pendant had history. Tyson and Mike had been co-owners of it for years. They'd passed it between themselves, giving it to whoever was about to go on a trip. They decided to give it to me before I left for Afghanistan. Now I couldn't find it.

'You have to find it,' I said. 'It has got to be here somewhere.'

It should have been in one of the two side-pockets of my pants. It wasn't. In fact, I couldn't even find the pockets. They'd been blown off in the blast.

'You need to find it,' I said. 'It's on the end of a necklace.'

The boys looked everywhere, metal detectors and all, but couldn't find it.

'There's shit everywhere,' one of them said. 'The ground's covered with shrapnel.'

I burst into tears. I was devastated that the pendant was gone.

***

'Argh!' A shot of pain snapped me out of my morphine-induced bliss.

They'd just rolled me onto the stretcher. 'Be careful!'

'Relax,' I was told. 'The chopper will be here soon. We're moving you to the extraction point.'

I then cracked a joke.

'Damn,' I said. 'They were brand new boots. Lucky I thought they were shit. I really didn't like those boots. The uncomfortable pieces of shit they were.'

Away from the pile of bloodied bandages, I was being stretchered across the desert. Two on each side, they moved as fast as they could.

'Don't you fucking drop me,' I yelled as the stretcher rocked. I reckon I said it another ten times.

We were on uneven ground, cutting across a sand hill, and I felt like I was going to roll out. The guys on my left were about two feet lower than the guys on my right. I didn't have my legs to keep me anchored. I started leaning towards my right, trying to help. I was probably hindering. Holding onto the right edge of the stretcher with all my might, looking up the hill, I saw a group of Afghan soldiers perched in a rocky outcrop. They were all just looking at me.

'Fuck you,' I screamed. 'Fuck you! You lazy pieces of shit. This is your fault. Fuck you and fuck your shithole of a country. Fight your own fucking war!'

I'd later regret screaming those words. But right there, on a stretcher with no legs, I was full of rage. I was full of pain. I needed someone to blame, so I blamed them.

'Fuck you!' I screamed again.

I was two metres away from the extraction point when someone asked me how I was doing. My rage had run out.

'It'll be all good, boys, I'll just get to the Paralympics, but it won't be in the green and gold, it'll be in the black and white.' They responded with a laugh. 'I suppose you can walk to the chopper then?' someone said.

***

We were about fifty metres from where the helicopter was expected to land. I was placed in a shelf-scrape next to a Bushmaster. There was a tarp over the top, but they positioned me in the only spot where the light came through. All I could see was bright light, the sun belting into my eyes.

I realised I'd knocked out my IV lines, either while trying to keep myself on the stretcher as they carted me across the hill, or when they put me on the ground.

I apologised profusely to Courty. 'Ah shit,' I said. 'So sorry, mate. You're going to have to do it again. Shit. Sorry. Sorry.'

I suddenly became concerned about Pitch. I thought I'd heard someone crying. Looked like a couple of soldiers were being consoled. Pitch was only twenty, so I feared he'd struggle to deal with what he'd just seen. I called Livo over.

'Mate, you gotta look after Pitch,' I said. 'Make sure he's okay.'

'Sweet, no worries. I'll keep an eye on him,' he said as he turned away.

And that's when I had an epiphany.

This is it. The end. I'm going to die.

I realised that I was in a bad way. I couldn't see or hear a rescue chopper. I thought I was done for.

'Livo,' I said.

He turned back and moved towards me.

'I don't want to die,' I said as I started to cry. 'I don't want to die.'

'You're not going to die,' he said. 'Help is coming. Relax. We've got it under control.'

I didn't believe him. He stood up and walked away. I then saw Pitch just outside the shelf-scrape. I called him over, not realising the enormity of what I was going to put on him.

'I need you to go on to my laptop and get my letters,' I said. 'There's a folder on the desktop and I need you to print all the letters out and get them to my family.'

'Don't be stupid,' he said. 'You won't need them. You'll be out of here in no time.'

I then noticed that Pitch had blood on his face. I thought it was mine. I reached up and tried to wipe it away but couldn't. I later found out it wasn't my blood. It was his. He'd been injured too.

And that's when I heard the choppers in the distance. Two Blackhawks thundering in.

***

The rotors picked up the scorching dirt and dust and spat them onto my naked body. Green smoke swirling, a Blackhawk attempting to land, I was using the foil blanket that had been covering my bloodied torso to shield my face. The hot baked dirt that was slapping into my bare skin should have hurt. But it didn't. I was completely numb. Peppered by rotor-wash – rocks and dirt shooting into my skin – I felt like I was being tickled. At least morphine was doing its job. I was no longer in any pain.

I pulled the thermal blanket from my face when the sandstorm suddenly stopped.

The helicopter had gone. All I could see was swirling green smoke and dust. No Blackhawk.

The storm resumed and grit smacked me in the head. I pulled the blanket back over my head to shield my eyes. I didn't find out until later that two US Army Blackhawk helicopters had been sent from TK to rescue me. The first had attempted to land but pulled out after being bullied by the wind. And that's when the second swooped, the pilot taking advantage of a small lull and attacking from a more wind-friendly angle.

I heard the voices next: someone screaming and someone else screaming back. I pulled the blanket from my eyes and saw the helicopter. It was about fifty metres away. The loadmaster was hanging out the side and shouting at a soldier on the ground.

'Ready?' the boys said.

But they lifted me without giving me the chance to respond. I bounced on the stretcher, up and down as they charged across the dirt and towards the chopper.

They slid me into the belly of the Blackhawk.

The loadmaster slammed the door shut and we took off. I suddenly felt like I was too close to the door. Like it had been shut on my legs. Like I'd have been dangling out the side of the chopper if the door wasn't closed. But it was.

Impossible.

It didn't make any sense. And then I remembered I didn't have legs. Not any more. I pushed myself up and saw that my knees were up against the door. I reached back, above my head, and grabbed the top of the stretcher. I reefed myself to the other door so it was against my head. Maybe I wanted to pretend that my legs were still there.

That's when I saw the medic. The newcomer grabbed my left arm and ripped the IVs clean out. Apparently, he wasn't happy with the way they'd been put in. I was. They'd saved my life. Anyway, he replaced them all.

He then had a look at my hand.

Hand? It's my legs, you idiot! I've lost my legs.

I had no idea, but my hand and arm had been injured too: broken bones, burns, and shrapnel stuck in my skin.

I suddenly became aware of my breathing. I was panting like I'd just finished a running race. I then noticed how dry my throat was, full of dust and not a drop of saliva.

'Water,' I said, weakly.

Seeing my lips move but not hearing a thing, the medic leaned in.

'WATER,' I said, as loud as I could.

He grabbed a bottle of water, removed the lid and put it in my hand. My good hand. I took a gulp and spat it straight out. I shook my head and went again, this time managing to swallow. Suddenly I wished I had spat that mouthful out too.

Idiot. Nil by mouth. You can't drink before surgery.

I have no idea why I had such a ridiculous thought. But I had it. And that's when I broke down. When I burst into tears again.

I ended up crying for about five minutes. Suddenly and inexplicably overwhelmed, I balled like a baby. Looking back, I think I let it all out because I realised I was going to be okay. Until this point I was completely committed to surviving. I was worried about tourniquets and IVs. About morphine and the extraction. But now I was in the hands of an expert, there was nothing left for me to do.

Except cry.

I only stopped crying because I passed out. Finally. I think I had prevented myself from passing out until this point because I felt I needed to help. Thought I'd never wake up if I went to sleep.

You'll be okay ... That's the last thing I remember thinking before losing consciousness. That I'd live. That life would go on.

***

CRACK! The sound of the door being reefed open woke me up. I didn't know where I was or what was happening. I didn't have a clue until I was being rolled under the rotor-blades, transferred onto a gurney and being pushed towards an ambulance.

IED. Hospital. Help.

I was only conscious for a moment, the world going black as soon as I was loaded into the back of the ambulance.

'What the fu—'

I lashed out, grabbing the first thing in front of me. Again, I had no idea where I was or what was happening. It didn't take me long to work it out. I was in a hospital and I was holding a fistful of one of the most senior Australian soldiers in Afghanistan.

Shit!

I quickly let go of the RSM, the man who had declared war on ASODs. I learned later that he jumped out of his skin and turned white when the seemingly lifeless body he was looking at suddenly started grabbing him by the shirt.

I passed out again.

'Hey, Kiwi.' A familiar voice brought me back.

I looked up and saw TJ, a medic I knew well.

'Hey, TJ. How are y—'

Anaesthetic. I was out again.

I later found out that one of my mates had worked on me without knowing who I was.

'Kiwi?' he asked TJ as I went to sleep.

He wiped some of the dirt and blood from my face.

'Oh fuck ... '

***

The boys would later tell me about the IED that I'd stepped on. Apparently, it was unusual and sophisticated. They believed the one that had taken my legs, and the others they found in the area, had all been built by the same bomb maker. He was using an uncommon compound that we don't often see and that didn't register on any of our explosion detection tests. His bombs employed a complicated chemistry of potassium chlorate rather than the stock-standard fertiliser.

As well as using this far more difficult and explosive cocktail, the sneaky fucker had also used carbon rods to make the trigger in the pressure plate. Most triggers are made with some sort of metal, so the carbon helped hide the trigger from detection. He'd taken the carbon rods from a D-cell battery and repurposed them for his deadly device.

He also had a strange signature. This particular bomb maker, the bloke who almost killed me, housed all of his battery packs in handmade wooden boxes. We can only presume it was a misguided attempt to mask the metal signature of his battery packs by covering them with wood, which, by the way, is impossible. I wore the box on my body after the blast, splinters all through my skin.

I have to say a big thanks to the blokes who saved my life. I wouldn't be here now if it wasn't for Pitch, who risked his own life by rushing to my aid. Who ignored procedures and protocol to give me first aid. The area around me should have been deemed unsafe following the blast. It should have been searched before anyone came near me.

All the soldiers who came into the blast zone after Pitch also risked their own safety to apply the lifesaving tourniquets and give me IV fluid and also comfort me in such a distressing time. They're the reason I'm still alive. I'd have bled out on the ground if I'd had to wait for them to search the area and deem it safe.

Then there was Courty. His ability to keep calm and ensure that everyone stayed on task also helped save me. He showed exceptional knowledge, skill and courage. I'd have been a goner without the IV.

Livo, Wertsy, Trooper Dane Woods and Private Ash Murtagh also put their lives on the line for me. They applied bandages, gave me encouragement and carried me to the extraction point. Livo held my hand the entire time I was being stretchered back to base.

Lieutenant Tony Harris, our patrol commander, also did his bit by keeping his cool. He was the one who made sure all the radio messages got through. He was the one who got the choppers to me.

And lastly, the chopper teams. The helicopters had come from TK. I was later told they were concerned about the threat of being shot down because of all the recent activity. Apparently, they were considering waiting for an Apache gunship to become available for a protecting escort. Thankfully they didn't. They chose to put themselves at risk to come for me. They got to me within forty-five minutes of the first call. They talk about the 'golden hour' when it comes to medivac rescues. The chance of survival is significantly increased if the injured person is delivered to hospital within an hour. The Blackhawk teams, including the Australian flight medic who treated me, knew they couldn't have done the job in that time had they waited for an Apache. So thanks to all. I'm eternally grateful.

The only person I blame for what happened to me is myself. I should have found the IED. I searched that area the previous day and missed it. In the end I'm glad that I was the one who stepped on it. I wouldn't have been able to forgive myself had someone else been injured or killed because I hadn't done my job properly.

16

SAVING SAPPER MCGRATH

I FINALLY WOKE UP. Heaved my heavy eyes open and looked into the fog. For a moment I didn't know where I was. Or what had happened.

I tried to wipe away the whitewash with the back of my eyelids.

Blink. Blink. Blink.

The fog began to clear. I saw white walls and single beds. I smelt bleach.

A hospital.

I looked down at my body. Towards my legs.

Gone.

I suddenly remembered everything: the blast, the initial treatment and the extraction. Everything up to hearing and seeing TJ. But while I knew I was in a hospital, I had no idea which hospital. I was facing a glass wall, which looked out onto a strange base. I wasn't in TK. I had no idea where I was. Or who the person next to me was. A blonde woman with blue eyes, wearing a dark green Australian Air Force flight suit, was sitting next to my bed reading a book.

'Where am I? What's going on?'

'Oh hi,' said the stranger as she put down her book. 'My name's Sally and I'm here to look after you. We're on Bagram Air Base about ninety kilometres north of Kabul. We'll be here for the next few hours. A medical extraction flight will then take us to Germany for further treatment. I'm a flight nurse and I'll be with you the whole time. I'm here to help and get you whatever you need.'

I looked at my legs again. What was left. Everything was missing below my knees, which were both wrapped up in heavy grey bandages. The bandages were clean, no blood, but a series of tubes was protruding from the bandages – drains I guessed; puss and infectious muck being pumped out.

I looked around the room and saw the other wounded soldiers. The room was full of injured men. It was a horror show. Blown up or shot, they wore slings and were wrapped in bandages. One soldier was wearing a halo brace on his leg to hold his shattered bone together. There were at least ten men, some more injured than me, some less, but all in pain and seriously hurt.

I soon worked out they were all American. I was the only Australian.

'Is Pitch okay?' I asked Sally. 'He isn't here too? Please tell me he didn't have to come here too.'

Sally assured me he was okay. She then told me about the eighteen hours I'd missed. And the two surgeries that had saved my life.

***

They'd operated on me in TK. In the first of the three lifesaving surgeries, they'd stopped the bleeding and given me blood. Although it was not a fully equipped hospital, the team of doctors clamped, cleaned and bandaged my wounds. They did enough to stabilise me and make sure I was well enough to be flown to a better-equipped hospital in Kandahar, about 160 kilometres south of Tarin Kowt.

Still completely unconscious, I was taken straight in for more emergency surgery when I arrived there. That surgery stabilised me to the point where I could be flown off to Bagram Air Base, about 500 kilometres to the north-east. There I'd wait for a flight out of Afghanistan.

I was out for all three surgeries and both flights. Bagram Air Base was about the size of Sydney airport. A huge facility with a huge hospital, it even had a KFC. I shit you not.

I was loaded onto a C-17 later that night for the eight-hour flight to Ramstein Air Base, a US facility near Kaiserslautern for yet more surgery. With Sally by my side, I was carried into the gigantic military medical plane and transferred to a bunk-like stretcher that was bolted to the wall. The worst of the wounded were double-stacked and strapped down; sixteen of us in all. The rest, those who didn't need to be horizontal, sat in seats. There were about thirty of them, faces wrapped in bandages, arms in slings, tubes, wires and monitors everywhere.

The sight of all the wounded soldiers was overwhelming. Horrifying. There were two guys up the front of the plane on ventilators, having surgery mid-flight.

It was the moment I realised how bad this war was. A whole plane full of shot and blown-up men. And this flight wasn't a one-off. Three planeloads of injured soldiers were flown out of Bagram that day. It was a huge reality check. The human toll of this war was suddenly and graphically revealed. I had no idea that so many soldiers were being injured until I boarded this flight. I was part of this war but had no idea things were this bad. That so many were being hurt, even killed. And this on top of the enormous toll on the Afghan people.

I drifted in and out of consciousness during the flight. Sally was by my side the entire time. Other than the two upfront, I was the only soldier with a full-time nurse. It wasn't because I was more injured than them, but because I was the only Aussie on the plane and it was policy to have an Australian medical officer with an Australian soldier.

We landed at Ramstein Air Base just on sunrise and were transferred to a bus that had been converted for medical escorts – basically, a really big ambulance. Landstuhl Hospital, another US military facility, was only a couple of kilometres away. I was taken to the ICU unit and transferred to a bed. A nurse came to greet me. I took one look at her and thought, *She's stunning!* Looked like I was going to live.

The nurse's name was Anna-Maria Saenz and she was a US Navy nurse. Anna-Maria had come in to relieve Sally, who went to take a well-deserved break. A doctor came in next and informed me that I required several more operations. That I'd be in and out of surgery for at least a week.

***

'Hi Mum,' I said after I finally got the opportunity to call home. 'I'm okay. I feel fine. I'm being looked after and everything is good. I'm alive. That's the main thing.'

It was both a short and strange call. There were no tears and little emotion. Just matter-of-fact. Mum also told me that she and Dad were about to leave for Germany. That they'd be by my side soon.

My parents had received a knock on the door just hours after the blast, at about the same time I was having my first operation. It was 9 pm in Brisbane, and Mum thought Brent, my cheeky teenage brother, was in some sort of trouble when she saw the uniformed men standing on her porch.

What's he done now? she thought, thinking the men were the Queensland Police.

She then realised the uniforms were military. I'm sure, for a moment at least, she thought the worst. Lieutenant Colonel Matthew Galton, the commanding officer of the 6th Engineer Support Regiment, and Captain Isaac Khan, the regiment's padre, were quick to tell her that I was alive. Injured and in a serious condition, but alive. I believe Mum took the difficult news well. She's a very strong person and has always been good in a crisis. Nothing seems to affect her. She just gets on with it.

Sophia, fourteen at the time, and Brent, eighteen, were also home. I'm not sure how they reacted. Dad, who worked in the mines, wasn't home. Mum called him with the bad news, which he didn't take so well. Dad is a very kind and emotional person, and he struggled to deal with it at first. He left work straight away and rushed home to be with the family. I later learned that Matt and Isaac were a huge help. They stayed with Mum and Dad and provided support and comfort as my parents came to terms with what had happened.

I hadn't spoken to Rachel yet. Mum told me she was also attempting to get to Germany. When Mum had given Rach the news, she was obviously shocked and upset, but aside from being the smartest woman I know, she's also one of the strongest. Right up there with my mum. She left Invercargill, a small town on the southern tip of New Zealand, where she was on a university placement, as soon as she found out, travelled north to a relative's house, and then on to Queenstown to spend time with some of my best mates from school and plan her trip to Germany.

***

I was wheeled into surgery about eight hours after my arrival in Germany. They cleaned out my wounds, removing all the dirt, splinters and shrapnel, to reduce the chance of infection.

I was introduced to the Australian trauma team that had been flown in to oversee my transition home after surgery. Alex Douglas, an Australian Air Force doctor specialising in ICU, anaesthetic and medical retrieval, was in charge, accompanied by two Australian trauma nurses. Alex explained she'd be taking over my treatment plan, and laid out the road ahead. She also told me that they were going to remove what was remaining of my lower right leg. The reason they were taking more of my limbs was that the bones below my right knee were splinters. There was nothing left down there that the doctors could use to form some sort of a functional limb, so the decision was to take it off at the knee and leave me with just the femur on the right and I'd keep my left knee and the tibia.

My parents arrived the next night. Mum came in and gave me a hug. She was fine but Dad was crying.

'I'll be okay,' I reassured him.

It was a little awkward hugging them both with all the tubes and wires. I had a central line, an IV line, a series of drains, a catheter, and I was hooked up to an ECG. I don't remember much else about our reunion. In fact, most of my stay in the hospital is a blur. I had several operations, in and out of surgery every thirty-six hours. I was loaded up on painkillers, the super-heavy type.

***

I was suddenly awake. Head off the pillow and scared stiff. I frantically reached for the call button. Terrified, I grabbed it and pressed, pressed and pressed.

The nurse rushed in and was soon standing beside my bed. 'What's wrong?' he said. 'What is it?'

At that point I realised I hadn't been blown up. Again.

I told the nurse that I'd been drifting off to sleep, exhausted. And then suddenly, I was back in Afghanistan. About to take my final step.

BOOOOM!

I was awake – but it wasn't over. I could feel the blast. My face felt like it was on fire. The shock was reverberating across my cheeks and in my head. I couldn't remember feeling anything on my face at the time of blast, but my brain had obviously stored the trauma and was now serving it back. It scared the absolute shit out of me. I wasn't in pain or covered in dirt, but I felt like I had just stepped on the IED again.

'You've been through some serious stuff,' the nurse said. 'It's normal. You're going to have plenty of bad dreams.'

Great. So PTSD would be my next hurdle.

I was taken out of the ICU after three days and probably three surgeries – I wasn't keeping count – and placed in a room with three Americans. I soon learned that they'd also been injured in an IED blast. They'd been driving along in a Humvee when they were hit. The guy across from me had some broken bones, nothing too serious. The guy on my left had injured his arm and leg, again not too bad. But the guy on my right was in a bad way. He'd been driving the vehicle and copped the worst of it. I will never forget the noises he made – or the smell of charred skin – when the medics came in to debride his burns. The screams chilled me to my core. Dried layers of skin and sores were ripped from his body, and the flesh underneath still stank of smoke. While there were no flames, not here in the hospital, he smelt like he was being burnt by a fresh fire. Being witness to his agony was probably the worst part of my ordeal. I just wanted his pain to stop.

When I was moved out of the ICU, I contacted Rachel. Off my face on opioids, I decided against making a phone call. Instead, I made a public post on her Facebook page.

Hey Rach, I'll call you soon. Just about to have a nap.

It was there for all to see. I called her later that day and she was obviously a bit bemused about my first communication to her since I was almost killed. But she quickly forgave me and told me she loved me. That she was sorry about what had happened but glad I was okay. She also told me she was having some trouble getting to Germany. Rachel didn't have an Australian passport. As a Kiwi, the Australian Government couldn't help her get the paperwork she needed to get into the hospital, which was on a US military base. I ended up telling her not to worry about coming. That I'd be home soon and there was nothing she could do here anyway. I was progressing well and had been told I might be able to fly back to Australia in a week. Taking up an offer from Defence HQ to speak to Dr Alex Douglas, Rachel was given an update on my condition and what was to come. Being a medical student, she had a few questions and Alex was able to provide clarification.

The doctors came in with my parents a couple of days after I left the ICU and drew the curtains.

'Okay, I'm going to remove your bandages and give you a look,' a doctor said.

I hadn't seen the extent of the damage yet, bandages always hiding the truth. And I didn't really want to. I wasn't ready to confront the full extent of my injuries. But I also knew this moment would come. That I'd see the damage done.

They slowly removed the bandages from my left leg first, layer by layer, reality a step closer with each unravelling.

'Okay,' the doctor said when the last bandage was removed. 'I'll explain what we've done.'

It wasn't a pretty sight, all bruises and wounds. The IED had devastated my left leg. But I did my best to look on the bright side. I knew it would have been a lot worse without the outstanding work of the doctors. They then started to remove the bandages on my other leg. The right leg. The bad leg.

I was expecting the worst.

I could see that the wound went right up to my groin before the bandages were fully removed. They'd packed that area with a long grey sheet of some sort. They told me the odd-looking bandage was to keep the wound clean and I'd require further surgery back in Australia. They kept unwinding the bandages and then I suddenly saw something familiar. Something on the end of my leg. A silver fern.

I'd had the Kiwi emblem tattooed on my right calf while based in Darwin. On my right calf, not on the flesh above my right knee. I was suddenly in shock. The replaced tattoo was a reality check. I was looking at a tattooed stub.

It broke me.

A shocking sight, I cried and cried and cried. I still find it hard to explain the emotions. Just six days before this moment, I was walking around a mountainside on healthy, strong legs. Now, looking down, I saw stitches, pumps and pipes, torn flesh and blood. I was suddenly devastated. Thinking ahead for the first time, I didn't know who I'd be or what life would be like.

I was lucky I had family and friends to support me. Once the army lifted an order restricting my contact to immediate family, a flood of uplifting messages came pouring in. I received beautiful notes of support and encouragement from all over the world. And I was finally able to speak to my engineering team, who were still in Afghanistan. Following my accident, they'd been deemed technically unoperational and were back on base in TK, so we arranged a time and got on the phone.

I spoke to all three of them: Livo, Wertsy and Pitch. I was relieved to learn that Pitch was okay. He told me he'd suffered a concussion and some minor cuts in the blast and had been airlifted to Kandahar for treatment. He played down his injuries. I would later learn that he'd spent two hours sitting on a hill after the incident in a near catatonic state.

Hearing their voices was a great feeling, as was knowing they were safe back in TK and away from that bloody checkpoint. I told them I was going well and would soon be heading home. I also told them about the US soldiers I'd just shared the room with, how badly some of them were hurt. I was about to tell them about all the injured soldiers on the plane, about the real cost of war, but I stopped myself. I didn't want them thinking about that. Not when they were still in Afghanistan. Still at war.

Instead I told them about the lost pendant. 'I think they found it in my leg,' I said. 'There's a bit of metal they can't explain stuck in my thigh and they reckon it could be the pendant. I'll never lose it again because they're not going to take it out. It is not doing any damage and they don't want to risk surgery so it's there for good.'

***

A day or so later they told me that the back-to-back surgeries, in and out, put under anaesthetic every thirty-six hours, were over. I was going home. Well, for now at least.

But before I left, I received some shocking news by phone.

'This is RSM of Joint Task Force 633,' the voice said down the line. 'I don't want to beat around the bush here, so I'll cut to the chase. I have very some bad news.'

My heart sank and my mind began to race. *What now. No. Not the boys. Not Livo. Not Wertsy. Not Pitch.*

'Last night there was an incident involving three Australian soldiers,' the voice continued. 'An Afghan soldier opened fire on Sapper James Martin, Lance Corporal Stjepan Milosevic and Private Robert Poate. The result was that they were killed in action and the incident is considered a green-on-blue. I understand you're from the same unit as Sapper Martin?'

'Yes, that's right, sir,' I replied.

He then asked if I'd known James Martin well. I told him I'd spent time with Marto in joint training exercises with the squadron. It was a horrible feeling to find out another soldier I knew had died in this war. But the way I felt would have been nothing compared to what their families were about to be put through.

I later learned that another two Australians had been killed in a separate incident on the same day. Lance Corporal Mervyn McDonald and Private Nathanael Galagher from the Special Operations Task Group had died in a helicopter crash.

It was a dark day for Australia. In fact, 30 August 2012 would be the darkest day in Australia's entire eleven-year campaign.

17

SURGERIES AND STITCHES

'DON'T TOUCH THE BACK OF MY LEGS,' I barked as the two Frankfurt airport employees approached the gurney. The wheelchair that would take me to the A380 was already waiting.

'Did you hear me?' I said after they both failed to reply.

One of them nodded.

'Do you understand?' I had the feeling that neither of them spoke English, but the man nodded again. Then they grabbed me.

'Ah! Fuck!'

It turned out neither of them did speak English. And they had both gone straight for the back of my legs, all freshly stitched and still stuffed with temporary packing. But the pain was soon forgotten and I smiled as I was wheeled onto the plane. I was going home.

My smile widened when I was pushed into the cabin. The first-class cabin.

I picked up a bottle of some sort from a compartment connected to my oversized and fully reclining seat. 'What's all this?' I asked Dr Alex, who was leading the trauma team that would escort me back to Australia.

'That's moisturiser,' she said. 'First time up the front?'

Sure was – I'd only ever flown economy. I thumbed my way through the VIP goodies: wipes, perfumes, toothpaste and soaps among the haul.

'I could get used to this,' I said as the flight attendant handed me a warm wet towel, perfume-scented and steaming.

We'd be flying first class all the way home. The trauma team and I.

Rachel didn't make it to Germany in the end. The army was just about to buy her a ticket when she learned I'd be coming home.

I turned my attention to the oversized LCD screen.

Alex slid over an elaborate drinks list and asked me if I'd like a drink.

'Not for me,' I said, explaining that I wouldn't drink while the rest of my section was still in Afghanistan. I would wait for them. I had nothing to celebrate until they got home.

I spent the first part of the flight writing in my notepad. I'm not sure why but I felt the need to write down everything that had happened. Everything I could recall. While some would want to forget an experience like this, I was determined to remember, partly so I'd never forget the heroic deeds of those who had helped me. I suppose it was also a form of therapy.

***

'What's this?' I asked when a staffer at Dubai airport handed me a shiny metal disc.

'Some sort of coin,' she shrugged. 'I was told to give it to you.'

I noticed it was a challenge coin, which is something soldiers exchange as a mark of friendship and respect. It turned out that the Kiwi commanders of the Dubai station had travelled to the airport after learning I'd be passing through. They couldn't get through security, so they passed on the coin instead. Legends. I was humbled by the gesture.

I began feeling a little anxious when I took my seat for the second leg: Dubai to Brisbane. I began thinking about how people would receive me. How they'd treat me. How they'd react when confronted with my disfigured body. Would they think less of me now that I didn't have legs?

Mostly I worried about Rachel. She'd been positive on the phone. Told me she loved me no matter what. But she hadn't seen me yet. Seen my full and shocking state. What would she think when she saw me being pushed towards her in a wheelchair, all bandages, catheter and a quarter of my body gone?

I tried not to be negative, but deep down I feared the relationship was over. More than feared it. I thought it was certain. So much so I was considering ending the relationship myself. Maybe as soon as I saw her. Which would be soon.

***

The plane began emptying out. One by one the passengers disembarked. I was helped into the aisle and then put into a chair. A wheelchair. I went numb as soon I was told that Rachel was waiting for me at the gate. She'd been given special clearance to meet me as soon as I exited the plane. They began pushing me down the aisle. Would I see the disappointment in her face? I wondered if she'd even recognise me. I was no longer the person she'd loved. Curtis McGrath never left the desert. I was a stranger, even to myself. We turned left. Towards the wide-open door. And there she was, white shirt and blue jeans, red hair falling down her porcelain perfect face, the love of my life.

And that's when I broke down. Cried. Balled. Suddenly I was back on the ground in Afghanistan. Just hit. World crashing down. Life over. I'd done a pretty good job keeping it all together. Until now ...

My tears were for Rachel, not for myself. I had let her down. Ruined everything. I'd never be able to give her the life she wanted. Deserved. Not now. Not without legs. She deserved more than half a man.

I cried even harder when she began rushing towards me. And even harder when she kissed me.

'Sorry,' I managed to blubber. 'I'm so sorry.'

She put her arms around me and hugged me as hard as she dared.

'Don't be stupid,' she fired. 'I'm not having that. You have nothing to be sorry for. Not now. Not ever.'

She silenced my tears with a second kiss, this one harder, longer, and laden with love.

I don't think we even spoke as they wheeled me through the airport. My condition spared me from the rigmarole.

There were no queues or bag checks. I was loaded into the back of an ambulance after leaving through the medical exit. The officer flicked on the emergency lights and pulled away from the kerb.

Next stop the Royal Brisbane Hospital, my new home.

***

The triage room would have been empty had it not been for some fellow soldiers. The one wearing the smile walked my way.

'I'm Captain Isaac Kahn,' he said before shaking my hand. 'I'm the padre, but don't worry. I'm not here to read you the Bible, well, unless you want me to, of course. No. I'm here to support you. A shoulder to lean on, if you will.'

I soon learned that Isaac had been at Rachel's side since she'd landed in Australia. Along with Gibbo, he'd been her rock. In fact, both the padre and Gibbo had been there for my entire family, doing whatever they could to make a horrible situation a little less horrible. Gibbo was a complete professional who knew what to say and when. He became more than a mate after the incident. He became family.

***

I was soon wheeled out of triage and pushed through the hospital, which was all white walls and smelling of bleach.

'This is you,' a voice said when the pushing finally stopped.

I was pleasantly surprised.

'Just me?' I enquired as I was pushed into an oversized room with just one bed. I wasn't expecting a private room, but that's what I got.

I began feeling a little hot as soon as I was transferred into the bed. Then a lot hot. Then boiling. I was soon covered in sweat.

'That's normal,' the doctor said when he arrived. 'And a good thing. It's a sign that you're healing. Your body is a remarkable thing and right now it's gone into overdrive to help you heal. It's pulling every bit of energy it can find and putting it into the healing process. Tapping into all your fat stores and burning them for energy.'

I guess it's easier than doing exercise, I thought.

The doctor was Associate Professor Daryl Wall, the head of trauma at Royal Brisbane Hospital. I liked him immediately.

Professor Wall didn't beat around the bush when he told me what I was in for. 'You know this isn't going to be easy, right?' he said. 'That it's going to be a long, difficult and painful road. You could be here for the rest of the year. Maybe longer. Everyone is different. It all depends on how you heal and what complications we face.'

He then went into detail. Spoke of surgeries and stitches. Skin grafts and specialists.

'Whatever it takes,' I said.

***

Mum and Dad came to see me later that evening. So did Brent, Sophia and Vic, my grandfather. Brent was a mess. He was crying before he even walked in. He was still very much the gentle kid who'd sit on the back of the go-kart that I never let him drive. Sophia held it together, as did Vic. I spent the evening relaying the information I'd been given earlier that day: the surgeries and the stitches; the skin grafts and the specialists; the long road ahead.

Another doctor came to see me the next day. She first talked about skin grafts, telling me they'd take skin from one part of my body and use it on another. My wounds weren't properly closed at this point. Everything was patched up and filled with packing. Temporary tubes sucking out fluids.

'A graft may not be sufficient for the end of your leg,' she continued. 'You may need a flap.'

I began thinking of a doggy door.

'It's when we take a large section of vascular skin from somewhere else on your body, usually your side or your thigh, and move it to the damaged area.'

I was told I wouldn't be able to move for at least two weeks if I had the 'flap' procedure. Any movement would bust the stitches and kill the skin before it took. She also said it was a high-risk surgery that was both long and complex.

I was soon told that I would need a flap, and that the long and complex surgery was going to be a ten-hour marathon. I was also told about the other surgeries I'd need, including having various nuts, bolts and screws put in my other leg.

I got to hang out with Rachel after I was given the rundown. I didn't have the courage to ask the question that would eventually have to be asked. To look her in the eyes and say, 'Can you love me like this?' Maybe I was being selfish. I just wanted to pretend it was all okay. Wanted to keep her for as long as possible. I feared she might bring it up herself. But she didn't. In fact, she didn't even ask me about the incident. I'm sure she was full of whats, whys and hows, but she decided to let me control the conversation. She didn't want me to relive my horror and had decided I would tell her in my own time. I thought that was very mature of her, given she was just twenty-four.

***

My first few days back in Australia were a haze. Drugged up on opiates, I drifted in and out. There always seemed to be someone in my room. Doctors, nurses, specialists and surgeons – it was a constant stream of white coats. And then there were my family and friends, in and out, a familiar face smiling at me whenever I opened my eyes. One of those faces belonged to Rachel, of course.

'You don't have to stay with me if you don't want to,' I said, eventually finding the courage to front up to my fear. I feared she was only there because she felt obliged. Not because she loved me. Not any more. How could she?

'I know what you must be thinking,' I said. 'I don't expect you to stay with me. There's no pressure. I won't think any less of you if this is too much.'

Rachel responded right away. 'No way,' she said, almost angrily, as she jumped from her seat. 'That's not going to happen. I'm not going anywhere. And you'll be the first person to know if I think things are becoming too much.'

With a kiss on the cheek, she exorcised my worst fear. She then pulled herself onto the bed and snuggled up next to me. It was then I decided everything was going to be okay.

***

'Do I really have to have this operation?' I asked a nurse as she wheeled me into the surgery. She responded by way of delivering me to the anaesthetist, who was waiting, needle in hand.

My next surgery was upon me before I knew it. And this was the operation I wasn't looking forward to. I didn't care about having a 'flap' sewn to my knee. But I did care that I'd spend the next two weeks lying completely still, constantly fearing that the slightest movement would rip the freshly sown vessels and skin from my leg and force the surgeon to start again.

'Relax,' the anaesthetist said. 'You're in good hands. Now count to ten.'

I didn't even know he'd put the cannula in my arm.

One, two, three, four, five ...

'What's the time?' I said, coming to.

'Just past 2 pm,' the nurse said as she looked at her wristwatch.

'Oh shit,' I said. 'What went wrong? Fifteen hours.' The surgery was only supposed to take eight hours.

The nurse laughed and then smiled.

'It took three hours. Not fifteen. You didn't need the flap, so they just had to close it up. You'll need some skin grafts later, but no need to worry about that now.'

It was the first really good medical news I'd received since losing my legs. I wouldn't have to worry about staying still for the next two weeks.

I called Rachel. She'd gone shopping with her mother in a bid to kill time, and was planning on being back when I came to.

'Where's my chocolate waffles?' I asked. 'You said you'd be here with Max Brenner when I woke up.'

'Why are you awake so early?'

I gave her the good news.

She was soon by my side, smiling, Max Brenner waffles in hand.

They were a welcome relief from the hospital food, of which I'd been eating plenty. I wasn't always hungry, but I ate everything I was given as I was conscious about my weight. I wanted to put as much back on as I could. I supplemented the hospital food with Footlongs from Subway, which was the only takeaway in Royal Brisbane.

Rachel left about two weeks after she arrived. Back to New Zealand. She had to get back to studying medicine.

'I'll be back as soon as I can,' she said after planting another kiss on my cheek.

I was okay when she left. There was nothing she could do physically, and while it was great to have her there emotionally, I didn't want to be interrupting her life.

She was back by my side two weeks later. There when I opened my eyes. I smiled when I saw her in the corner of the room, glasses and serious face on, sitting in a chair reading a textbook. I'm not sure how she managed to both keep up with her studies and look after me. She's a remarkable woman.

***

Rachel joined me for my first trip to the physio clinic. It proved to be a landmark moment in my recovery, as it was the first time I was able to get into the wheelchair without help.

'Right,' the physio said after she told me how to use the transfer board. 'Let's do this.'

I pushed myself onto the board and slid down from the bed and onto the seat.

'Well done!' Rachel said after I made it into the wheelchair.

I didn't reply. I just looked at the floor.

'What's wrong?' she asked.

'Na, nothing,' I lied.

I was suddenly overcome by sadness. The act of putting myself into the wheelchair made me realise I was a disabled person. It was a hard thing to comprehend. A month earlier, I'd been fit and healthy. I was ninety kilograms and muscled. And now I weighed fifty kilograms wringing wet. All skin and bone, withering in a wheelchair. It suddenly became too much.

'I don't want to go through this,' I said as I began to cry. 'Why me? What did I do to deserve this?'

It was my lowest point since arriving in hospital.

Rachel stepped in and gave me a big hug as the physio left the room. 'We'll get through this. We just need to get a start. Let's do this.'

The physio returned to the room a few minutes later.

'You back with us?' she asked.

I nodded as I wiped my face.

'Well, let's get into it.'

The clinic was just a big room with a smattering of gym equipment, things like hand grinders, bikes and benches. I was handed the transfer board and asked to move myself onto a half Swiss ball. I managed to get myself out of the chair and onto the top of the ball without difficulty.

'Steady yourself,' the physio said as I wobbled.

It was difficult to remain balanced now that I didn't have legs. I shuffled around on my bum until I felt I had a good base and then stiffened my core. I had to strain just to hold myself straight. Once I was stable, the physio produced a tennis ball. She told me we were going to play a game of catch. I felt a little offended. Catch was a game for toddlers. She softly threw the ball my way and I caught it. Just. Throwing it back proved even more difficult. I was suddenly overcome by anger. I couldn't understand why something so easy was so hard. I was about to tell the physio I was done. I wanted to give up, go back to my bed and do nothing for the rest of my life. I didn't want to have to relearn how to throw a ball. It was demeaning.

But then I looked at Rachel. Saw her willing me on with her eyes.

I had an epiphany. It was then and there that I realised I had only two options. The first was to give up. To say this is too much and quit life. To ... I really don't know what I'd have done had I taken that path. The second was to become the best person I could be. To make it my mission to live the best life I could. To do everything I was asked and accept every challenge with a smile.

'I guess I just have to do this,' I said to Rachel. 'All of it. It's the only way I'm ever going to get better.'

That was the moment I made the commitment to do anything and everything I could to recover, both physically and mentally. To not only do what was asked of me but to do more.

'Let's go,' I said to the physio as I turned away from Rachel. 'Throw me that damn ball.'

It was the best decision I ever made, because I'm sure it was what kept me sane. I had a purpose again. And I gave it my all.

***

'You ready?' Mum said as she entered the hospital room. 'We've picked a good day for it. It's beautiful out there.'

It was time for my first day trip, a lunch in Brisbane with my family. To be honest, though, I wasn't that keen on leaving the hospital.

'Awesome,' I said, putting on a brave face as I was transferred into my wheelchair. 'It'll be good to get some fresh air.'

I looked down at my legs.

'Pass me that blanket,' I said to Dad as I pointed back towards the bed.

I grabbed it and covered my lower body, not ready to have the world see what I had become. I wanted to hide. I wasn't ready to face the enquiring eyes. My arm was still damaged, so Dad had to push me through the hospital and to the car.

'This will be nice,' Mum said.

I nodded but was apprehensive. Still, it was nice to get outside. Out of the sterile hospital, where everything was clean, white and smelling of bleach.

I slid over the transfer board and into the car, a red XR6 Falcon. Yep. Suddenly Dad was a Ford man. I strapped myself into the front seat and went to reach down for the little bar that pushes the seat back.

'Won't be needing that,' I said, after realising I'd never have to worry about leg room again.

This was my first time back in a car and I hadn't expected anything to be different. But it was. I was shot forward as soon as Dad braked. He didn't slam on the brakes, just came to a gentle stop at the first set of lights. I'd automatically attempted to brace myself with my legs and, without them, I was sent forward by the minor force. I had no idea how important legs were for balancing yourself in a car. Even going around corners was a battle. I had to hold onto the dash or push against the window.

I felt exposed as soon as we left the car. Transferred back into my wheelchair, I tried to hide under my blanket, but it didn't work. People were looking at me. Turning their heads as we passed.

Why me? Why did this have to happen to me?

I suddenly felt sorry for myself. I wanted to be normal. Wanted to be the same as all the people who were walking past. It was nice to be out with the family, but going out in public just made me realise that my life was forever changed. I was different. And always would be.

***

Despite being mostly restricted to my bed for six weeks, I was never bored. Between all the doctors and surgeries, visits from family, friends and the army, I seemed to have no free time.

My New Zealand schoolmates Mike, Tyson and Ryan came to see me while I was in Royal Brisbane. The hospital allowed them to stay back well past visiting time so we could watch a game of rugby on the TV. It was the All Blacks, of course. I can't remember the game, but I can safely say the All Blacks won. They always did.

Mike asked me about my injuries. I proceeded to list them all.

'Oh, my dick,' I said. 'I forgot about my dick.'

'Your dick?'

'Yeah. My dick.'

Not sure why I decided to tell him about the injury, but I did. Just blurted it out.

'You want me to show you?' I continued.

Mike was quick to say no.

I was very lucky to have only sustained a cut to my manhood. I didn't realise how lucky I'd been until I came across a statistic that revealed nine out of ten British soldiers who lose permanent sexual function end up taking their own lives.

On a lighter note, it was also about this time that I went to the toilet by myself for the first time. You wouldn't think it would be something to get excited about, a landmark moment, but it was. I had to take every victory. No matter how small.

18

COFFEE AND CAKE

I SPENT SIX WEEKS in Royal Brisbane before being transferred to Greenslopes Private Hospital. This was where the new Curtis McGrath was born. A Curtis McGrath who moved into Greenslopes didn't feel sorry for himself or want to quit. Nor did he hide. The new Curtis McGrath welcomed challenges. He not only wanted to live but wanted to succeed. Maybe even conquer.

With all the major surgeries done – now five in total – I was moved into Greenslopes towards the end of 2012 to step up my rehabilitation.

I was taken to the Rehabilitation Ward for a scheduled rehab session almost as soon as I arrived.

'Nup,' I said, looking around. 'This is not for me. Take me back to my room.'

I didn't mean to be rude, but I knew straight away that an environment such as this would set my rehabilitation back.

Aside from the fact that everyone there was well over fifty, the equipment wasn't suited to me. It was all designed for its clientele, the elderly, mostly recovering from strokes and falls. There was no way I'd have been able to push myself in such an environment. It was just depressing.

Thankfully, Jess the physio agreed that I wouldn't have been able to motivate myself in that ward. I was allowed to do my rehab in my room, which was transformed into a gym perfectly suited to my needs. Weights, balls, bands ... I had everything I required. And having all the gear gave me the ability to train whenever I liked. I only had a one-hour physio session each day, but the equipment allowed me to get serious about building my body. And serious I got. I used every spare moment I had to get stronger. To improve myself. In between appointments and medical reviews, I pushed, pulled, lifted and sometimes even squeezed. I couldn't even pick up a coin when I arrived, so I spent a lot of time squeezing a specially developed hand putty to strengthen my grip. It was tedious, but I was determined to leave no stone unturned. That's if I could pick it up and turn it!

I found this period of my recovery even more demanding than the last. I was pretty much a passenger through the surgeries. All drugged up and laid up. Now I actually had to contribute to the process. I was busy too. I was always being treated or speaking to someone about my treatment. I still had a steady stream of friends and family coming to visit. My army commanding officer would come to see me every couple of days. I looked forward to getting news about what was happening in Afghanistan. He knew I was still emotionally attached to the deployment, and provided me with small pieces of information that helped ease my anguish.

I was able to stay in touch with the boys, who were still on the ground in Afghanistan. I chatted to them on Facebook Messenger, and got the odd phone call, too. Their deployment was coming to a close. Not a lot was happening over there. Winter was coming and things were quietening down. Still, I was concerned, not just because of the threat they faced but also because of what had happened to me. They might not have sustained serious physical damage in the explosion, but they'd been wounded all the same. Not physically but mentally. I was almost certain that they'd all be suffering from some degree of PTSD. I always put on a brave face when I typed or talked. I didn't want them worrying about me. Especially while facing deadly threats. I couldn't wait to see them all again. To have that first beer.

I did as much as eight hours a day of physio. I made it my mission. Slowly my strength returned. Bit by bit. Lift by lift. Squeeze by squeeze. And my confidence grew with my body. So much so that I was ready for my first solo mission a couple of weeks into my stay.

***

I slid down the transfer board, from the bed and into the chair. I had this bit mastered. I then reached towards the bedside table, opened the drawer and grabbed a handful of coins. Yes. I finally had the strength to do something as simple as pick up money. I placed my hands on top of the wheels, gripped the rubber in my slightly sweaty palms, and took one look at the call button I didn't need – not today – before setting off.

I pushed: once, twice, out the door. I felt a sense of empowerment as I wheeled myself down the corridor towards the nurse's station.

'I'm just heading down to get a coffee,' I declared when I reached the countertop.

'You need some help?

'Na, I'm sweet,' I said with pride before I pushed.

Hudsons Coffee, ground floor, Greenslopes, was the destination I chose for my first solo mission in a wheelchair.

I continued down the corridor, pressed the lift button and wheeled myself into the lift. But when the lift doors opened and I pushed myself into the foyer, the anxiety started. This was the first time I'd had to face the public on my own, without a chaperone. It was just me, myself and I. People would look at me. I still didn't know how I even viewed myself, let alone how others would see me. I pushed myself into the hospital foyer knowing I didn't have anybody to hide behind. I also knew it was a fear I had to face.

I kept my head down and pushed on. People looked at me. But I made it to Hudsons. I sat in front of the counter waiting for someone to take my order. It took the lady a little while to notice I was there. I had to remind myself that I was no longer six foot three. I ordered a flat white and a slice of banana bread.

'Need a hand?' she asked as she placed the coffee and cake on the countertop.

'Na, all good. Thanks.'

I grabbed the banana bread and put it on my lap. I then reached for the coffee. Yep. All good. I could do it on my own. Time to go. And that's when I realised I needed both of my hands to push. Mmm. A cupholder would be nice.

My only option was to hold the coffee cup between my legs. I knew that was going to be a problem. I'd already transferred the cup from my right hand into to my left because of how hot it was. But my only other choice was asking for help, and I wasn't going to do that. So, I put the cup between my legs and pushed off. Back towards the lift.

What started as uncomfortable soon became almost unbearable, especially when I had to reposition the cup to keep it stable. Yep. I had to push the cup right up against my balls to stop it from tipping. Anyway, whatever discomfort I experienced was worth it, because I made it back to my room without having to ask for help.

Buying coffee and cake might not sound like a big deal, but it felt like a major achievement after being completely reliant on others since the blast. Until now I could not satisfy even my most basic need without help. So, with slightly burnt balls, I tucked in.

Needless to say, it was the best coffee and cake I'd ever had.

***

Marry her. The thought came to me while I was lying in bed.

Do it.

It wouldn't go away.

She loves you. You love her. Why wait?

It started as a suggestion and then turned into a demand.

Do it. Now. What are you waiting for?

I called my Dad when I decided the come-from-nowhere suggestion had a point. A good one.

'Hey Dad,' I said. 'I think I want to marry Rachel. What do you think?'

Dad replied immediately. 'I think that's the best idea you've ever had.'

'Okay,' I said. 'Do you know anything about rings?'

I told Dad he'd have to go out and get it for me. While I could now go and buy coffee and cake, I was a long way from going to Prouds to buy an engagement ring. I would have sent Dad out to buy a ring there and then had he not offered to bring in a catalogue. He came in with it a few days later, but I didn't even look at it.

'I've changed my mind,' I said. 'I don't think now is the right time.'

Mostly the decision was selfless. I didn't want to pressure Rachel into marrying me. I didn't want her to say yes out of pity or obligation. Part of the decision was also selfish. I was only young. Just twenty-four. Did I really want to commit to marriage? The catalogue ended up in the bin.

***

'Hi, my name is Jens,' said the softly spoken man. 'I'm going to make you some new legs.'

Jens (pronounced Yens) Baufeldt is a prosthetist. He had travelled up from Sydney to Brisbane at army expense to begin the process that would eventually see me fitted with artificial legs. After speaking to the doctors who had overseen my surgeries and recovery so far, he talked me through the process. I soon learned the important part of the prosthesis was the socket, the part that meets the body. I also learned that the quality of the socket would be determined by the fitting. He told me that the fitting could not be done until the part of the body that contacted the socket was healed, clean and fully closed.

We talked about the phases I'd have to go through. He said that I had to do a lot of preparation before the fitting. That I'd have to strengthen the parts of my body that I'd need for both balance and power. Those muscles were mostly in my core. My lower back would be worked like never before. He gave me a list of exercises.

Jens kept in touch by way of phone, calling to check on my progress.

'Curtis, I have some good news,' he said during one call. 'I've spoken to the doctors and we've agreed you'll be ready to leave hospital in November. Provided all goes well, that's when you'll be fitted with your prostheses.'

It should have been the news I was desperate to hear – but it wasn't. While part of me wanted to move on, had had enough of doctors, nurses and hospitals, another part of me was terrified of being alone. My freedom and independence were going to come by way of having my security blanket ripped away. No call buttons, no check-ins, no meals delivered to my bed. I didn't know if I was ready to be independent. I liked having a medical team at my beck and call as much as I hated it. I also liked the thought of sleeping in my own bed as much as I hated it. But it was inevitable. My only option was to steel myself for what was to come.

***

The day finally arrived.

'Time to go,' said Dad. 'You got everything?'

It was 16 November, eighty-eight days since I took my last step. Since then, I'd undergone nine operations in three different countries. I'd been in six different hospitals. Now it was time to go home, a place I hadn't seen since June. It had been 160 days since I walked out that door. Since I said my goodbyes and headed off to war. It was difficult knowing that I wouldn't be walking back through that door. No. I would be wheeled.

I was apprehensive. Not only had I become accustomed to 24/7 care and support, I also didn't want to be a burden on my family. I didn't want them resenting me because I was too much work. My apprehension grew during the car ride.

'Here we are,' Dad said as we pulled into the driveway. 'Must feel good to be home.'

I knew I should have been excited, but I wasn't. I transferred myself onto my chair and began pushing myself towards the freshly installed ramp.

'It's all been taken care of,' Dad said. 'They put in ramps, widened the doors and built you a new bathroom.'

The Department of Veterans' Affairs had paid to make the entire house wheelchair-accessible. They widened the door frames, installed a shower chair, put in grab bars, and built ramps. I wouldn't have been able to go home if the modifications hadn't been made. You don't realise how wide a wheelchair is until you're in one, knocking skin off your knuckles as you squeeze through doorways.

Despite my initial reservations, I felt comfortable as soon as I pushed myself through the door. While I didn't have all the doctors and nurses, I did have my family. I also had my own bed, which was what I'd been looking forward to most after spending three months lying on glorified gurneys.

***

While I'd been apathetic about returning home, I was utterly excited about getting my legs. It was hard to believe that I'd be able to walk again. I'm not sure how I'd have got through this had I sustained this injury in another time. Been one of the poor buggers who lost their legs in World War I. The prospect of being able to walk again gave me hope. Even when I was lying on the ground, dust cloud rising, blood gushing, I thought of prostheses. I knew, no matter how bad the injury turned out, that I'd one day be able to walk. Not once did I think that I wouldn't. I suppose that's strange given the extent of my injuries, but I'm not sure I could have resigned myself to life in a wheelchair. And now the day I'd been looking forward to had finally arrived.

Rachel and my parents accompanied me to Sydney for my prostheses fitting. We flew from Brisbane and then drove to Baulkham Hills for my appointment with Jens.

Jens showed me the two prostheses he would fit to what remained of my legs. Built by a German company called Ottobock, the prostheses were top of the line. One of them, however, was far more advanced than the other, given it included an artificial knee.

The prosthesis I'd use as a right leg was called an X2. Worth about $180,000, it was equipped with four microprocessors and sixteen sensors. The X2 was developed by Ottobock in collaboration with the US military. I did some research before I arrived and learned that the US Defense Department had spent $680 million to help develop the product. I didn't know why my new leg would need Bluetooth, but I thought it was cool that it did. I was also intrigued by the 'stumble recovery' feature. Apparently, the artificial knee was so advanced that it could stop a fall by correcting a misstep. Both of the prostheses were military grade. They had encrypted electronics that could not be hacked or detected, both of which would be vital in a war zone. The X2 was also the first artificial knee capable of both climbing and descending steps.

'Okay, nice and slow,' Jens said after attaching the custom-built prosthetics.

And then, with the help of parallel bars, I stood. Upright and back to my old height for the first time since the blast. I turned to Rachel, and looked at her, standing eye to eye for the first time since the incident. We then hugged standing up, me taller than her again. Rachel had a tear in her eye.

'Let's get a photo,' I said.

And we did. But the jubilation was short-lived.

'Something's wrong,' I said to Jens.

The left prosthetic was uncomfortable as soon as I put it on. Uncomfortable quickly turned to painful. It was now almost unbearable. Holding on to the parallel bars, I shuffled around, trying to make the prosthetic comfortable.

'Ahh,' I uttered as I was hit by a lightning bolt of pain. 'This isn't right.'

Jens urged me to persevere.

I was struck again; this time it felt as though I'd been stabbed.

'No,' I said, as I pushed up on the bars and took the weight away from my legs. 'This isn't right. Can't be right.'

Jens got to work and examined both the prosthetics and legs. As I mentioned earlier, the socket was the most important part of the prosthetic. It wasn't the technology, the carbon fibre or the radio encryption, it was the section of hardened plastic that joined my body to the mechanical legs. And even though the socket had been custom made for my leg, I could not put any weight down without being stabbed by pain. I asked Jens if there was a problem with the socket.

'I don't think so,' he said. He quickly determined that I had a troublesome nerve right where the socket contacted my leg.

Jens encouraged me to continue. He told me the nerve would help and the pain would slowly go away. So I got back up, determined to take my first step. I steadied myself and tried to block out the pain. And then I took a deep breath.

I took a step.

It hurt like hell. It also felt awkward. I would have fallen over had it not been for the bars I was grasping.

I took another step.

'That's it,' I said. 'I'm done.'

I was completely deflated. Don't get me wrong, standing up was amazing. To be back at eye level with another adult made me feel normal, if only for a moment. But I was really expecting to walk out of that room. Legs on, walking like I had before. I had no idea that I'd be limited to just two steps.

Jens both comforted and encouraged me. He told me it would be a process and that we would progress further the following day, when I was scheduled to come back and see him.

Rachel was amazing. She told me she'd be with me every step of the way. She also said she believed in me and that she knew I had the strength to conquer not only this but anything. I probably would have not gone back the next day had it not been for this remarkable woman.

***

Day two was not much better. The prosthetic was every bit as painful. I had to tell myself that this was just part of the process. That I'd have to learn how to manage the pain. So I persevered. Expectation dialled down, I followed Jens's instructions. I went to the bar.

One ...

Two ...

Three ...

Four ...

The pain was horrid but I persevered, largely thanks to Rachel, who reassured, motivated and comforted. She was incredible. Again.

I took more steps on day three. I also moved away from the bars and walked with the aid of crutches. I had to come to terms with the new challenge I was facing. Walking was going to take time. Aside from the pain, I'd have to learn the limitations of my new device. I'd also have to become familiar with my terrain. I never knew how rough the world was until I began walking on artificial legs. Walking in the flat clinic was hard enough. I learnt that even a slight change in the surface, like going from a tiled area to a carpeted area, affected the use of the prosthetic legs, so let's not get me started on a sandy beach ...

And the movements I'd use to drive the legs were both new and foreign. It's quite difficult to explain, let alone do. It was not just a matter of walking but was a combination of balance, power and momentum. I had to lift first and then both swing and drive. The movements had to be controlled and precise. I also had to trust the prosthetics. Again, a strange feeling, but each step felt a little like I was about to jump off a cliff. I had to trust that the hunk of carbon fibre I was about to put my weight on would do its job and I wouldn't fall flat on my face.

***

While talking about pain, now might be a good time to tell you about the strangest of them all – phantom pain.

It comes from nowhere. Sudden. Sharp. Much like the pain I just described. But unlike the pain that struck the end of my leg, this pain strikes in parts of your body you no longer have. It strikes in limbs long lost or paralysed. I first experienced it around this time. Out of nowhere it came. It felt like someone was hammering a nail into my foot. But I no longer had a foot. I had to do some research following the episode to make sure I wasn't going mad.

A reasonable person might say that this phenomenon can't exist. Pain in a limb you no longer have? Absurd. But I can tell you that phantom pain is real and can be excruciating. I'm very lucky that I don't get it often. I'm also lucky it's not as severe as it might be. I've met a number of people who have horror stories when it comes to this bizarre ailment.

There is no definitive explanation, but the consensus is that phantom pain is caused by severed nerves attempting to repair and regrow.

I returned home to Brisbane with my prosthetic legs both determined and deterred. My mood changed by the moment. Undecided, I stopped thinking about my legs and turned my full attention to the day I'd been waiting for above all. Ryan Werts, Mac Pitcher, Daniel Livesay and Solomon Hanks were almost on their way home. In fact, they'd be back in Australia in just five days, safe and sound, their deployment in Afghanistan over. And I'd planned a little surprise ...

19

LEGS FIXED, HEART BROKEN

'KIWI!' WERTSY WAS THE FIRST to spot me and he beamed. 'What the? No way. I thought you were still in hospital.'

I stood tall and proud, a tear of joy escaping, even though I was doing my best not to cry. Wertsy looked at me slightly confused, partly because I told him I wouldn't be at Brisbane airport for the homecoming, but mostly because I was standing.

'No way,' Livo beamed when he caught on. 'It's Kiwi.'

And that's when they all rushed in. Wertsy, Livo, Pitch and Sol, all streaming across the aerobridge, only moments after they'd exited the plane.

'Easy, boys,' I said as they gave me the best damn group hug I'd ever had. 'Just got these legs.'

I'd been waiting for this moment since the incident. I'd spent every day worrying about them and wishing they were home. And here they were. All fit. All healthy. Safe. It was some moment. Especially given the pain I went through to make it happen.

My plan had been simple. After telling them I was still laid up in hospital, I was going be standing outside the plane door to meet them as soon as they stepped off the military chartered flight from Afghanistan. No wheelchair. No crutches. I'd be standing on the legs they didn't even know I had. Problem was, I couldn't walk very far. After five days of relentless practice, I was still measuring my distance in steps. So I had to alter my plan and take both a wheelchair and a pair of crutches to the airport. And I'm glad I did, because the arrival gate was on the far side of the terminal.

I got rid of the wheelchair but had to use the crutches to stand when I reached the plane. I was actually late and was a little embarrassed to find the airline had held the passengers on the flight just for me. But I'm glad they did. I can still remember the looks in their eyes, first surprise and then joy. Then more surprise. The last time they saw me was when I was being loaded into that helicopter. Blood everywhere, legs gone, no idea whether I'd even survive.

We then had our reunion. Hugs and handshakes followed by beers. I kept that promise I made to not have a drink until I was with them. I cracked my first cold one a moment after arriving with them at the airport bar. We then caught up, chatting as we sipped. Even though it wasn't my usual brand, beer had never tasted so good.

They were all more interested in asking about me then talking about themselves or their deployment. They wanted to know how I was and how they could help. I assured them that I was all okay. I wanted to make that point because I didn't want them thinking they had to worry about me. Nor did I want them to treat me any differently from how they had before. The trauma I went through was not mine alone. They also shared in it and I knew they'd have been affected by it. I wanted to do whatever I could to make sure they weren't suffering from that fateful day on the hill.

I remember wondering why I didn't have PTSD. I wasn't having flashbacks. Loud, sudden noises were not making me wince, let alone jump. I wasn't even having nightmares. In fact, I was sleeping better than I ever had. Surely I had to have PTSD. Right? But I didn't. And it worried me. I thought something was wrong with me. I thought that it was abnormal not to be having even the slightest of symptoms.

Was I broken? Devoid of emotion. Reduced to a machine?

I ended up asking a nurse about it. She suggested I see a psychologist, which I did. Following an exhausting chat, he told me he thought I was fine. Nothing to indicate an issue. But he did warn me that I was not yet out of the woods.

The official welcome-home parade was held at Enoggera Barracks two days after the boys returned home. I can't tell you how proud I was when I was told I'd be included in that parade. I no longer felt like I was part of that deployment and I expected the fact that I couldn't march would rule me out. But the army gave special dispensation for me to join the march in a wheelchair.

Wheelchair?

Yeah. Right.

There was no way I was going to be wheeled out onto the parade ground. I didn't want anyone's sympathy. I didn't even want to use crutches. Problem was I could hardly walk. In another admirable act, the army gave the boys permission to help me. They'd be allowed to fall behind the march and hold me up if need be.

All my family and friends were watching on when I walked out. Mates by my side, there for me but not yet needed, I walked tall and proud.

Everyone was clapping and cheering. It was some moment. Some day. I was later told there wasn't a dry eye in the crowd when I stepped onto the parade ground. It was also the end of a chapter. While I was still employed by the army, I knew I'd never be a soldier again. Although I hadn't ruled out staying in the Defence Force, I knew I'd never be fit for combat and could never be a combat engineer. I was a soldier no more.

I ended up walking 300 metres, which was at least three times my previous best. But it hurt like hell and the boys were almost carrying me towards the end.

I was in agony that night and I began to worry. Perhaps I'd never be able to walk a meaningful distance on my own. The pain was so immense, I dreaded the thought of having to walk again. And no one could tell me if it would ever get any better.

***

I continued my rehabilitation, and went as hard as I could. I spent at least four hours a day in the army rehabilitation clinic at Enoggera, pulling and pushing. Lifting and lugging. I also swam. I felt comfortable the very first time I went back into the water. I actually challenged Rachel to a fifty-metre race and I beat her. I felt like the man I was before. I also did whatever I could at home. And slowly my strength returned.

Slowly I put on weight. But while my body was getting bigger and stronger, walking wasn't getting any easier.

I also started going out in public. Sometimes aided by crutches, sometimes without, I did regular things, even though I knew I was not a regular person. Not any more.

'That's the guy from TV,' a woman at the local shopping centre said. 'The bloke with the metal legs.'

The media had given my story quite a bit of coverage. I allowed both TV New Zealand and *60 Minutes* to film various stages of my recovery, and it had made me a familiar face. I'd pretend I hadn't been noticed. I'd avoid making eye contact, keep my head down and hope they'd walk on by. But most didn't.

'I'd just like to thank you for both your service and your sacrifice,' they'd say. 'You're an inspiration.'

I never felt comfortable with the gratitude. It was unwarranted. I hadn't served them. Not really. I'd become a soldier to serve myself. It was a career, not a charity. I'd ended up serving others, even though it was not my motivation when I enlisted. I'd served the people of Timor by giving them water. I'd served the people of Afghanistan by clearing bombs. I'd served my fellow soldiers by backing them up. By being their mate. But I didn't feel like I'd served Australia. And certainly not the elderly shoppers who were stopping me in the mall. It felt even more awkward when they offered me money.

'Take this,' a woman said as she handed me a twenty-dollar note. 'Just a little thank you. I know what you've been through.'

I tried to give it back but she refused. And she was not alone. The unwanted donations occurred almost daily.

'What happened to you?' That was the question they'd ask. Always. Almost as soon as they saw my prosthetic legs. I didn't mind telling them my story at first, but when asked each and every day, answering became a chore. I had to catch a taxi to and from Enoggera each day to do my rehab. While every driver was different, the question was always the same.

'What happened to you?'

That's part of the reason why I decided I wanted to drive. I knew that there were devices that allowed the disabled to drive, but I wasn't sure how to go about getting those modifications or the licence to use them.

Like everything else, it was a process. It began with driver training. I took lessons and underwent assessments with an instructor at Enoggera. I had to not only learn but master driving a car without using my feet, by steering, accelerating and braking with my hands. It doesn't sound that difficult, but I also had to use those same hands to do all the things they'd normally do. To indicate, to turn the windscreen wipers on and off, to operate the radio. It took some getting used to.

There are a few different car hand-control devices. The device I learned on was called a push/pat. The accelerator on a push/pat is located on a lever under the steering wheel. Using your right hand, you pat down on that lever to accelerate. The brake is attached to the same lever. But rather than pat down, you push it. Using a 'spinner knob', you steer the car with your left hand. It took a little time to get used to using the brake and the accelerator lever. To work out how hard you had to push or pull to get the desired response.

Around the same time, I was introduced to a charity that would change my life. Called Mates4Mates, it's operated by ADF veterans *for* ADF veterans. An organisation outside the military, its objective is to provide support and rehabilitation to anyone who has served. Its members attempt to bring you and your family together, mainly by way of organising activities. And we're not just talking about a trip to the park. The activity that caught my eye was a Bass Strait crossing in a kayak.

I thought that sounded pretty cool. I'd enjoyed my time in a kayak back at school in New Zealand, and I also thought it was something I'd be able to do. I asked Dad if he'd do it with me, and he agreed. So we both signed up, even though we had no idea what we were actually signing up for. I was back to my normal weight, almost ninety kilograms and I felt fit and strong. I was confident I'd be able to complete the trip, even when they told us we'd be paddling from Sydney to Brisbane instead, a total distance of around 900 kilometres. I thought I was up to the task. Having reached all my rehabilitation goals, I was as strong as I used to be, even stronger in some parts. My medical team both approved and encouraged the expedition.

Dad and I started training together. We did a swimming test first. I had no hesitation. And I think I surprised a lot of people. I jumped into the pool and went for it. I did my laps. No legs. No problem. I actually enjoyed swimming because I didn't need my artificial legs. They were still hurting me so much, I didn't even want to put them on.

***

'This isn't right,' I said to Jens, again, calling him after a particularly bad day. 'It can't be. It's not getting better. I'm fitter, stronger, but I can't walk any further. It's not working for me. There's no improvement with my nerves, my distance, or the pain.'

I'd tried everything. Even padded the socket with everything from foam to an old sock.

'Okay,' he said. 'Come back to Sydney. Let's see if we can work it out.'

So off I went. To go through the process again. Unlike last time, my expectations were low, but I wasn't looking for a miracle, just an improvement. I'd have been happy with just a little less pain.

Jens produced a new socket, freshly moulded and taken from a new cast. He attached the new leg and handed me a pair of crutches.

'Mate, this is it,' I said as soon as I stood. I took a couple of steps to confirm what I already sensed. 'You've nailed it."

There was no pain. None. It was a game-changer. It was exactly what I'd expected the first time I went in.

'How does it feel?' Jens asked.

'Fucking amazing. I won't be needing these anymore,' I said as I threw the crutches away.

Jens smiled.

'Where's the toilet?' I asked, not that I needed to go.

Jens pointed the way.

I walked myself to the toilet. No crutches, all on my own. I then stood in front of the toilet, unzipped and did my first standing-up piss since the IED took my legs. It was the best damn piss I've ever had. I smiled like a kid at Christmas. I was back on top of the world, which is not a good place to be when it all comes crashing down.

***

I was about to go out to dinner when my phone rang. Restaurant booked, new and pain-free legs on. Dad was attempting to load the family into the car when Rachel's name flashed up on my screen.

'Give me a minute,' I said to Dad.

I smiled as I answered the call, excited as always to hear from my girl. I knew something was wrong as soon as she spoke. I could hear it in her voice.

'What's up,' I said. 'What's wrong?'

Her reply broke my heart.

'This isn't working,' Rachel said. 'It's been two years and I can't keep going for another three. It's too much.'

I should have known it was coming. How could it not have been coming, given our relationship had become a long-distance affair. While I was living in Brisbane, Rachel was living in New Zealand, and her studies were all-demanding and completely time-consuming. She had a placement in Wellington Hospital as part of her course. The distance and the demands of her career and my recovery kept us apart. We were only catching up in person every six weeks or so. We hadn't seen each other for almost three months when that devastating phone call came.

'I can't do this any more,' Rachel said. 'I can't see how we can have a relationship when you live in another country.'

She was right. But still it hurt like hell. My rock. The shining light on my darkest day. The one who had got me through all of this was now leaving me.

An easy solution would have been for me to move back to New Zealand, but that wasn't possible. Not with my medical situation or my employment. All of my doctors, specialists and support were in Australia. I was also still employed by the Australian Army. And it was the Australian Army that paid for all my medical care.

Rachel made it clear that she wasn't ending the relationship because of my disability. She didn't love me any less without legs. And while the thought did cross my mind, I believed she was genuine. It was all about distance and different paths. She knew she'd have to move to Australia to be with me and she couldn't because her dream was 3000 kilometres away in New Zealand. She couldn't move to Australia now because of her studies and placement, and maybe not ever because of her career.

I ended up going to the dinner. I didn't speak throughout the meal. I was determined not to ruin this family affair, but my emotions got the better of me. I started crying during dessert. Cried even more when I explained why. Mum left her seat and gave me a big hug. Rocked me until the tears stopped. I'd been in a breakup before – but nothing like this. I just could not imagine my life without her. And in my mind, it was over. For good. She'd made that clear. There were no maybes or who-knows during the conversation. It was a breakup, not a break. And I was broken too. Again.

I feared that I might be single for ever. That no one else would love me. I wasn't the man I used to be. It was a fear I'd not had to confront. Not really. The fleeting thought I had when I arrived back in Australia was fast swatted away when Rachel told me she loved me no matter what. I certainly hadn't thought about dating. I was numb.

But as they say, life goes on. It was time to find a new love. And I'd soon find one. I was about to fall in love again. Not with a woman, but with a sport.

***

The Sydney-to-Brisbane kayaking adventure commenced shortly after the breakup. Sixteen of us started the journey under the Harbour Bridge, before paddling past Circular Quay and the Opera House. Sydney certainly looked stunning.

Me and Dad. A billion-dollar view. It was, at the very least, a distraction from the hurt of losing Rachel.

I loved being out on the water, at least at first. The world looks different from there: cliffs, bridges and buildings are all so big when you're so low and feeling so small. I found the paddling easy. Paddle in, paddle out, I slid across the calm ocean like greased glass. Sydney to Brisbane? Piece of piss.

At first, I enjoyed the slight up and down, almost lulling, the gentle puffs of sea spray cooling my face. But soon the sea rolled, the small swells breaking against our bow. Now the molehills felt like mountains.

After finally rounding Sydney Heads, we were on the open ocean. Now it felt like my paddles were dragging through concrete. And the sea spray that at first soothed now slapped, like buckets of water were being constantly hurled in my face. I was rooted.

'You good?' asked Dad after I stopped.

'No,' I said. 'I'm stuffed.'

'Me too,' he said. 'What have we got ourselves into?'

Dad was struggling as much as me. And strangely, that made me feel better. I wasn't rooted because of my disability or because I was unfit. I was rooted because this was hard. And hard was just a challenge. So Dad and I put our paddles back into the concrete and struggled on.

I can't tell you how glad we were when we finally reached checkpoint one, at Terrigal on the NSW Central Coast.

'Sixty kilometres down,' Dad said. 'Only 840 kilometres or so to go.'

I soon learned that it's a very long way from Sydney to Brisbane by water. The kayaking was both mentally and physically exhausting. Paddling up to sixty kilometres a day, in all conditions, I pushed my body to its limits. My mind too.

We began each day of paddling at sunrise and finished around 4 pm when we reached our daily destination, where we'd stay in the local holiday park. Up the coast we went, Nelson Bay, Forster, Port Macquarie, Nambucca Heads, Coffs Harbour.

The ocean was pretty calm all the way up – until we reached Byron Bay. There we were confronted by potentially boat-tipping waves. But I chipped away, stroke by stroke, day by day, and Brisbane slowly drew closer.

Twenty-one days after we left Sydney, we finally reached our destination. I felt hugely proud. I was also proud of Dad, who defied his age to conquer the feat as if he was a young man. The long days at sea had been tough, but the experience had been invaluable. I got so much satisfaction from pushing and proving myself, and now I knew I could do amazing things if I put my mind to it. Sure, there were some things I couldn't do without legs, but there were also plenty of things I could. I'd just heaved myself through 900 kilometres of ocean. My body wasn't broken. It was strong. Ready for anything.

Apart from wheelchair basketball. It turns out I was crap at that. I'd been invited to go to the Marine Corps Trials in San Diego later that year. The Marine Corps Trials is a Paralympic-style invitation-only event involving more than 300 wounded, ill and injured US Marines and international competitors. Participants are organised into four competing teams: two active-duty teams, a Marine veteran team, and an international team of wounded warriors from US allies.

I'd been invited to compete in the allied team. I jumped at the chance because, just six months into my recovery, it was a good opportunity to see where I was at and whether I had a future as an athlete.

There was a range of sports on offer, but I chose to compete in wheelchair basketball, swimming and archery. They were the sports that appealed to me and the sports I thought I could do well in. They were also quite different from each other, so I thought I'd have to be okay in at least one of them. I wasn't. Especially basketball.

'What was that?' screamed the coach. 'Fucking terrible.' The coach of the team was an American guy and he ripped into me as soon as I got into my wheelchair and made my way onto the court. To be fair, I wasn't very good. I couldn't shoot to save my life. Sitting in a wheelchair, the basket looked as though it was bolted to the top of a skyscraper. I could shoot okay standing up, but I was shocking from the chair. Still, this bloke was full-on. I'd just met him and he was shouting, screaming and swearing.

I ignored the first tirade.

'Seriously,' he said as he blew his whistle. 'Not even close. You shouldn't be on my court.'

'Fuck you,' I muttered under my breath as I wheeled my way off the court. I hadn't come here to be abused by some bloke who thought he was coaching in the NBA. I put my legs on, stood up and walked off. Until now, I have never given him or basketball another thought.

I was much better at swimming. While I didn't set any records, I did manage to win a couple of medals. I was proud of my performance and thought I might even have a future in the pool.

And then there was archery. I don't know if I was any good at it, but I found the process of going through the shot to be quite therapeutic. I certainly enjoyed it more than shooting a rifle in the army. My teacher encouraged me, which contributed to the positive experience.

All in all, I enjoyed the event, the people and the competition. I left wanting to explore both swimming and archery, the latter so much that I even bought myself a top-of-the-line archery set, which I'd end up using just twice before selling it.

I was also interested in running but I didn't have a pair of running blades. Rachel had done a lot of research on them, but I still hadn't committed to getting a pair. I didn't think my legs were stable enough at that point to be able to run on a pair of blades.

Rachel and I ended up staying in touch, speaking on the phone every now and then. I found it difficult, but not as difficult as it would have been had we severed all ties. Hopefully, we'd be friends for life.

20

PADDLING ON

WHEN I RETURNED HOME from San Diego, I began to enquire about the Paralympics and what sports were available. I was thinking about what I might be good at. To begin with, I made those enquiries through Paralympics New Zealand, not Australia. I wanted to represent New Zealand and, after some initial emails and conversations, I was invited to head over the ditch to try a few sports and have a look at the facilities and the general set-up. On the recommendation of Hadleigh Pierson, who identified talent for Paralympics New Zealand, I went to Dunedin.

This particular program was focused on track sports: running, jumping and throwing. I wasn't particularly interested in anything but running – and I still wasn't ready to attach a pair of blades. Still, I was here and willing to give anything a go, so I did javelin and shotput, which I didn't enjoy or excel at. While I was never going to have a future in those disciplines, it was invaluable to not only get to watch the top-class athletes but also meet them. It allowed me to get an up-close look at what was required to be a success in terms of performance, conditioning and mental frame.

The woman running the program sensed my apathy for the athletics-based field sports. 'We have a canoeing program, too,' she said. 'Not here. Not now. But we'll be running a program in a month if you'd like to come back over for that.'

'Shit yeah,' I said.

***

I was back in New Zealand soon enough and put straight into a full-blown Olympic K1, which is a skinny and long kayak, 38 centimetres wide at its broadest part. It is a fairly unstable craft, certainly not for a beginner, and I had visions of tipping the damn thing as soon as I got in. With legs back on the shore and unable to help me, I steeled and then steadied myself. Aside from not wanting to be embarrassed, it was also the middle of winter. The water was only a few degrees above freezing – a further incentive not to get wet. But I was surprised to discover how good my balance was. All that time sitting on Swiss balls and working hard to strengthen my core had given me the stability I needed to keep the competition craft upright and afloat. The Sydney-to-Brisbane event had also paid off. The biggest challenge was the steering. Without legs, I couldn't use the foot-operated rudder.

'You stayed in?' one of the coaches said when I made it back dry. He looked surprised. 'Everyone falls in first try. You might have found yourself a sport.'

We also did some testing. Strength, mobility, reactions ... stuff like that. It all suggested I had some potential. Maybe even some talent. That coach may have been right. Perhaps this was my sport. Maybe even my new love.

I made some enquiries when I got home. Initially, I was interested in slalom kayaking, which is navigating through gates in white water. Alas, it was not a Paralympic discipline. I wanted to choose a sport that would allow me to compete at the pinnacle of disabled sport, so I crossed that one off the list. The only paddling-based discipline I could find on the Paralympic list was called Paracanoe V1. After a little research I learned that a V1 is an outrigger canoe, not a kayak. A V1 is more like a traditional-style canoe, and you use one blade to propel it instead of two.

The data from the testing came back and I did pretty well. I sent some emails to New Zealand and asked whether my results would apply to this boat. I was told that while a V1 was quite different from a kayak, the testing I'd done could be transferred.

I told them I was keen to proceed.

'So when are you moving to New Zealand?'

Another curveball.

'Ah ... About that ... '

I told them it was going to be very difficult. I was not yet a full year into my recovery, and I couldn't see myself relocating given that all my doctors, physios and everyone else who cared for me were in Australia. I also didn't know whether it would affect my employment with the army, which was still paying me, even though I wasn't turning up to work as such. The New Zealand administrators told me that it would still be possible for me to compete for New

Zealand, but it came with a caveat. They could not support me financially. I'd need to pay for my travel, equipment and coaching. *Not so bad*, I thought ...

***

I signed on to become an extra in the movie *Unbroken* after receiving a text message from a friend of a friend. An American war movie based on a non-fiction book written by Laura Hillenbrand, it was being filmed in south-east Queensland and they were looking for veterans for a prisoner-of-war scene. It sounded pretty good to me. A week or two of work. Good money. It sounded even better when I learned Angelina Jolie was the director.

I wanted to prepare as best as I could, so I bought the book and ploughed through the incredible story of Louie Zamperini in four days. I was quite excited about being involved and getting a behind-the-scenes look at how a Hollywood blockbuster is made.

The scene I was set to be in was to be filmed on an old dock beside the Brisbane River. The industrial complex had been transformed into a Japanese war camp circa 1943. I was one of 250 extras hired to be POWs. I felt out of place as soon as I arrived. All the others appeared to have prepared for the role, not just by reading the book but by dieting to resemble a POW. All skin and bone. I was up to about ninety-five kilograms with my legs on by this time, and hardly looked like a starving soldier who had been kept in a cage. I reckon they'd have sent me straight home had I not been an amputee, which they required for the scene.

I fast found the work pretty dull. I sat in an antique

wheelchair, doing mostly nothing. The days were long and filming was sparse, as we waited around, bored, hot and uncomfortable. I was dressed in heavy khakis and covered in make-up that looked like dirt.

It was during one of those long breaks that the director introduced herself. 'Hey, I'm Angelina.' She shook my hand. 'Nice to meet you.'

There wasn't much more to the exchange, but it made my day.

My dreams of becoming a Hollywood star were crushed when I was omitted from the final cut. Yep. Too big. But while I was the wrong size and shape to play a POW, I was now perfectly built for something else. Paddling.

***

Living in Australia and competing for New Zealand was going to be possible. But I would have to find my own coach and pay him or her, buy my own equipment and also pay for my travel. I was still earning a good wage from the army and had some money saved. I was prepared to invest it in both myself and my dream. On the advice of the officials back in New Zealand, I travelled down to the Gold Coast to meet the Australian paracanoe coach, Andrea Wood. She showed me the facilities and discussed my options.

'Yeah, I can work with that,' she said after I went for a paddle. 'You have some potential.'

Andrea discussed a potential training program, hours and days, what she'd expect of me, and the targets we'd work towards. It all sounded great. But when I worked it all out, I figured it was going to cost me in excess of $500 a week for coaching, equipment and travel. Andrea also told me that as the Australian coach, she wouldn't be available to me during competitions.

'Well, I'm not 100 per cent set on competing for New Zealand,' I said. 'I've lived in Australia half my life ... '

Yep. There you have it. It was me, a bloke called Kiwi, suggesting he was willing to wear the green and gold. An All Blacks tragic who considered himself a Kiwi through and through was open to competing against New Zealand ... as an Australian.

It wasn't just the money, it would have been a logistical nightmare. All those trips back and forth to New Zealand, to competitions, and I wouldn't be travelling light. Aside from the boat and the paddles, I'd be taking two sets of legs and a wheelchair.

There was also the issue of medical support and funding. I knew I'd be in good hands, with help only a call away if I got into trouble while training in Australia. But in New Zealand? I didn't even know where to start.

While not committing to a country, I decided Andrea would be my coach. So I joined her squad and started thinking about moving to the Gold Coast. Getting my own place.

***

'I miss you,' Rachel said as we began one of our phone calls, which had become more daily than weekly.

'I miss you too.'

'Then what are we doing?' she asked. 'Let's get back together. To hell with the other stuff; we'll worry about that later.'

And with that I had my girl back. Together again. Me and Rach.

It was another month or so until we saw each other in the flesh, when Rachel came over to help me move to the Gold Coast around December 2013. After telling my parents about my dream to become a Paralympic paddler, I rented a two-bedroom apartment near the beach. Rachel, who had started another medical placement at a hospital in Wellington, made the trip over to help me pack what little I owned into boxes and bags.

I wouldn't say it was an emotional reunion. Not overtly anyway. There were no tears or bearhugs. We kind of just picked up where we'd left off. It was like we'd never broken up. We didn't really talk too much about what had happened. Or what would happen. We were still in the same geographical predicament that caused the separation, but for now we didn't care. We were just happy to be together. It was meant to be. The rest would work itself out.

I was about to turn twenty-six and life was good. I had my girl and my own place. I now turned my attention to what I said on the stretcher on that fateful day in Afghanistan. 'You'll see me in the Paralympics ... '

***

I began training on 4 January 2014. It was the date I officially became an athlete. Boat under my bum, paddle in hand, I embarked on what would be my next great adventure.

Things didn't begin well. The training was a lot harder than I expected, mostly because of the heat. Without all the skin that used to be on my legs, I don't cool down as I should. Skin serves a vital function. It combines with glands in the body to expel heat by way of evaporation. Our skin sweats out the heat. And I was missing a shit-tonne of skin. So my core temperature rose fast and cooled slowly. Exerting myself in the tropical heat of the Gold Coast was both a shock and a challenge. I knew there was no medical solution and it was something I'd just have to endure. So I got on with it. I managed the situation as best I could by hydrating and avoiding wearing colours like black, which draw in the heat.

The V1 is also a difficult beast. Seven point three metres long, no rudder and light, it is a handful. The biggest challenge, without a doubt, was steering. With all direction provided by the paddle, I struggled to keep the thing straight. Despite my best efforts I was always pulling the boat to the left. Steering the V1 with a paddle is a fine art. The angle of the paddle as it hits the water needs to be precise, as does the follow-through. I was also getting pulled into the wash of others. I struggled for weeks.

I trained alongside Glenn Pyne, another double amputee who just happened to be the best Australian paddler in my class. A schoolteacher by trade, the then 50-odd-year-old took me under his wing, even though I was going to be his competition. And he gave me the pointer that set me straight. Noticing I had a problem with steering, Glenn showed me a paddling technique that corrected the fault. Thanks, mate. Glenn, along with Andrea, gave me the foundations I'd need to be a success.

So it was a little awkward to have to race against Glenn in my first competitive event: the Queensland Canoe Sprint Championships. Glenn wasn't just competition, he was my *only* competition. We were the only two people in Australia who competed in our disability class. So we put our friendship on hold for the 200-metre race. And in the first real indication that I'd chosen the right sport, I won. I did it in a decent time too.

I went back to training motivated and ready to rip. I was determined to take the next step, which was to make the Australian team. While the Queensland Canoe Sprint Championships was not a qualification event, the next two races were.

With my first win under my belt, I went off to the Oceania Championships the following month and repeated my first-up feat. Up against Glenn again, I proved the first result was no fluke. A month later I made it three from three when I won the Australian Championship. I also won a spot on the Australian team.

I was inducted in what was a rather underwhelming ceremony on a dock in Adelaide. At the completion of the event, a spokesperson stood and looked at a list.

'These are the people who have been selected in the Australian team,' he said.

There was no fanfare, just names read out, all matter-of fact. I was still overwhelmed with pride. Pumped. Stoked. Super happy. One step closer to my dream.

My life was moving ahead full steam. I was given a further shot when I found out the Australian Army was giving me 'elite sportsperson status', something I hadn't even known existed. It meant my place of work was officially on the water. My service to the army would be by way of sport. The commanding officer of my unit was instrumental in ensuring I got the right administrative backing to achieve my goal of becoming a sporting champion. All I had to do was report to the unit every three months.

I stepped up my training after the Australian season closed. I started doing ten sessions a week: three in the gym, seven in the water. I had to be as fit as possible. As fast as possible.

I was about to take on the world.

***

The first things I packed were my water legs. Basic, no microchips or Bluetooth, they were metal poles with plastic feet and the knee a glorified door hinge. I placed them in one of the two oversized suitcases I would be taking to Moscow, for my first-ever international event.

I took a moment to look at the prosthetics I'd be wearing to compete at the 2014 ICF Canoe Sprint World Championship. Was this real? Was I really going to a world title race? I had only been paddling for seven months. I couldn't believe things had happened this fast. What felt like such a distant dream was suddenly here, all the more real now I was packing to fly to Russia.

As proud as I was anxious, I continued to pack, which was a sport in its own right. Water legs safe and secure, I placed a spare set of fully functioning military-grade Ottobock prostheses in the suitcase. I was given a duplicate pair of prostheses to supplement the everyday pair I owned. I used them as a back-up, in case anything on my main set broke, so I decided it would be a good idea to take them with me. Then in went the other leg-related items: six knee liners, six knee sleeves, two 4-millimetre Allen keys and two battery chargers. I also threw in a handful of valves. All in all, the bag contained more than thirty kilograms of gear.

My other bag was light in comparison. Filled with jumpers, jackets and competition wear, it was standard travel size. I also had to take two paddles and a wheelchair. While I'd long ago ditched the crutches, I still used a wheelchair. Even though I'd become proficient on the prosthetics, they were not appropriate for long-term use. Despite a near perfect fit, they were both awkward and uncomfortable, and became painful after about an hour. So I used them only when needed: to cook or clean, to reach for something high, or when I left the house.

My chair is a fixed-frame rather than folding type. I find it quite easy to move and I'd become proficient in using it to get around. There aren't too many things I can't do while in my wheelchair and, for those things that prove problematic, the legs are both easy and quick to attach, although putting shoes on the plastic feet can be a pain.

I also packed an assortment of other competition-related gear. Things like water bottles and GPS, a physio roller and stretch bands. Thankfully I didn't have to worry about my boat: the 7.3-metre craft had been freighted ahead and was already in Russia.

I met my new team at the airport. There were plenty of people around to help with the gear, but I wanted to carry it all myself. Legs on and walking tall, I managed to get the entire load onto a single trolley. I smiled when the check-in lady asked me if my wheelchair was a bike, proud that I had managed the feat so well that my injury had gone unnoticed. When I boarded the flight with the Australian team, I was beaming with pride, other passengers looking at me because I was wearing an Australian polo, not because I'd lost my legs.

It was all smooth sailing until we arrived in Russia.

'What do you mean?' I said when a customs official told me they'd confiscated one of the suitcases. 'My legs and paddles are in that case.'

Yep. I was told I could not have the suitcase that contained not only the water legs I'd need for the race, but also my spare set, and the battery charger I'd need for the legs I had on.

Guy Powers, who had taken over as head coach while Andrea was on maternity leave, stepped in when he saw I was about to lose my shit. He had no luck either. We were told we'd have to come back the next day. I didn't end up getting the suitcase until the night before my first race. Guy had to beg and maybe even pay the officials to release it. Yep. A bribe. I shouldn't have been surprised – after all, this is common in Russia.

Armed with water legs and ready to race, I was blown away by the course. It was brand new and state of the art. No expense spared. Turns out the Russian vice president, a former national kayaker who still enjoyed a paddle, had a bit to do with it. He convinced Vladimir Putin to open the vault to pay for his pet project.

I was also surprised by the weather. I always thought Russia would be a cold place, all snowstorms and blizzards, even in summer. I could not have been more wrong. It was at least 35 degrees and humid as hell. I wouldn't need all those jumpers and jackets I'd packed in my second suitcase.

When my heat was called, I put my canoe in the water and paddled my way to the start line. Heading towards the automatic starting gate, which is called a start bucket, I was glad the now-empty lane next to me was not occupied by the reigning world champion, who had been reclassified before the race. Scheduled to race in VL2, which is the class for people with mid-level disabilities like myself, the champion had been reclassified to VL3, which was for lower-level disabilities – things such as a single amputation rather than double.

I placed the nose of my canoe in the bucket and waited for it to drop. Connected to a metal frame, the bucket would disappear under the water when the race went green.

Ready. Set. Go …

Bucket gone and canoe set free, I slammed my paddle into the water to the left and stroked twice. Then I pulled it out and jammed it into the water on my right. Another two strokes. I was using a paddling style known as the traditional Tahitian. Using a short, single paddle, I'd stroke on both sides of the boat. A couple of times on the right and then, as the boat started to change course, I'd move to the left. I was the only person in my class using this style. All the others were using a longer paddle to make either a 'J' or 'C' stroke, and all their paddling was done on one side.

I had no idea which was proving most effective given I was looking down the lane. I didn't turn my head around until I'd reached the line. I was surprised not to see anyone in front. I turned around. There they were. All behind me. I'd won.

I was stoked to have won, but celebrated only by way of a fist pump followed by a smile. While it was nice to have won the heat, the final was still to come. I watched on as a British paddler named Jon Young took out the other heat. He was both experienced and fast. He was also the man I'd have to beat in the final. I went to bed that night playing out the race in my head. I'd have to be flawless. Perfect. Execute every stroke and every change perfectly.

I woke up pumped. An international final. My first international final. In Moscow! Again, I paddled out to the start line and moved towards the bucket. The Lane 5 bucket. Lane 5 was pole position, the top spot, the best lane. I'd secured top billing after recording the fastest time in the heats. I put the bow of the boat in the bucket and told myself I belonged, my lane number a validation of all the work I'd done to get there.

Ready. Set. Go!

The bucket dropped and I took off. I went hard, gave it my all. Again, I only focused on myself, head down and all hard work. But this time I couldn't help myself sneaking a glance out the corner of my eye as a powered my way towards the finish line.

No one. Nothing. I was all on my own.

So I pushed. Went as hard as I could. And a couple of strokes later I was a world champion.

Holy shit! I was completely surprised. I hadn't expected this. Not yet. The shock continued when I learned I'd set the world's fastest time. I went into the event thinking I had potential. I'd leave with a gold medal and a world's fastest time.

Walking legs back on, I stood proud and tall as I received that medal. It was put around my neck just eight months after I picked up a paddle and exactly two years since I stepped on that IED. In a bizarre coincidence, the final took place on the anniversary of the worst day of my life: 23 August 2012

Now, exactly twenty-four months on, I was celebrating my biggest-ever achievement. What a turnaround.

My dream of making the Paralympics was no longer a dream. It was now a possibility. As was winning gold.

It was also my mission.

21
INVICTUS

I WENT STRAIGHT FROM MOSCOW to Rio de Janeiro in Brazil for another competition, which also happened to be a World Championship event. Run by a different governing body, but essentially the same sport, it was the 2014 World Outrigger Championships. I was excited to go, not just because it was another chance to compete on the world stage, but also because I'd never been to South America. It was also where the Paralympics would be held in 2016 so it was an opportunity to get a look at the place and the people.

Located in Copacabana, under the shadow cast by the Christ the Redeemer statue, the regatta course was underwhelming despite the spectacular scene. With less than two years to go until both the Olympics and Paralympics, they'd only got as far as putting some buoys in, and even those weren't straight. They hadn't even removed all the weed from the water, which would have been a disaster in a kayak.

Thankfully I was in a canoe, and the weed didn't prove to be an issue as I doubled up and won another gold medal. Not content with winning my event, I entered myself into the able-bodied race, where I'd compete against the best outrigger paddlers in the world. I wouldn't say that I registered for races because I wanted to compare myself against the world's best. It was more a case of just wanting another opportunity to race. I had no doubt that it would make me a better paddler. And it gave me a chance to learn from the best. I performed pretty well, finishing eighth.

All in all, it was a good early introduction to Brazil, the place that would make or break my dream. The people, the climate, the course, the competition: I got a good taste of what to expect in 2016.

***

I celebrated my success by travelling to New Zealand to spend a week with Rachel. I would have stayed longer but I had to jet off to another event – the inaugural Invictus Games. Inspired by a visit to the US Department of Defense's Wounded Warrior Games, Prince Harry launched the Invictus Foundation in 2013 and had a hands-on role in planning the inaugural event in London. A soldier himself, a captain who had toured Afghanistan twice, Prince Harry made the Invictus Games his cause.

He saw the power of sport and the opportunities it could provide to those who had been injured while serving their countries. I found out I'd be the captain of the very first Australian Invictus Games team while I was competing in Brazil. I'm not sure why I was selected among a host of worthy candidates. I guess I was an example of a person who had used sport as an inspiration to recover from a devastating injury. Whatever the reason, I was both surprised and proud.

I flew over separately from the team as I was in New Zealand. Rachel came too, and we couldn't believe the fanfare. Everyone in London knew it was on. Needless to say, Prince Harry had some pull.

With paddling not being offered, the sports I'd compete in would be swimming and archery. I'd done them before at the Marine Trials, so they were a natural choice. While I enjoyed archery, I didn't progress very far, but I did beat one of the top-seeds in what came as a major surprise to both me and him. I felt a little bit bad about knocking him out, because he was far better than me and the favourite to win gold. But I'm a competitive bastard and took my opportunity to beat him when he was having a bad day.

All the athletes and their family members were invited to a function at the US ambassador's house after my day of archery. I ended up running late, as the archery had gone over time. I could see the mansion called Winfield House from the road. The Neo-Georgian mansion boasts, among other things, thirty-five bedrooms.

Rachel and I walked through the towering gate and started up the driveway.

'Have a look at this.' I pointed at the collection of cars parked on the lawn. Ferraris, Lamborghinis and McLarens. I stopped beside an antique Aston Martin, silver, immaculate and almost sixty years old. 'That's a DB5. Like the one James Bond drove in *Goldfinger*.'

Turns out it wasn't just *like* the one Bond drove in *Goldfinger.* It *was* the one Bond drove in *Goldfinger.* It had an estimated value of more than $5 million.

I turned my attention towards the band.

'Wow, that sounds all right,' I said as we walked across the immaculately manicured lawn, which just happened to be the second-biggest private lawn in London, twelve acres in total.

The band, still out of our sight, was playing a Foo Fighters song.

'Sounds just like the real thing,' I continued.

Turns out it was the real thing. I was stunned to see Dave Grohl on the lawn with his band, belting out 'The Pretender'. I'd been expecting a cover band. I was standing jaw agape, staring at the rock god when I was interrupted.

'G'day mate,' Prince Harry said as he approached.

'Oh,' I blurted. 'Hey bro.'

Rachel went white.

As a soldier employed by a Commonwealth country, I was obliged under the rules of service to address any member of the royal family formally. I should have said, 'Good evening, Your Royal Highness'. Instead, I said 'Hey bro'. What was I thinking?

While I'd have been sent off to the Tower of London 200 years earlier for making that remark, Prince Harry didn't bat an eyelid. I ended up meeting him several times over the following few years and got to know him reasonably well. Despite being one of the most famous men in the world, he's just a normal dude. A good guy.

When this function was over – it was one of many star-studded events I'd attend during the Invictus Games – I continued to compete, this time in the pool. I felt far more comfortable in the water than I had on the archery range, and ended up doing quite well. I actually left London with three medals: two silver and a bronze.

While Rachel had to fly back to New Zealand to continue her studies, at the conclusion of the games I went to France and then Belgium with members of the RSL team to visit some famous World War I battlefields. It was a humbling experience and a trip I will never forget. I'd urge every Australian to visit places like Villers-Bretonneux and the Somme. I hadn't fully understood the scope of the Anzacs' sacrifice.

Then, with 2014 done and dusted, I flew home. It had been the best year of my life. Amazing. To think I'd been lying in a hospital bed just two years earlier. I never in my wildest dreams thought I'd be introduced to Prince Harry as a world champion. I felt like I'd won Lotto. Life was good. Maybe even better than before.

What could possibly go wrong?

***

Andrea, back in her role as head coach after maternity leave, called me as I was getting ready for bed. It was 9 pm. A Sunday night.

'This can't be good,' I said as I answered my phone, thinking she was going to cancel our session scheduled for 5.30 am the following day.

'It's not. I've got some bad news. Something I want to tell you before you find out ... '

Maybe she'd quit. Would I have to find a new coach?

'The International Paralympic Committee has just removed the V1 canoe from the Paralympic Games,' she said.

'Bullshit,' I interrupted. 'No way. You're kidding me, right?'

'No. Afraid not. I just got a call. It's official. The V1 is being replaced by the kayak, the K1.'

I was in disbelief. The Paralympics were just eighteen months away.

'They can't do that,' I fired. 'We're about to go to a qualifying race. What about all the work we've done? They can't expect me to start from scratch. Is there anything we can do?'

'Afraid not,' Andrea deadpanned. 'They've made their decision.'

She explained why they'd scrapped the outrigger canoe and replaced it with the kayak. It was because of an issue with the classification system, which needed an overhaul.

At this point I should talk a little more about the classification system and its importance in my sport. As I've mentioned, there are three classifications in each paracanoe discipline, which relate to the level of disability of the athlete. Firstly, the 'para' in Paralympic doesn't mean paraplegic. It means parallel, in that the Paralympics run alongside the Olympic Games. The Paralympics is the Olympics for athletes with a disability. The devil is in the detail.

What makes a person disabled?

Missing legs? Of course.

Missing an arm? Yep.

How about a finger? It does.

While all of these conditions represent a clear disability, is it fair to pit someone who is missing a finger against someone missing a leg? Probably not. But what if the sport was archery? The person missing the finger might be at a disadvantage. And that's why the classification system is so complex, depending on both the disability and the sport in which the athlete competes.

With the three disability classes in my sports, each classification reflects the severity of the disability, with 1 for the most affected and 3 for the least affected. I'm in 2, the middle, which some people find strange because I am missing legs, not arms. But those people don't know how important legs are in my sport. A lot of the power in a paddle stroke comes from the legs. Leg drives kick in after the catch, which is when the paddle hits the water. They then push the power generated from that drive into the core, into the arms, into the paddle and finally into the water. All I'm saying is that the classification system is complex. And while I agreed with the reasons they gave for scrapping my boat, I didn't agree with the timing. We were three weeks away from the first qualifying event, and the only thing that could have stopped me from qualifying was a major injury. Now I had to start from scratch. Go from a canoe to a kayak.

But aren't they the same thing? Well, I might have thought so too had I not been in both. They're not the same thing. Not at all. The only thing they share in common is the water in which they race. They're vastly different sports.

Don't believe me? You will when you read about the world champion canoer who couldn't even stay in the kayak, let alone race it.

***

I went to training the next day and took my canoe as if I hadn't been told that I'd just wasted over a year of my life. And I was fine until I began paddling in, session over, only reality ahead.

'What's the point?' I muttered under my breath as I dragged the canoe onto the beach.

I was suddenly furious. I kicked the canoe with my metal leg. Raging, I lifted my paddle into the air as I thought about all the training, all the time, all the resources that had been wasted preparing me for something that no longer existed. I was about to bring the paddle down, wanted to smash my boat to bits. I'm not sure how I stopped myself, but I did. With gritted teeth, I washed down my boat and packed it away. I then jumped in my car and drove home, no goodbyes or see-you-laters. I stewed as I drove.

The year 2015 had started on such a high. The year I'd qualify for the Paralympics. I'd upped my training, lost weight and increased my strength. Now competent in my craft, the basics down, I was going to fine-tune and work on all the extra things that would help me go faster. I'd been in for a good year. I'd already competed in Sydney and was looking ahead to the world championship, this year in Milan.

And then came that call. That decision. Everything had been for nothing.

Andrea called not long after I arrived home. 'You want to come back for a 10 am session in the kayak?' Andrea asked. 'We might as well get stuck straight in.'

I decided it was something I needed to do. My anger wasn't going to get me to the Paralympics. I thought about it as I drove back. With the nationals just three weeks away, I had to become not only proficient in a kayak but also fast. In order to qualify for the world championships, I'd have to set an international-standard time. I'd essentially miss an entire season if I failed to set that time. And while I'd still have an opportunity to qualify for the Paralympics the following year, I knew the next three weeks were make-or-break.

I hesitantly put the kayak in the water. It was the first time I'd been in one since I did the test in New Zealand, when I'd done nothing more than float and keep it upright. I wasn't so lucky this time.

I fell in the water after only a few strokes. I went under and, at least for a moment, I didn't want to come back up. I was utterly embarrassed. Here I was, a world champion, and I could not even stay in my boat. It was completely deflating. I thought I was past this, training wheels long ago thrown in the bin. I took a gulp of air when I surfaced. My shame turned to anger.

I grabbed the boat and began swimming back to shore. Dragged it as I stroked, determined as I'd ever been. I wanted to get to the Paralympics and this was the only way. I figured I'd conquered the V1 and I could conquer this. I didn't think I'd be able to get anywhere near the international time, but I was going to give it a go. If I failed I'd stay in Australia and train on my own. Get ready for the following year.

I repeated the process for an hour. I'd paddle out towards the middle, fall out, swim back, and then do it all again. *Paddle, sink, swim.* A race kayak is not a boat you can roll over and get back into. They fill with water, so you need to drag them back to shore and empty them first. I was doing more swimming than paddling.

I couldn't believe how difficult this boat was to balance. I was amazed I'd kept it upright in New Zealand. The V1 has an outrigger, a float connected to the left side of the boat that helps keep the boat stable, making it almost impossible to flip. The kayak – narrow, long and without a float – is harder to keep upright. I had two options: keep on going or quit. And I'm not the quitting type, as you may have already worked out.

Thoroughly exhausted but as determined as I was deterred, I decided to go to the gym. Hard work was the only thing that would get me where I needed to be.

My phone rang when I got home. Andrea. Again. 'Want to do another session this afternoon?' she asked.

'Yep.' I went back for another hour of *paddle, sink and swim.*

***

I did three sessions the following day. *Paddle, sink, swim.* But I was getting a little further each time I emptied the water from the boat and went back out. Soon fifty metres became sixty metres. Then sixty metres became seventy metres. After a week, three sessions a day, I got to a point where I was actually able to keep the craft stable enough to join the rest of the squad. While far from fast, I could sit at the back of the group and paddle behind them. I bobbed around in their wash, which highlighted my next hurdle – steering. As I mentioned, the kayak is steered by a foot-operated rudder or tiller bar. That proved a problem, as I didn't have a foot. So I went about teaching myself to steer with the paddle, just using my weight and the paddle to keep my boat straight.

The three weeks leading up to the nationals were exhausting, both mentally and physically. I ended up having to swim about a kilometre each session to get myself back to shore. But I got better and better, and was encouraged after we did a trial race. It turned out I was only one second away from the time I needed to set.

When I arrived in Sydney for the nationals, I didn't know what to expect. Getting close to the international time had given me a little confidence, but even making the time didn't mean I'd qualify for the world championships. Not if I didn't also win. I looked at the competition as I moved towards the line. They were all guys I'd never raced against. I was told a guy named Sam was the one to beat. Apparently, he was the best in my class. After winning my first race a month earlier, I lined up against him for a head-to-head battle for an Australian spot. The winner would be off to the world championships in Milan, provided they set the minimum qualifying time.

I managed to both beat him and make the time. Just, in both instances. And I managed to do what I thought would prove impossible. I'd not only learned a new sport in three weeks but I'd made the Australian team. I'd kept my Paralympic dream alive. Still, I had a lot of work to do. Standing in front of me and my golden dream was a six-time KL2 champion: an Austrian by the name of Markus Mendy Swoboda.

22

THE SHARK AND THE IRON COWBOY

I TRIED NOT TO LET THEM intimidate me as I made my way towards the line for my first world championship final in a kayak, even though one of them was circling like a shark and another banging his boat as if he were a wild beast.

I'm not exaggerating.

Having arrived in Milan for the ICF Canoe Sprint Championships, I got through my heat and was now paddling in the warm-up area, edging towards the gates. The shark was Markus Mendy Swoboda, the six-time KL2 champion, and the beast was Fernando Rufino de Paulo, a former pro bodybuilder who still benched 300 pounds for breakfast and was known as the Iron Cowboy.

Markus launched into a sprint, before suddenly performing a U-turn and was now paddling away from the gate. Towards me. He weaved his way through the competitors, going left and right, performing a series of elaborate turns.

Then he got to me; left, right, behind, and then back in front.

Markus lost both legs after a farming accident when he was seven. He took up Paracanoe when he was ten and was now a master of his craft. He'd been so good that he'd made the able-bodied Austrian Under-23 team before deciding to become a para-athlete. Now twenty-five, he'd spent fifteen years competing in a kayak and he moved the boat like it was an extension of his body. I was still struggling to steer mine straight, and right now he was giving me an up-close-and-personal demonstration of his incredible skill. I don't know whether he was trying to intimidate the competition, but it was working.

And then there was the Iron Cowboy. He screamed so loudly and suddenly that I almost fell out of my boat. He screamed again, banging his boat as he did so. I can't tell you what he was screaming because it was in Portuguese, but I got the message all the same. Fernando, Markus's biggest rival, was here to win.

My new competitors were nothing like the men I'd gone up against in the canoe. But, while slightly intimidated, this is where I wanted to be. I did my best to ignore both of them as I moved into the gate, turning my attention to the job ahead. I had to fully focus on my start because it was my weakness. I was a strong finisher after working hard on my endurance, but still struggled when it came to getting out of the gates. And that was a big problem in a 200-metre race that is over in just forty-five seconds or so.

Shit! I'm here. I'm really here, I said to myself. I was about to race for a K1 world title.

I lined up right next to Markus in the second-best lane. I put my nose in the gate and immediately struggled to balance the boat. This was the most difficult part of the race. I was still learning how to maintain my balance while sitting still. I was okay as soon as I got going, as the kayak becomes more stable with speed.

I was still upright and in the boat when the bucket dropped. I dug my paddle in and got going. Markus was already gone. He got off to a flyer. So did everyone else.

While I had given away an advantage, I went as hard as I could, knowing my best was to come. I began feeling comfortable as I got into my stroke and started gaining momentum. And then, one by one, I started picking off the field.

I saw Fernando in my peripheral vision. He was in front of me but not by much. I dug a little deeper. We were soon neck and neck. I dug even deeper and pipped him at the post. While I beat the Brazilian, I didn't catch Markus. He won the race, finishing about half a second in front of everyone else.

I was second. It felt every inch as good as a win. I'd won a silver medal just three months after I'd been kicking my canoe, my Paralympic dream in disarray thanks to a rule change. I had gone from three sessions a day just trying to stay in the boat to winning a silver medal at the World Championships. I was back on track. I was pumped.

I won my second gold medal in the outrigger canoe. It ended up being a little too easy for my liking, because I was one of the few athletes who chose to compete now it was not a Paralympic sport. While most brushed it to concentrate on the K1, I figured it was still an opportunity to compete for a prestigious title. I also wanted to defend my crown, and took great pride in both competing in and winning the race. Rachel and my parents were there, and winning a gold medal in front of them was an unforgettable moment.

***

Following a quick trip around Italy with Rachel for a much-needed break, I travelled over to Brazil for the Paralympic test event in Rio. It was an exclusive event, with only a few in my class invited. My focus was to further familiarise myself with the place, the people and the course, eighteen months ahead of the games.

The venue was still in no shape to host a world-class event. While the lanes were now straight, the course was still very much under construction. Since 2014, when I was last there, they'd only managed to add start gates and an unanchored pontoon. The 'lake', or lagoon, was quite different from the other venues I'd been to. Most of the lakes we compete on are straight, purpose-built channels. The one in Rio was a big, open, love heart–shaped body of water. It made paddling a challenge, with unusual winds and waves. There was also still a large amount of weed, which was a major concern now I was in a craft with a rudder, even though I kept mine locked straight.

On the water, the results were a repeat of the world championships, with Markus winning and me coming second. He finished about half a second in front of me again. In distance, half a second translates to about half a boat length. While only about three metres, it's a fair margin in a 200-metre race. While it was clear that I had some work to do, I didn't think making up that margin was beyond me. I knew I could find speed, especially in my start, and I was confident of being able to bridge that gap before my next trip to Brazil.

The big unknown was whether Markus had anything in reserve. Was he just doing what he had to do to win? I also had to assume that, like me, he'd improve. But by how much? While he was a veteran, I was new to the sport. I figured that meant I had more untapped potential than him. At least I hoped it did.

The games were still a long way off. I hadn't even qualified yet. While I'd won Australia a spot by coming second in Milan, I'd have to win the Australian Championships the following year to book my own spot.

***

Rachel and I were seeing each other every six weeks or so. While both busy, with me competing and her finishing her med-school marathon, we were managing our long-distance relationship. We kept in touch with daily phone calls, messages and video chats. And with her schedule and mine, we figured our relationship would have been no different had we lived in the same house.

We got an opportunity to test that theory a few months later when Rachel finished med school and moved to Australia. She'd made a lot of sacrifices for me since Afghanistan, and this was another one. Having completed her Bachelors of Medicine and Surgery, she'd knocked back an opportunity to work in a big hospital in Auckland, where many of her friends were going. On arriving in Australia, she went to the Gold

Coast University Hospital to meet the administrators, but she didn't have an offer and was stepping into the unknown.

I don't think I pressured Rachel to make the move and I'd like to think she made the decision on her own. But regardless of how it played out, I was absolutely stoked to finally have her by my side. It was the next step, exciting and new. It gave me a stability I'd never had. I now had my girl, my job and my dream. I felt completely supported in every aspect of my life.

And Rachel ended up getting a job at the Gold Coast University Hospital, beating a host of applicants to become one of just a few international graduates employed by the new, world-class hospital.

***

I was as happy on the water as I was at home. Everything was on track, stroke by stroke, improving every day. I was in the best shape of my life when my chance to qualify for the Paralympics finally came around. Finding ways to work both smarter and harder in the gym – and refining my diet – I was both lean and strong. I'd dropped four kilograms but managed to gain muscle.

The National Championships were held in Perth and I blitzed the field with a complete performance that included a new and improved start. I went faster over 200 metres than anyone had before. The time, however, was not officially recognised as a world record because you need to have three nations represented in a race for it to qualify.

I'd found a way to push myself to this time even though there was little in the way of competition. Without strong competitors, I motivated myself in other ways. I think my biggest competitor has always been myself. I have motivated myself to new bests by creating my own competition. But Markus was also providing motivation at this event, even though he was overseas. I thought about how hard he was training and what times he was setting. I wondered who would have won – me or him – if he was in Perth. It was hard to judge on time alone, because conditions had been fast; with the famous Fremantle doctor sea breeze at my back, and the water flowing towards the line.

Either way I was happy. I'd not only qualified for my first Paralympic Games but had done it with a record-breaking time, albeit unofficial. It felt awesome. I'd achieved the goal I set when I was lying on a gurney in Afghanistan. Still, I didn't celebrate. I moved on to my next and upgraded goal: a Paralympic gold medal.

***

'Hurry up, Australia!' the official yelled over the PA. 'This is your fault.'

I turned to the rescue crew who had pulled me out of the water and put me in the safety boat.

'You need to tip out the water,' I screamed. 'Come on. I'm about to be disqualified.'

My World Championship bid began with a disaster when I fell out of the boat during a false-start catastrophe. Having arrived in Duisburg, Germany, following a whirlwind trip to Orlando for the Invictus Games, and itching to take on Markus, I was in the drink. My competition was set to end before it began.

The horror show began at the gates. With Markus in the other heat, I was determined to improve my start. I'd been working hard on this, and saw the heat as an ideal test. I moved into my gate, Lane 5, and lined up next to an Italian guy who was considered the sport's best starter. I was going to try to go with him.

Ready. Set …

The Italian went. I went too. Only problem was the bucket didn't move.

There had been no *Go*.

It was two strokes before I realised I'd jumped the start.

Oh shit!

I'd pre-empted that start and driven the nose of my boat into the bucket before it dropped. The gate that held the bucket was flexing forward. There was nothing I could do. I was flung back and into the water, the gate eating the force of the three rowers who had gone early and spitting it back in my face. I was upended. Underwater for the first time in my racing career, I fumbled for the strap that was holding me in my craft. I'd drown if I didn't get myself out. I found the buckle fast and freed myself – but the drama had just begun.

Thankful to be pulled into the safety boat, I quickly learned that the rescue crew had no idea about my sport. They didn't have a clue how to right my boat, empty it, and get it back to me.

They looked at me with blank faces so I pushed them out of the way, jumped in and did it myself.

'Last chance Australia,' the official yelled.

My boat was still half full but I was out of time. I moved towards the line. The water was about three inches deep and sloshed about, back and forth. Aside from that, my rudder had been knocked and was no longer locked straight. But I'd avoided disqualification. Just. And even handicapped by the weight of the water and a boat that wouldn't steer straight, I won my heat. It was time to meet Markus.

***

I went out to the warm-up area when the final was called. I ignored the shark as he circled, concentrating on myself. Determined not to repeat my heat horror show, I practised my starts. I couldn't afford another blunder. I was confident of getting it right by the time I moved into the bucket. In Lane 7, right beside Markus, I listened hard, paddle cocked and ready to fire.

Ready. Set ...

This time I waited.

Go.

While the bucket didn't get me, Markus did. But not by much. I was pleasantly surprised to see how close he was, all the work I'd been doing to improve my start had paid off when it mattered. Leading by a full boat length at our other races, Markus was only half a length in front of me by the time I got up to speed and into my stroke. I was in the race.

There was only three metres in, with the best part of my race still to come. I steamed down the lake, the gap narrowing with every stroke. My hands started to tingle when I drew level with the six-time champion. Suddenly I felt like I didn't have the strength to hold my paddle. With the finish line in sight, I found the steel and the power to blast my way home.

It took me a moment to realise I'd won. Even longer to realise I was now a K1 world champion. I'd done it. Beaten

Markus. Delivered him his first defeat in seven years. It didn't sink in until I walked onto the podium to collect my gold medal.

'So you have finally learned how to start,' Markus said as he faced up to his first defeat. He remained dignified as he took his place on the unfamiliar second step of the podium, and I could see that while he was disappointed, he hadn't lost any of his determination.

I was both stoked and surprised. I hadn't been expecting to beat Markus. Not yet. This victory had been planned for later in the year. At the Paralympics. I ended up wondering whether it would hurt me. Had I just lit a fire? Awoken the beast in Markus?

Later that night I thought back to the podium. To that comment. It wasn't a declaration of resignation. It was a declaration of war. He'd looked like a man determined, not defeated, as he accepted his silver medal. I knew he was going to train harder than he ever had. I'd given him a motivation he hadn't had for seven years. I also wondered if he'd been foxing. Maybe he'd realised I was his Paralympic competition after the time I'd set in Perth, and he'd let me win in a ploy to make me overconfident. In any case, I wasn't going to be lulled into a false sense of security. I knew what I had to do, and nobody was going to stop me.

***

Fresh from the world championships, I decided to step it up. Even though my training had been good, I knew I could do more. I could go faster. And I thought the best way to do it was to train in a more focused environment.

The able-bodied Australian team had gone overseas to ramp up their preparation for the Olympics, which would begin in Rio a month ahead of the Paralympics. While the men's canoe/kayak team was in Hungary, the women had gone to Italy, which is also where our pre-Paralympic camp would be. I was on par with the women when it came to speed, so I asked if I could go over to Italy three weeks ahead of schedule to train with them.

I thought training in Italy with the women would improve my performance. First, it would get me away from the distractions at home: media requests, friends and family. I was only interested in using my time to go faster. Sport can be a selfish pursuit. Secondly, I'd be able to learn from these amazing athletes. I'd already established a good relationship with one, Naomi Flood. She was an experienced Olympian and a hell of a paddler. She was also happy to take me under her wing.

I arrived in Milan on 26 July. Training alongside Floody was brilliant. She knew how to push me. She also helped me fine-tune my diet and gave advice on everything from stretching to sleep. I'd trained with the women before, so I felt completely comfortable with them. My body was in great shape, holding up to the training load. I was fast and strong. I was also happy and in a good place.

I'd already been training for three weeks in Italy when the Paralympic team arrived to begin its three-week camp. I wished my mate Floody and the rest of the women's team all the best and continued training with her lessons learned. Floody represented Australia a week or so later. We got together as a team in the gym and watched not only Floody but all the women compete. They did us proud.

In the camp, there was a lot of excitement, which grew

as the Paralympics neared. It reached fever pitch when it was finally time for us to leave. I could hardly believe I was on my way to Brazil. To Rio. To compete at the Paralympic Games.

We flew from Milan to Rio via Portugal. 'Sir, would you like to come into the cockpit,' an air steward asked as the first leg of the journey drew to a close. 'The captain has invited you in for the landing.'

Needless to say, I replied 'Hell yeah!' I'm not sure how the invitation came about, but it was a thrill to get the chance to ride at the very front. My passion for aircraft was still strong, and I watched in awe as the captain and his co-pilot gently placed 50,000 kilograms of speeding metal onto a dime after a three metres per second fall.

Darkness had descended by the time we reached Rio. A mass of volunteers, unmissable in their yellow-and-orange shirts, were waiting in the terminal to meet us, armed with bottles of water and smiles. There were more volunteers in the airport than passengers. There was no escaping them or the fact that the Paralympics were set to begin. Posters, streamers and promotional material were everywhere. The volunteers ushered us through the crowds and into a nearby terminal, which had been turned into an accreditation centre.

Eventually we were processed, and now with lanyards bearing our credentials and swipe cards to get free products from Coke machines, we were escorted by the volunteers to a bus.

We rolled into the village that would be our home for the next eleven days. It resembled a small city: a cluster of towering apartment blocks wedged between a lake and a highway. Located in Barra da Tijuca in western Rio, the Paralympic section of the village consisted of thirty-one apartment blocks. There were more than 15,000 apartments inside, some specially modified for both the disabled and visually impaired.

It was some sight, blocks about fifty storeys high, flags hanging off nearly every balcony. It wasn't hard to work out where the Dutch were staying, given every accessible surface of their apartments had been draped in orange.

The village was happening. People everywhere. Coming from every corner of the globe and suffering all manner of disability. It was quite confronting at first to be surrounded by more fellow disabled people than I'd never seen in one place. I remember checking out all the different types of prostheses and mobility devices. I stopped a guy to ask him about his scooter, which was completely cool. It was both new and interesting to be a majority rather than a minority. There was no worrying about people looking at me – instead I had to be careful not to look at others.

My first impressions soured not long after I checked into my room. On the surface everything appeared okay – all new, clean and furniture fine. But it became evident there were some issues when I had to use the toilet. A little sign in the bathroom told me I wasn't allowed to flush anything other than human waste down the toilet. And I mean anything. Not even toilet paper. The sign informed me that I was to put my used toilet paper in the bin. Yes. Yuk.

I was aware that there would be some issues in the village because of a funding controversy. In a poor decision that led to disabled athletes being put below the able-bodied, the Brazilian committee had taken money from the Paralympics budget and put it into the Olympics budget. The Paralympics wouldn't even have gone ahead had they not found money just two weeks before the competition was due to start. And while they got the money and finished the village in time, everything was slapped together. The non-toilet-paper flushing toilets were the result of the small-bore plumbing pipe they'd used to save money.

Thanks to my time in the army, putting shitty paper in a bin didn't bother me too much. I'd burned tonnes of raw sewage while serving in Timor. Still, I wouldn't have been too happy if I was one of the American athletes who ended up with shit seeping down their walls. Yes, both walls and ceiling ended up covered in crap after the Irish team, located in the apartments above, blocked all the pipes by flushing their toilet paper.

Aside from the odd exposed wire and burst pipe, the rest of the village was okay. The dining hall was located in a tent about 300 metres long and 100 metres wide. It dwarfed any tent I'd ever seen, even while in the army. Again, my time as a soldier served me well, given I was completely used to mass feeds. For those who didn't like the long queues and bains-marie, there was a 24-hour McDonald's located in the village. And it was free. The store offered all-you-can-eat McDonalds, at no charge, which I thought was strange given we were athletes. I found it even stranger that the McDonald's Barra da Tijucas was always packed, athletes lining up out the door to get a diet-busting feed.

I thought the prosthetic clinic, located near the dining hall, was far more useful than the free fast food. Especially for me, given Jens was working in the facility, which was run and staffed by Ottobock. It was pretty cool to have my 'leg man' and friend in Rio, knowing I had both support and expert advice should anything go wrong with my gear.

23

LONG AND STRONG

DAY ONE BEGAN WHEN the alarm went off at 4.30 am. Despite not having to be at the course at any particular time, I convinced the team we had to get into a race day routine. We'd need to be at Rodrigo de Freitas Lagoon in Ipanema, the venue for all sprint kayak and canoe events, by 8 am when competition began. And even though it was only a 45-minute drive, that meant leaving at 5 am to allow for traffic. We'd been told it could take up to three hours to get there on a bad day, and I successfully argued that we should factor in the worst-case scenario, even for non-time-sensitive training. We all needed to be completely prepared and conditioned come competition time.

I exited the bus and marvelled at the facility. I couldn't believe it was the same place I'd visited less than a year before. I'd doubted it would even be finished, let alone the world-class facility I was now looking at. Aside from straight lanes and anchored pontoons, there were also grandstands, windboard and towers. The transformation was remarkable.

But while the facility was immaculate, the water was not. 'Ready to get Zika?' someone remarked as we walked towards the lake.

Zika virus had been one of the big talking points leading into the games. A mosquito-borne virus, Zika had originated in Brazil and spread to other parts of the Americas. We were told to take a number of precautions, which included wearing long-sleeved shirts, applying insect repellent and sanitising straight after leaving the water. I wasn't particularly worried. Zika was really only dangerous if you were pregnant.

While there wasn't a mosquito in sight, the water quality was poor: murky and more brown than blue. That was due to the lack of sanitation in the homes around the city.

Because of its unique layout and its position near the coast, the course was susceptible to wind. While most sprint kayakers train on glass-like surfaces, this course could become rough, all whitecaps and waves.

But then the wind turned the course into a washing machine on the final day of practice. With heats set to start the following day, we were invited out to the course for start-gate practice. A lot of people opted out because of the wild conditions, but I wasn't going to miss the opportunity. It would become especially valuable if the roaring wind returned the following day. I wasn't surprised to find Markus out on the water. A complete pro, he was one of the three athletes outside the Aussie team who decided to brave the conditions and prepare as planned.

I was used to choppy conditions because I trained on the Gold Coast, an open body of water susceptible to wind. This was rough, but I managed to stay in my boat and got through my routine. I felt completely prepared and comfortable with the start-gate procedure by the time I paddled back to land. Rain, hail or shine, I'd be ready come race time.

The night before the heat was like any other: a meal, followed by a phone call to Rachel, some television and then bed. I slept like a baby, not waking until my alarm sounded at 4.30 am. I threw back the cover, jumped into my chair and rolled onto the balcony. All calm. No wind. Not even a breeze. Those who hadn't trained had dodged a bullet. Still, it didn't matter. I was prepared for whatever.

I never felt pressure going into the heats. No nerves. Nothing. I geared up and got on the water when it was time for my heat. I treated it like any other race. Or I did until I got to the line.

'Smash 'em, *Kiwi*!'

I turned towards the stands after hearing someone yell my name. It didn't take me long to spot them. My mates. Decked out in green and gold, holding beers and flags, my cheer squad was in full force. I saw Livo and Wertsy: the two men who had been by my side on my darkest day had travelled all the way to Brazil to be by my side again. Gibbo, my old roomie and Timor drinking buddy, was there too. I saw Mike and Tyson, my mates through thick and thin; our friendship had started at school and not only survived but had grown stronger since I left New Zealand. They were there for me as always. I then saw Mum, Dad and Sophia. My family. The ones who made me the man I was. Brent would have been there too, but he'd just become engaged and had commitments at home. Finally, I saw Rach. The love of my life. A cheer started up.

'Ooh, ah, Curt McGrath! Ooh, ah, Curt McGrath! Ooh, ah, Curt McGrath!'

I wanted to wave but didn't. Couldn't. Instead, I smiled.

Ready. Set ...

Crap!

The bucket dropped while I was thinking about my family and friends. About the effort they'd made to be here. I hadn't even heard the starter call 'hold your boats'. Just go. I'd missed the start.

I dug my paddle in and got going. Thank God this wasn't the final. I'd given away a fair margin but I didn't panic. Markus wasn't in my heat, I didn't need to win to progress, and my back end was still to come. I was pretty sure I could mow them down. And I did. Easily.

With my spot in the final booked, I gave myself a kick in the bum for my bad start. A rookie mistake: I'd let my guard down and been distracted. I vowed not to repeat the error. Lesson learned, I then had a laugh about the state of my mates. I could see they were drunk even from the water. My suspicions were confirmed when I got to see them after warm-down. They weren't just drunk but completely smashed. Turns out they'd pulled an all-nighter. Apparently, Brazil was putting on one hell of a party.

It was great to catch up with the boys and my family, even though we only had five minutes together. It was the first time I'd seen any of them since leaving for Italy. And the boys would have won a gold medal for drinking had that been included as a sport.

***

I spent the evening like every other night before: dinner, a phone chat with Rachel, some TV and bed. Again, I wasn't nervous. Again, I was out like a light. I didn't toss and turn, go through scenarios or play the race out in my head. I went straight to sleep.

I was wide awake and raring to go as soon as the alarm went off at 4.30 am. I boarded the bus after a light breakfast at the dining hall, just like every day since I arrived. Traffic was light and we arrived early for my 10 am race, the 200-metre KL2 final. I had plenty of time to gear up and warm up.

I entered the Australian team tent, located behind one of the four grandstands, at 9 am. Beginning with what I call my 'land warm-up', I grabbed a medicine ball, some stretch bands and a series of rollers. I then rolled, pulled and stretched, loosening up my joints and warming up my muscles.

Come 9.15 and it was time to put on my race uniform, which consisted of a green-and-gold race singlet, an under-top, shorts and a hat. Once dressed, I grabbed my sunglasses, which I always wear when I'm racing, and my lanyard. Warmed up and gear on, I took my paddle and bottle of water and left the tent. It was time to check my boat at boat control.

I walked over to the team rack where all the boats were stored. I pulled down my twelve-kilogram carbon-fibre Plastex sprint kayak. I checked the rudder first, as always. My biggest fear in using a fixed rudder – I steer with my paddle and hips – is that it will be knocked out of place overnight and I won't notice until I'm racing. So I always thoroughly check the position first.

'All good,' I said to Andrea after checking the rudder then the rest of the boat.

Andrea picked up the boat and carried it over to the accreditation area. I handed my lanyard over to her and waited as an official checked the number on my ID against the number I wore on my back. He then turned his attention to my boat, checking all the modifications were approved and legal.

'Okay,' the official. 'You're good to go.'

I placed myself on the ground when I reached the pontoon, removed my legs and then swung myself into the kayak.

All strapped in after securing myself with the snowboard style buckles, I took a sip of water before putting the bottle between my legs.

'You know what to do … ' Andrea said as I pushed off. 'And remember to enjoy it.'

That's when I noticed the 'tingles', first in my hands and then in my belly. I was suddenly nervous.

Why now? I'd never really felt nervous before a race. While I often got nervous tingles in my hand during a race, I'd never had them before the start. It was a shock, especially considering I'd been completely relaxed throughout my whole Paralympic campaign. I thought I was going to get through nerve-free.

I was wrong. I put the paddle across my lap and shook my hands. It didn't help. Neither did taking a deep breath. I moved into my 'on-water warm-up', hoping some paddling would work. I started with a 1000-metre paddle, slow and steady, checking the rudder was good and that I could steer straight. I worried that the nerves would affect my race, which only made them worse. I moved into some power paddling, fast and hard, short spurts of speed. Still the nerves remained. I was getting anxious, the start line nearing with every stroke. I moved into the final phase of my warm-up, practising my starts. I tried to wash away the nerves with a swig of water, the liquid wetting my dry mouth but not curing anything else.

Oh well.

I moved into my lane and paddled my way into the final section of water before the gate. And just like that my nerves were gone.

Thank God.

It was weird how they just vanished – not that I was about to complain. I was filled with a fresh blast of confidence as I continued towards my gate. Nerves gone, no excuses, it was back to business. I turned my mind towards my start, vowing not to be distracted, urging myself to get it right. My mates were no less drunk than the day before and just as loud, but today I'd be listening only to the starter's call. I moved into the gate and placed my nose into the start-gate bucket.

'Hold your boats.'

Kayak balanced, paddle cocked and ready to fire, I was all ears.

Ready ...

I listened hard and looked straight ahead.

Set ...

I could no longer hear the crowd, the only voice in the stadium-like course belonging to the starter.

Go!

I had a really good start. Nailed it. Not early, not late, only a slight wobble as I moved into my stroke. It was my best-ever getaway. Perfect. Or so I thought. Through the corner of my eye, I saw a bow in front of mine. About a quarter of a length in front. The man in that boat was Markus. Of course it was Markus. He'd gunned his way out of the gate to make my perfect start merely good. I sneaked another look at the fifty-metre mark as I searched for rhythm. I hadn't gained. No. Not an inch. In fact, he'd extended his lead to half a boat length. It was time to get to work. It was going to be tough but tough was good. I'd been in a worse position at the world championships and mown him down. I vowed to do it again.

Close enough to hear his heaving breath and his paddle slapping the water, I fully focused on myself. I made sure I grabbed as much water as possible with every plunge of the paddle, made sure my stroke was both powerful and technically correct. I couldn't unleash yet. I had to time my run. I was tempted to chase but I didn't. I knew that would have been a fatal mistake. I paddled my own race. 'Long and strong.'

Assistant coach Guy Powers' words were in my head. Our game plan. I couldn't win the race at this point, but I could lose it. I had to resist the temptation to try to overtake Markus now and risk burning myself out. So I stuck to the script.

I sneaked another look when I hit 100 metres. I'd almost drawn level with him. I changed nothing.

I didn't know where Markus was when I entered the final phase of the race. And I didn't care. It was all about me. Into the final fifty metres, where I was always at my best, I was only worried about giving it my all. I'd worry about the result only when I'd crossed the finish line.

Forty metres ...

I could see nothing but unbroken water in front.

Thirty metres ...

I suspected I was in front but didn't want to interrupt my stroke by sneaking a peak.

Twenty metres ...

My muscles screamed as the lactic acid pulled. I ignored the pain.

Ten metres ...

I could see the finish line. My body urged me to back down, telling me I'd done enough to win. I ignored the soft option and tried to find even more. I continued all the way to the line.

Beep.

And then an extra two strokes, just in case.

The beeping sound of the electronic finishing system didn't register with my brain until after my final stroke.

The beep, my beep, was the first beep. I'd won! I put the paddle across my lap and took a deep breath as I heard another beep.

Second. Markus.

Then came a series of beeps, rapid fire as the rest of the field crossed the line. I let out a big breath and then put my head down. I thought I'd have been pumped in a moment like this, full of adrenaline and emotion, but instead of fist pumps and celebratory shouts, I dipped my head. I was suddenly calm. All still.

It took me a moment to realise what I was feeling. It was as if a heavy blanket had just been pulled away. I hadn't realised how much pressure I'd put on myself until that moment. Hadn't realised that it had started in the moments after I stepped on the IED, when I told everyone I was going to be a Paralympian. That pressure grew during my recovery, each milestone moment removing an excuse or a reason to back out. It intensified when I began competing, and reached fever pitch when I upgraded my goal to not just becoming a Paralympian but becoming a Paralympic gold medallist. No one ever pressured me, said 'Hey didn't you say you were going to become a Paralympian?' Nothing like that. The pressure was of my own making.

And now that pressure was gone.

Head still down, I turned my attention to the memorial bracelet I was wearing on my wrist. Black and made of steel, it was produced to both honour and remember the soldiers who had been killed on my deployment. I'd been wearing it since 2012. It was my way of taking the fallen on a journey they'd been denied. On a journey I was almost denied. The forty-one Australian men who had been killed in Afghanistan had been my source of inspiration; and the band was a constant reminder that I'd been given an opportunity taken away from them.

I reached down and pulled it off my wrist as I thought about the brave men. Guys like James Martin, Darren Smith, Richard Atkinson, Jamie Larcombe and Scott Smith. I decided that this moment was for them and I went to put it into the water. It would be my tribute. I stopped myself when I thought about the water. I didn't want to leave them here. Not in this murky, possibly virus-riddled lake. They deserved better. I put the band back on my wrist.

And that's when I finally looked up. But still I didn't celebrate. Not after seeing Markus. He was shattered, looking as if he was about to cry. I paddled towards him and wrapped my arms around him when I arrived.

'This sport wouldn't be here today if it wasn't for you,' I said. 'You're a true legend.'

I'm not sure what he replied, or if he even said anything. I think he'd have struggled to get a word out. I patted him on the back and attempted to compose myself as I paddled towards the pontoon.

'Well done, mate,' I said as I saw Nick Beighton exiting his boat. I realised he'd finished third.

Nick and I had a lot in common, given he'd also lost both his legs to an IED while serving in Afghanistan. He'd been a British Army captain. We shared a similar story and now we'd be sharing a Paralympic podium.

My team manager, Christine Bain, who we called Bainer, was the first Australian to greet me. She handed me a jacket, a pair of shorts, my legs and a big hug of congratulations. My coach was next in line to give me a hug. I was then pulled away and ushered off into a media zone, and soon a microphone was in my face.

'Is it a dream come true?'

'How much does this mean?'

'How does it feel?'

I responded on autopilot – answers made up on the spot because I still didn't know how or what I felt.

I watched the last race of the day before putting on my shorts and jacket. I was then summoned to the podium. Subdued and slightly numb since crossing the finish line, I exploded with emotion as soon as I saw my friends and family. Mum, Dad, Sophia, Rach and the boys – yep, drunk of course – were in the crowd that had gathered around the podium for the ceremony. I suddenly wanted to celebrate.

I ran over to Rachel first, and we hugged and kissed. I didn't notice she was crying until after the embrace.

'I'm so proud of you,' she said.

And now I was proud too. Finally, a feeling other than relief.

***

I spoke further to Markus as we waited for the medal ceremony. He told me he wasn't happy with his start, which came as a surprise. It looked pretty good from where I was sitting.

'There was too much pressure on me,' he said. 'And I was nervous.'

I was also surprised to hear that a six-time world champion had been nervous before the race. But I suppose there was a lot of pressure on him. He'd been the red-hot Paralympic favourite until I came along. He was supposed to be a sure thing. It must have been hard for him to take. I later learned he'd been working so hard that he lost too much weight. He went crazy with both his training and his nutrition, and overstepped the mark. Pressure can do that. I felt a little sorry for him, but in sport there could only be one winner and today that was me.

Markus, Nick and I watched the other ceremonies as we waited for ours to be called. At last it was our turn. I stood on my legs, proud and tall as I accepted my Paralympic gold medal. Maybe there was even a little tear in my eye as the Australian flag was raised and the national anthem was played. I was still a Kiwi by birth, but very much an Aussie when it came to my chosen sport. This medal was for all the people who had supported me to get to this moment.

This medal was for Australia.

The celebration began as soon as I stepped off the podium. My family and friends were there to greet with handshakes, hugs and high-fives, followed by a few beers behind the grandstand. Mum and Dad told me they were proud. Rachel stood by my side wearing a gigantic smile. We had a lot to catch up on.

***

With my gear packed up and shipped home for me, and my medal around my neck, we made our way towards the hotel that would host the team function. Along the way, I was stopped by strangers, a seemingly endless supply of people asking me for photos. I was happy to oblige.

I'd booked a room in the hotel where the function was to be held. After dropping off our gear and checking out the room, Rachel and I went to the roof, just me and her, for a quiet beer. We didn't say much. Just sat hand in hand, enjoying the moment as we took in the view.

The party lasted all night, so I wasn't particularly flash when I got up at 6 am for a live TV cross back to Australia.

Two days later, I was sitting in a bar with my mates. 'What are you doing?' I said to my team manager as she began removing the long line of empties from the table. 'We don't mind the mess.'

She ignored me and continued to clean. I was sitting in the bar, feeling a little strange to be wearing the team polo that she'd asked me to wear. 'Just in case anyone wants an interview,' she'd said. I thought it had been a weird request, as was her sudden urge to clean. The penny dropped when I saw the camera crew walking towards the bar. They were following the Australian chef de mission, Kate McLoughlin, who just happened to be holding an Australian flag.

With the cameras rolling and now pointing in my direction, Kate stood in front of me, flag in hand and asked me if I'd like to be the Australian flag bearer for the closing ceremony. Wow. I hadn't seen this coming. It was my debut games. My first medal. Not usually emotional, I began tearing up. This was a big deal. Such an honour. I was sure there were others who deserved this more. Men like Kurt Fearnley or Ryley Batt. Ladies like Ellie Cole or Liesl Tesch. Legends. My heroes. I was deeply humbled and incredibly proud just to be considered, let alone asked. It meant even more to me than winning the medal.

With the wheelchair I'd used for the opening ceremony back in my room, I walked proud holding the Australian flag high as I helped close the games. Afghanistan but a distant memory.

I was no longer Curtis McGrath the soldier.

I was no longer Curtis McGrath the amputee.

I was now Curtis McGrath the Paralympian.

It felt good.

24

ROYALS AND RINGS

THERE WAS NO FANFARE when we returned home. No tickertape parades. No celebrations. Being a Paralympian is very different from being an Olympian. I arrived back on the Gold Coast and returned home as if it were from any other event.

While I did some extra media over the following days, headlined by an appearance on Channel Ten's *The Project*, my life was pretty much the same as before I left. Having a gold medal on my mantelpiece didn't change a thing. That was a little bit of a letdown, as my manager at the time had promised me the world. He said sponsors would be lining up to sign me after I won gold. But there were no big cash deals. No free products. Not even an email.

The only thing that changed was that I was doing more public speaking. The only source of income I'd ever had outside of the army, public speaking was something I'd started not long after recovering. Fellow army veteran Ben Roberts Smith had encouraged me to become a public speaker and then mentored me after a chance meeting at the army gym. I remember the day I first met him vividly because he'd been hitting the punching bag so hard that the entire building had been shaking. With Ben's help, I was being booked about once every month or so. That became a lot more frequent after I won my medal. I was mostly hired by companies as a motivational speaker, and would go to conferences to talk to staff.

For a time, I considered having a break from my sport. I toyed with the idea of taking a year off and doing something else. I wasn't burnt out, nor had I fallen out of love with paddling, but having achieved my goal I did wonder whether I should pursue something else. But I decided that all I knew was paddling, so I turned up to training when the new season began.

And I continued where I left off, winning all my races and then going on to defend my world titles in both the kayak and the canoe. Both titles came a little too easily. While I'd continued training with intensity and challenging myself to improve, many of my rivals seemed to be going through the motions. With the next Paralympics three years away, they looked as though they'd taken a long break and had not prepared properly. Markus was not in competition mode and was way off his best for the world titles, held in the Czech Republic. My great rival looked like he'd been enjoying himself instead of training. And good on him. I'd considered doing the same, but my nature prevented me from doing anything other than give it my all.

My best memories of 2017 were on land, headlined by a diamond ring and followed by a national speech. But first, a right royal occasion.

Named as an ambassador for the next Invictus Games, I was flown down to Sydney to join Prince Harry on a promotional tour. He'd flown in to announce Sydney would be hosting the games in 2018, and I became part of his three-day media blitz. It was a huge honour to be an ambassador for a movement I believed in. I joined Harry for a series of interviews. We spent a lot of time together, and my opinion of him, formed during the first Invictus Games in London, didn't change. Prince Harry was down to earth and appeared to be every inch the normal bloke. I ended up giving it to him about the rugby because the British Lions were touring New Zealand at the time and were being flogged – in the first Test at least. I think he enjoyed the banter. I don't think he was used to being sledged.

The next big highlight was when I was asked to deliver the national address at the Australian War Memorial on Anzac Day. I was a little overwhelmed when first asked. I didn't think I deserved the honour, given all the people who had made the speech before me were national heroes. But I also didn't think I could decline. I was anxious even before I accepted, and damn nervous after I did. I would be delivering a speech in front of 40,000 people on Australia's most sacred day. I'd be standing on the steps of the War Memorial, all eyes on me, my speech broadcast live on national TV.

What would I say?

Following some more advice from Ben, who had given the national address just two years before, I employed a speechwriter to help. I didn't want to take my chances writing something myself for such an important occasion. I also went to Canberra for some media training. It was a little overwhelming, too, because the highest-serving enlisted soldier in the Australian Army came to meet me. Regimental Sergeant Major of the Army Donald Spinks AM greeted me and asked me whether I had a ceremonial service uniform. I not only didn't have one but didn't know what it was. So he organised to have me taken off and fitted for the most extravagant suit I'd ever seen. Think of the gear Tom Cruise wore in *Top Gun*.

Even with the speech written for me and my Tom Cruise suit, I was fretting. It was such a big deal and I didn't want to stuff up. I held my breath as I walked up to the rostrum. It was dark and raining, and when I looked out into the crowd I could see only shadows. The lights that had been set up for TV were blazing in my eyes. It was also silent. Forty thousand people in front of me, and I felt like I was completely alone. I started and didn't stop until I was done. And I got through without a hitch. It was some moment. A proud moment.

A further highlight came when I went to the Invictus Games in Toronto to play wheelchair rugby. I'd always wanted to have a crack at that sport but had been worried about getting injured. But now strong and fully recovered, and with the Paralympics three years away, I signed on. And I had a blast. It was as brutal as it was fun, and I loved it. It was the first contact sport I'd played since I was injured, all bash and crash, and I wasn't bad at it either. So much so I reckon I would have taken it up as my full-time sport had I been eligible to play it at the Paralympics. Unfortunately for me, the sport is only open to those have a disability or injury that affects three limbs or more.

I've saved the best highlight of 2017 for last.

I'd organised for Rachel to come and meet me in Toronto for the games. Having already bought the ring – with Tyson's help and advice – I was going to ask her to marry me. Yep. It was finally time. There were no doubts on my side. None. Rachel was the one for me. I knew it straight after my injury and nothing had changed. We worked. Everything worked. Our relationship had gone from strength to strength since the injury. I felt like we were living our lives together, not individually. We were a team. I decided we needed to make it official.

I think Rachel was onto it as soon as she arrived. Wanting to make it a surprise, I'd booked all the accommodation and flights, which was a bit of a giveaway. She met me in Toronto as planned and from there we travelled to Banff. With fresh snow on the ground, we checked in to the fanciest hotel I'd been able to find. It was picturesque. Perfect. It was also within walking distance of a gondola lift that went up to a spectacular lookout. I threw the ring into my pocket before suggesting we go up to the lookout. I also popped a GoPro video camera in there so I could record the moment. Sitting on the gondola on our way up, I reached into my pocket.

'Oh,' Rach exclaimed, big grin on her face. She stopped there when she saw I'd pulled out the GoPro.

We exited the gondola and I scanned the scene, looking for the perfect spot. It was all okay but not what I'd pictured. I hadn't planned to go to the top of the lookout because of all the stairs. I hated stairs. Really struggled with them. But for this I would persevere.

'Let's go up there,' I said. 'We have to get some photos before the sun goes down.'

It was perfect. Right on sunset, not a cloud in the sky and a stunning view. I went to my pocket, this time pulling out a ring instead of a video camera. I got down on my knee.

'Yes,' she said, before I even asked.

My family were as stoked as we were. They loved Rachel too. They were excited about the prospect of the wedding and wanted to support us in any way they could. Rachel's family were also pleased. They were very happy to know we'd be making the relationship both official and legitimate. Mostly people said 'about time', which was a fair assessment.

***

Some good news came at the end of 2017 when the V1 outrigger canoe was put back into the Paralympic program, after they'd sorted out the classification problems. As part of the reclassification I was placed in the highest category. While I was in VL2 before, I'd now be competing VL3 against the fastest guys. Still, it gave me the opportunity to compete for two medals at the 2020 Tokyo Paralympic Games.

I knew I could both train and compete for two disciplines. I didn't think adding the V1 would affect what I was doing in the K1. And I'd kept on competing in both even after V1 was scrapped from Rio. I also didn't have a problem in being re-classified, as my times were the fastest across all three classes, so this would be a great opportunity to stand on the podium twice.

Both my training program and my confidence in competing in both disciplines were confirmed in 2018 when I won both the VL3 200 metres and the KL2 200 metres at the Sprint World Championships, which were held in Montemor-o-Velho, Portugal. I set a world-record time in the VL3 and took my tally of world championship gold medals to eight. I was at the top of my game. And again my competitors, including Markus, were off the pace.

Away from the water, 2018 was my busiest year yet. I was being booked for public-speaking engagements every other week, and I also landed a part-time job guest-presenting on lifestyle programs at Channel 7. It was an opportunity that popped up and I decided to give it a go. While a TV gig might be a dream job for some, I felt awkward and unnatural. It wasn't really my cup of tea.

I also did a lot of work in my role as an Invictus Games ambassador both in the lead-up to and during the Sydney event, which began in October. I racked up a fair few frequent flyer points travelling to and from Sydney. While I didn't compete in the games, as competitors must retire after three events to give others a shot, my schedule was jam-packed. Aside from fronting the press and speaking at functions in my role as an ambassador, I worked as a commentator for the ABC. It was a whirlwind of non-stop work, a great experience and a taste of what might be down the track when I hang up the paddle. The games themselves were a huge success. Sydney really supported them, and the entire nation was exposed to what is an important, worthy and powerful cause.

A lot of the success I was enjoying off the water was thanks to a remarkable man named John Dunlop, who came into my life in 2017. I met John at a Legacy charity function and he immediately took an interest in my sport, my story and my career. He offered to look over my business documents and eventually became my manager. I'd split with my previous manager earlier that year and John was a godsend. The executive director of sponsor strategy firm FrontRow Group, he came through almost immediately by getting me my first official sponsorship, with business insurance group Aon Australia. John would become a mate as much as a manager, as would his wife, TV journalist and presenter Melissa Doyle, who needs little more by way of introduction.

***

My time in the army officially ended in 2018. My twelve-year career as a soldier was over when I was given a medical discharge. It wasn't a big deal given that I'd not really been a soldier since the incident. While I officially remained part of the army and had been drawing a wage, I had first been given time off to recover, then had been given elite athlete status, which had allowed me to serve through my sport. Since 2012, I'd made only sporadic visits to the base and dealt with my superiors only on occasion, such as when I was asked to speak at the Australian War Memorial on Anzac Day. Getting my medical discharge was a bit of a process. In addition to the paperwork, I had to attend a series of 'transition' seminars. I also had to have all my injuries recorded, confirmed and verified. I have nothing but good things to say about the Australian Army. It supported me both during and after my recovery, and was always there for me in every way.

My discharge was inevitable given my injuries, but no one ever pressured me into applying for it. They allowed me to take my time, to get my life in order and put my post-military career in place first. I wouldn't have been able to pursue my Paralympic dream without their support and understanding.

Rachel and I were planning to get married the following year. I tried to keep that ball in her court, as wedding planning is not my sport. Originally, we were going to get married in Queenstown, but it would be a logistical nightmare going back and forth to pick things like flowers, food and napkins, things I wasn't really interested in. We then considered Tasmania, but eventually settled on the NSW North Coast. We found a picturesque homestead on an old sugar plantation in Kingscliff, just south of the Queensland border. Close enough to the Gold Coast for all the planning trips, it was perfect. We locked in both the venue and the date, and got to the flowers, food and napkins ...

25

HONEYMOON OVER, PARALYMPICS POSTPONED

MY HANDS BEGAN SHAKING just a few words in.

'It's strange. I do a fair bit of speaking, but for this I'm a bit nervous, because this is the first groom's speech I've ever made.'

My throat began to swell. 'Since 2010, it's been a remarkable time with Rachel, and you all here today have had some part in making our love grow and our happy life together. It's an honour to have you all here and share this day with Rachel and me.'

I looked around the room – all friends and family, no strangers. They'd travelled from far and wide to be in northern NSW for my wedding. Turning towards the front, I acknowledged my parents with a nervous smile before struggling to get out the words.

'I'm so very proud to be your son. You've shown me how to love and be loved.'

Tears welled in my eyes but I didn't wipe them away. I didn't want Mum and Dad to know I was struggling.

I took a deep breath before turning to my right. Towards Mike and Tyson. Towards Gibbo and my Olympic kayaking mate Loccy Tame. My groomsmen.

'These boys have had my back for a very long time, giving me sound advice, whether it be the selection of Sonny Bill Williams to the Rugby World Cup All Blacks squad or some home modifications, or on a deployment in a faraway land. Your wisdom and counsel are always welcomed. An example of that counsel was when Gibbo advised me to write some letters to my loved ones in the event that I didn't come home from Afghanistan. It's difficult to write these letters, but as you write them it makes you think about who and what's important in your life.'

I turned to Rachel, my bride, and I could no longer hold back the tears. 'Rachel, you look absolutely beautiful, today and every day. You've done an amazing job creating a day that I'll remember forever.'

I attempted to compose myself. I was a professional public speaker, but right now I was a blubbering mess. I'd nailed the speech in front of the mirror, practising it at least fifteen times. But now the tears were flowing and my words were choked.

'They say distance makes the heart grow fonder. When you add in a war zone, an IED blast and a medical degree, not to mention the hours that come with being a doctor or an athlete, well, it's true that the love we have has only become stronger.'

This was harder than delivering the Anzac Day speech. On that day, there were 40,000 people on the steps of the War Memorial, but they were just faces in a crowd, strangers. Now, here I was, for the first time, addressing the most important people in my life, all together in one room.

'To finish off, I'll quote my old mate William Shakespeare. "My heart is ever at your service." I Love You Rachel.'

This was my proudest day. Forget the medals, forget the accolades, marrying Rach was my greatest achievement.

***

I married my sweetheart on 8 June 2019, and aside from the rain, which we were forced to brave during the ceremony, it was perfect. I had skipped a competition in Europe before the wedding to ensure everything went to plan. I actually had to apply to the Paddle Australia board for permission, and some didn't understand that my wedding was more important to me than a European competition that didn't count towards Paralympic selection. But after some initial resistance, I got the go-ahead to stay in Australia, and I trained on my own, right up until the moment my guests started to arrive.

I still had to squeeze in a bucks' party, however. We had it at the Star Gold Coast casino complex. The boys were shouting all the rounds, a steady stream of schooners delivered to my hand. I didn't need to leave my chair.

But sometimes I like to do the shouting myself, even at my own bucks'. I guess that's because people are always buying me drinks.

'Na, mate ... I've got 'em,' they always say. 'Sit back. Relax.' It's unintentional and, to be honest, unwanted sympathy. A kindness offered because of my condition.

'No, it's my shout,' I say. 'I'm good. *I've* got 'em.'

By the time it got to my shout on the night of my bucks', I was already tipsy. But I successfully navigated my way through a heaving mass to get to the bar and buy a round. I started back with the first two schooners, which was all I could hold. Even now, halfway drunk, I was walking just fine. I don't find it any more difficult to walk when I'm affected by alcohol. In fact, I reckon able-bodied people are affected more because they don't have to think about what they're doing when they walk. I'm so in tune with my artificial legs because I have to be. Walking is always a conscious process for me – even after six beers.

So I took note of the drunk girl ahead. Swaying and slurring, she was a human hazard. I adjusted my path and went around her. I was approaching the tabled section and was clear of her after a few steps. Well ... I thought I was.

Whack! She tripped on my foot and I went over.

The first of the two schooner glasses hit the table as I went down. The other landed in a man's lap. A very big man's lap.

The very big and heavily tattooed man was now soaked.

I pulled myself up. 'Umm ...' I started. But when I saw the anger in his eyes I was speechless. He was red with rage and with fists clenched he jumped out of his seat.

I braced myself for the punch.

And then he saw my legs. 'Oh,' he said, sheepishly.

'Sorry, mate,' I interjected.

'Na, na. All good. You need a hand?' Then he offered to buy me a drink.

I'm sure he would have belted me had he not seen my legs. That's why I always wear shorts. While some might want to hide a disability like mine, I always make sure my artificial legs are on show. I only wear long pants when I have to – for a black-tie event, for example. It's not so much to avoid confrontation but more to stop people asking me why I walk funny. I'm not ashamed that I have no legs. It is what it is, and I am what I am.

It backfires occasionally, mostly when I'm around kids. Recently a little girl walked straight up to me and pointed. 'Why do you have robot legs?' she asked.

As for falls, well I go down when I'm sober too. I take a tumble at least once a month. While the legs and the high-tech knee are great, even with the anti-stumble feature, falling is inevitable. Just a part of the deal. And while I wouldn't say I have mastered the art of falling over, I have learned to do a bit of a roll that stops me from breaking bones.

The bucks' night continued. And so did the drinking, but I didn't go back to the bar. I ended up pretty pissed. I would say I ended up legless if I hadn't started that way!

***

Rachel and I honeymooned in Tasmania. Two weeks, just the two of us. Well, aside from all the devil-worshippers.

'You here for Dark Mofo?' an airport staffer asked us when we landed in Hobart.

'What the? Dark Mofo? What's that?'

'It's an arts festival,' he explained. 'A satanic arts festival. Black art they call it.'

Rachel went white.

'Oh, nothing to worry about,' he continued. 'It's all a bit of a laugh. Just a big party with lots of good food.'

Wary of anyone wearing black, we checked in to our five-star hotel before spending the next two weeks eating and drinking our way through Tasmania. Champagne, shucked oysters and salmon. I indulged. Overindulged.

I didn't realise how much I'd consumed until I got back into the water to begin preparing for the world titles, which were just six weeks away. I quickly came to the stark realisation that I was in the worst shape I'd been in since I started in the sport. Overweight and unfit, I struggled through the sessions.

I decided I needed help and went to see an exercise physiologist. She told me the fastest way to get back to my competition weight was to train in a heat tent. So that's what I did.

The heat tent was a temperature-controlled altitude chamber containing exercise equipment, including a rowing machine suitable for my use. With the heat dialled up to almost 40 degrees and the humidity at 80 per cent, I did a series of hour-long sessions on the rowing machine. It was utter torture. During my first session, I almost passed out after forty minutes, but when I discovered I'd lost half a kilo, I went back.

By the time I arrived in Szeged, Hungary, for the world titles, I was back in shape. I was about to attempt to qualify for the 2020 Paralympic Games, but despite having dropped the weight, I was nervous. Taking four weeks off for my wedding had me fretting, and I wasn't as fit or as strong as I could have been or should have been.

So I was anxious when I discovered that both Markus 'the shark' Swoboda and Fernando Rufino de Paulo, the Iron Cowboy, were in my heat.

I was concerned about losing my first kayak race since 2015. Thankfully, that wasn't the case. I won and won quite well. I got off to a good start, which was a surprise given my lack of conditioning, and I came home strong. I felt a lot better, especially after seeing that my time was not too far away from my best.

But the nerves resurfaced when a new contender emerged in the other heat. Federico Mancarella from Italy had always been a fast starter, But in this race, he got off to the fastest start I'd ever seen and went on to blitz the field. He almost beat the time I'd set, and would have if he hadn't cruised his way towards and over the line.

I didn't know if I could beat Mancarella. I went into the final telling myself not to worry. That all I had to do was finish in the top six to qualify for the Paralympics.

Fighting self-doubt for the first time, I didn't start as strongly as I should have. But while I didn't have a great start, by the time I reached the 100-metre mark I was only about a boat length behind the Italian, who had blasted his way out of the blocks. I had no idea where Markus or Fernando were, and focused only on the boat in front. My self-doubt had disappeared. Coming into the strongest part of my race and seeing the Italian fading, I decided I could win. And I did. But it was close. I beat Federico by just 0.45 of a second. I actually thought he had beaten me until I saw the result. It was only a final push that saved me from defeat.

I also won gold in the canoe, but I was not at my best. Some of my competitors had upped their game and I had to fight. Thankfully I'd done enough work to win my events and qualify for my second Paralympic Games.

I was relieved but still dirty on myself for not being at my best, and vowed never to enter another competition underprepared.

***

I headed over to Japan almost as soon as I got back. Unpacking and repacking in quick succession, I flew out with the team for the Olympic and Paralympic test event. With the Tokyo games now just eighteen months away, we'd been invited to check out the city and try out the event facilities.

We did some sightseeing and attended a sumo wrestling tournament, then headed out to the course. I wasn't surprised to see everything was well on track. While the South Americans were known for being a little disorganised, the Japanese had a reputation for being both efficient and diligent. In fact, the venue wasn't just on track but complete. All done, eighteen months before the games were due to start.

The only thing that was a surprise was the direction of the wind. While we'd all expected the location of the course and the typical weather patterns would be conducive to tail winds, we were confronted by a head wind. But it was good to be surprised now rather than on the day of the event.

The lake was also full of fish. Big fish. We voiced our concerns about the prospect of being hit in the face by a salmon and were assured the fish would be removed before the games.

Most of those racing had been my competition at the World Championships. But this race didn't mean anything.

There was nothing on the line; it was just a chance to paddle the course. That didn't make it any better when I lost. Yep. I was defeated for the first time since 2015. The man who beat me wasn't Markus, or the fast-starting Mancarella. No. Instead it was Fernando Rufino de Paulo, the Iron Cowboy. Back in the sport and looking bigger and stronger than ever, the Brazilian weightlifter pipped me at the line. I think it had a lot to do with the headwind, with his size and power helping him in difficult conditions. But still, I had lost. I was unimpressed and I now had work to do.

I don't like losing. So I entered 2020 determined to train harder than ever before. I had no excuses now. This was a Paralympic year. My year. Nothing was going to stop me. Famous last words ...

***

It was February 2020 and I was standing on a stage in front of a crowd of 400 or so, there for the Gold Coast Sports Stars Awards. I was there to accept the award for Para Sports Star of the Year.

The host fired off a couple of questions. 'How do you feel? What's ahead? And then he asked me about the virus. 'What do you make of this COVID thing?'

'I don't think it's anything to be worried about,' I said.

I continued, dismissing it as another SARS. It would be confined and dealt with, and life and sport would go on, full steam ahead.

The first case of COVID-19 had been identified in Australia the month before, but I wasn't concerned. My life hadn't changed and I didn't expect it to. I'd train, travel and compete. And come August I'd be in Tokyo, competing for Paralympic gold.

And I continued on that basis, following the finely tuned training program I'd set. All schedules and benchmarks were designed so my body would be perfectly built for peak performance in August. I trained and I worked, looking forward to what would be my busiest ever year. Aside from the competitions, headlined by the Paralympics of course, I had locked in almost ten months of paid work. I would be flat out with speaking engagements and sponsor commitments. Quotes had been sent out and contracts had been signed. Future income had been pencilled in.

On 17 March, I was sitting in a café in the Sydney CBD after the second competition of the year, the national titles. I had performed well, winning both my events. I was waiting to meet a mate. We'd been developing some motivational workshops in Sydney. I was thumbing my phone, scrolling through the news.

'Tasmania borders shut, other states expected to follow.'

That's when I knew this COVID thing was not just another SARS.

'I think I better get out of here,' I said to my mate when she arrived. 'They reckon Queensland might shut its borders too. Sorry, but I can't risk being stuck here.'

And so I packed my bags, jumped in the car and drove all the way back to Queensland. As predicted, the Queensland border was shut, although not until 26 March. By then most of the country was in lockdown, Western Australia, the Northern Territory and South Australia all closing their borders just a few days after Tasmania.

COVID hit hard and fast. It went from a non-issue to an international crisis in the space of a few weeks. Industries were suddenly shut down and stimulus packages announced. Australian sporting codes suspended competitions. I braced myself. It would only be a matter of time until my sport was suspended too. And I didn't have to wait long. On 25 March I received an email informing me that the Olympics had been postponed.

I didn't agree with the decision – at least not at first. I thought that with strict COVID protocols and procedures, the games could have still gone ahead. The decision they'd made would affect so many lives. While I'd be okay, given I had other streams of income and activities away from my sport, many didn't. Some athletes need the games to be able to continue with their sport. Without sponsors and the games, they'd be forced to look for jobs that probably wouldn't even exist because the virus had also shut down half the working world.

Things changed even more when all the COVID restrictions were announced. Until then I had been training almost as normal. I'd stuck to my program and continued with my plan. But then we were told that we were limited to training in pairs. That's when I ripped up my most important ever training program. The one that was going to win me another Paralympic gold – or two. It was useless now that gyms were closed, the door to the high-performance training centre locked shut. Useless now that I could only paddle with a single partner.

Suddenly thrown into uncharted waters, coaches and athletes debated over the phone and by way of Zoom, attempting to come up with a new training plan. But it soon became evident that there was no way we could replicate our training program with all the COVID restrictions, protocols and doubt surrounding events. All I could do was stay fit and strong. So I went out on the water and paddled on my own and bought a home gym.

I pretty soon decided the decision to postpone the Tokyo games was right. I realised that had they gone ahead, it wouldn't have been a level playing field. Some countries were more affected by COVID than others, which would mean there'd be a discrepancy in preparations. Athletes in countries that hadn't been affected by the virus could train as usual, while athletes in heavily affected countries might not be able to train at all. I thought about the man who was shaping up as my main rival: Federico Mancarella. In that first wave, Italy had been devastated by the virus. There was no way he wouldn't have been affected, and I didn't want to race him if he'd been denied the opportunity to be at his best. It wouldn't have been fair. And fairness is the foundation of the games.

Knowing the games had been delayed by a year made it a challenge to train, even when the restrictions were eased. We'd always trained in cycles, based on what was ahead. So neither the coaches nor the athletes were sure how to go about it under these new and strange circumstances.

A lot of the information we received came via the Olympics. We just had to assume it would relate to us. We didn't have any specific protocols or plan for the Paralympics.

I decided to take a break in August 2020. With nothing confirmed until the following year, there was no need to be in competition shape. I also needed a breather. So I put my kayak on the rack and limited my training to the home gym.

And that's where I suffered the injury that threatened to set me back.

I was doing my daily circuit when I was struck down by elbow pain. It wasn't excruciating, certainly not a getting-your-legs-blown-off pain, but it was a concern, nonetheless, considering I needed that elbow to paddle.

I learned that I had a thing called 'golfer's elbow'. The scans showed I had some minor ligament damage. While it was not the end of the world, more of an annoyance, I struggled to get on top of it. It ended up being a frustrating injury I couldn't shake.

In October, we were given dates for all the competitions that would precede the Paralympics. And there were plenty of dates, with all the cancelled competitions rescheduled and jam-packed into a revised eight-month calendar.

It was going to be a tough eight months, especially when we learned we'd be unable to attend any of the international competitions because of travel restrictions placed on Australians.

We devised a training plan and I got back into a more normalised routine. But I was anxious heading into my first post-COVID competition, which was a state championship in Queensland, held in February 2021. Aside from my general fitness and preparation, I worried about whether my elbow would hold up, and whether it would affect my performance. It was a bit of an unknown, because we don't really do race simulation or sprints at training until very late in the season before a World Champ meet.

While the elbow did affect me during long, slow sessions, I suspected it would not be an issue in a sprint. And thankfully it wasn't. I won both my races and also set fast times. I felt so much better after that event, both my anxiety gone and my training validated. I was very much looking forward to competing in the nationals, which were scheduled for Sydney in March 2021.

Enter COVID. Again.

While not a nation-stopping crisis like the year before, my sport was again affected when an outbreak in Melbourne sent the city into lockdown. With the Melbourne-based athletes unable to compete, the nationals were turned into an Olympic and Paralympic COVID protocol rehearsal. While we still raced, the competition was more about getting used to the unique restrictions and procedures we would face in Japan.

Meanwhile, Rachel, now a doctor working in intensive care, would be on the front line if there was a COVID outbreak in south-east Queensland. She was pretty busy with work, but I had a new little mate to keep me company when she wasn't around, a field retriever puppy named Theo. He was a godsend during the long months leading up to the Tokyo Paralympics, and reminded me every day to take a little time to smell the roses (or, in his case, the lamp posts). I needed that little bit of time out each day, because preparing for the Paralympics under COVID was already presenting challenges.

26

FINISHING WITH A FAIRY TALE

'NOT AGAIN,' I SAID TO RACHEL. I was scrolling through the news on my phone. It wasn't good. In fact, the news from India was dire. The country was being ravaged by a new strain of COVID-19. More than 400,000 cases had been reported in a week and thousands were dying every day.

It was May 2021, with just four months to go until the start of the Paralympic Games in Tokyo – the games that had already been rescheduled once, thanks to the coronavirus pandemic.

I hadn't considered that the event I'd now been preparing for and basing my entire life around for almost five years would be delayed again. But now there was a new variant of the virus called Delta, which was at least 50 per cent more contagious than the version of the virus that had caused the previous postponement.

It was heartbreaking to hear of so many sick and dying, all those families losing loved ones, and health workers risking their lives to save others. But I have to confess that, at the same time, the thought that the games I'd been working towards for five years might again be postponed was gut-wrenching.

But no. The games wouldn't be postponed. Not now that the world wore face masks and everyone used hand sanitiser. Not in a world of social distancing, contact tracing, isolation and vaccines. So I stuck with the plan.

Two months later, Delta had been detected in almost 100 countries, including Japan. On 8 July, Japan recorded more than 800,000 cases. With just 15 per cent of the Japanese population vaccinated, the government declared a national state of emergency.

'Not again,' I said to Rachel. It looked like the games would surely be postponed. But in conjunction with the International Olympic Committee, Japan banned spectators for both the Olympics and the Paralympics and issued refunds. The games would go on.

Fast forward a couple of weeks and the Olympic Games were set to begin. As I had before Rio, I'd been training with some of the women's Olympic paddle team, this time Alyce Wood and Alyssa Bull. Saying goodbye to them, with hugs and best wishes, and knowing the Olympics was about to open, should have been reassuring. It wasn't.

The Australian Olympic paddle team were part of an international group of almost 92,000 people – athletes, coaches, support staff and media – who were on their way to Japan. They would all be living together in the Olympic Village, using the same lifts and eating in the same dining hall. The odds that at least one of them would bring the virus with them were high. The odds that someone would contract the virus while there were higher. And forget odds – bets on whether or not the Paralympics would go ahead after an Olympic outbreak were off. If there was an outbreak, the Paralympics would be shut down. Guaranteed.

I decided I had to stop worrying. I had to presume the games would go ahead. I couldn't let the prospect of another postponement derail my training. Not now. Not after almost five years of giving it my all. I decided to erase words like coronavirus and Delta from my vocabulary, but I couldn't. Not when the new strain hit Australia and NSW went into lockdown, forcing Rachel to move out of our home.

She was working in the Intensive Care Unit at Tweed Hospital, which is located on the NSW side of the Queensland–NSW border. She was concerned she'd contract the virus and pass it on to me. She was also concerned that I might be forced into quarantine on suspicion of having contact with someone who'd been working in a COVID-affected state. So after we both decided I couldn't afford to be exposed to even a slight risk, Rachel moved out to live with a friend. I would spend my last couple of weeks in Australia alone, with just my best mate, Theo the retriever, for company.

I found the water was the best place to be during this time. As soon as I grabbed my paddle, I forgot about everything that was happening in the world and everything that *could* happen. Luckily, my training wasn't affected at all. I'd been able to stick to my program and had switched from the longer-style endurance work to the shorter-style sprint training.

But watching the Olympics from my lounge was a little bit nerve-racking. I would wait for the broadcasters to interrupt an event with the breaking news that an athlete had tested positive for Delta. I was almost certain it would happen. And it did.

'Not again,' I said, to myself this time, when news broke that an athlete had tested positive to the virus during the final week of the games.

I waited for the outbreak. Waited for the Paralympic Games to be cancelled. But neither happened, thank goodness. By the time the Australian team had arrived home on 3 August, more than 200 people connected to the games had tested positive to the virus, twenty-three of them athletes. It sounds like a big number and would have been scary for every one of them, but given almost 92,000 people had flown into Tokyo for the games, as well as the thousands of Japanese workers and volunteers, it was an impressive effort.

Still, we were all relieved when told the Paralympics, five years in the making, would go ahead. It would begin on 24 August, two weeks after the close of the Olympics, as scheduled.

Training wise, I was spending a lot of time working on my starts. The 10-kilometre efforts were all in the bank, and I had tapered down to doing simulated race starts and 250-metre sprints. Now the outrigger or Va'a canoe had been included as a Paralympic event, I was preparing for that event in addition to the kayak. I was really excited about being able to compete in the boat I started in, but I also had to do a lot of work to get ready for the race. While I had continued competing in world championships after the shock decision to remove the canoe from the Paralympic program six years earlier, I hadn't been able to compete in any of the international events since the first outbreak of COVID, and I was a little concerned that I'd be off the pace. All the athletes in Europe had continued to compete, and the British canoe team in particular had emerged as a serious force. A guy called Stuart Wood was blitzing it, and he had me doubting myself.

I spent a lot of time in the canoe trying to perfect my stroke. Without a rudder, the canoe is steered by way of a single paddle. While it's faster to keep that paddle on one side – your most powerful side, which in my case is to the left of my boat – you need to periodically change sides to correct the direction of the boat. The changes have to be performed both quickly and powerfully. The paddle is literally heaved from the water and flung across the top of the boat to the other side before being plunged back into the water, all in about half a second. It's a manoeuvre that requires a good grip, precision and a heap of practice. The key to recording a good time is limiting those changes.

All was going well. And then I threw my paddle. I was executing a change when the paddle slipped from my grasp and went hurtling through the air.

It had been five years since I'd thrown a paddle. It's easy to do and I'd done it a lot when I started. As I paddled over with my hands to retrieve it, I shook it off as a freak occurrence. It was nothing to worry about. I hadn't done it for five years and wouldn't do it again for another five years.

'Shit,' I screamed two weeks later when I threw the paddle again. This time Channel Nine cameras happened to be filming.

That's when I began to panic. I could no longer say it had been a one-off, and I began to worry that there was a problem with my technique. But the games were about to start, so there was little I could do except worry. I imagined myself doing it in the race. Sitting helpless at the halfway mark in the final as my paddle hurtled across the lanes. It was a horrifying prospect.

I did my best to exorcise those thoughts and put it down to a lack of concentration. I vowed to be fully focused on every movement I would make. I had to be completely precise and thorough in every detail of my performance. Every movement had to be completely correct, even if it came at the expense of speed and time. I figured it was better to go a little slower and finish the race rather than blast my way to a place called shit creek and be up there without a paddle.

***

It was weird to watch the Paralympics opening ceremony from my lounge room in Queensland. I felt like an outsider and wanted to be there. But with COVID still a major concern, the Australian paddle team had made the decision to delay our arrival as long as possible. I didn't necessarily agree with the decision and would have liked to have had the opportunity to train in race conditions, but I understood why it was made.

Saying goodbye to Rachel was even stranger. Wearing facemasks, we met in a park to say our farewells. I couldn't even hug her, let alone give her a kiss, due to the COVID risk.

'You've got this,' she said, farewelling me with a wave instead of a kiss. 'You've given it your all for five years for this moment. For *your* moment. Now go get 'em.'

The games had been going for almost a week by the time we arrived in Tokyo. After a horrendous four hours of admin and COVID checks at the airport, we arrived at the Paralympic Village.

I was immediately astounded by the heat. I knew Tokyo was hot at this time of year but I wasn't prepared for the humidity. It was well over 90 per cent and the temperature was in the high thirties. By the time I got through another round of COVID checks and was taken to my room, I was soaked with sweat.

I was sharing with Dylan Littlehales, another Australian paddler. Our room was located in a fifteen-storey building that had been covered in green and gold. Apart from a few athletes from a handful of smaller nations, the entire building was occupied by the 179 Aussies who had come to compete.

Later that day, we went out to the course, called Sea Forrest Waterway, for a bit of a float. Boats checked and gear good, I had a light paddle to familiarise myself with both the course and the conditions. As I mentioned it was hot. There was also some wind, as the course was located in the middle of the harbour and was exposed to the elements. When it came to the condition of the course, I would have to be prepared for anything.

I was feeling very comfortable at the end of the day. I went to bed – which was rock hard and the worst thing in an otherwise immaculate village. I felt my starts were good, my conditioning was great and my mind was clear. I was ready to roll.

***

When I arrived at the course for day one of competition, I was greeted by mist and drizzle. I was ready for a big day of racing, beginning with my KL2 heat and finishing with my return to the canoe in VL3.

I geared up for the KL2, choosing the orange-lens sunglasses due to the lack of light. Then I checked my boat, giving it a thorough once-over: screws, bindings, body and rudder. With everything tight, intact and in place, the kayak was good to go. So was I.

After checking in, I boarded my craft and paddled to the warm-up area. It was shaping up as an easy heat, with Fernando Rufino de Paulo, aka the Cowboy, who I now considered my biggest rival, Federico Mancarella, the fast-starting Italian, and Markus Swoboda all in the other heat. I was, however, up against Mykola Syniuk, an up-and-coming Ukrainian paddler.

I was full of confidence and determined to make an early mark. I thought I could take a big step towards winning gold if I could undermine the confidence of my competition by setting the fastest time.

My water warm-up went well. I felt fresh as I practised my starts. Had no nerves as I perfected my stroke. I paddled over to a rubbish station to throw out my water bottle. Plastic gone and ready to race, I then performed a snappy, fast, left-hand turn and started towards the line.

Ready. Set. Go!

And with that my Tokyo Paralympics campaign was underway.

I got off to a great start. I felt strong. Felt like the race was already mine. I ignored the fact that my boat seemed to jump out a little off-centre, putting it down to my stroke or the way the boat was positioned. I was all head down and doing the work.

I was closing in on the lead when it all went to hell. Noticing my boat was veering to the right, I lifted my hip and redistributed my weight in a bid to correct my path. If I had legs, I would have been able to use the rudder. My body adjustment didn't help, so I tried a double stroke on the left, but that didn't do enough to correct the boat either. It was then I realised that if I kept on paddling, I'd be in the next lane. That would mean an automatic disqualification from the entire event, so I stopped paddling and drifted my way across the line to finish third. The race was won by Mykola Syniuk, who went straight through to the final.

Even before I checked to confirm, I knew I'd had a problem with the rudder. As I mentioned previously, I fix my rudder, and I suspected it had been knocked off-centre. I thought back to the sharp turn I made after throwing out my water bottle and realised the force of the snappy move could have been enough to nudge the rudder out of place.

Luckily, it wasn't the end of the world. Everyone qualifies for the semi-final bar those who win the heat and those who are disqualified. I would get a second chance.

***

With just seventy minutes to go before my VL3 heat, I had to quickly shake off a feeling of frustration. I did that by checking my canoe and only thinking about what was to come rather than what had gone. But I felt a lot of uncertainty about my next race. For one thing, it was hard to tell who my rivals would be in the VL3, because I hadn't competed against many of them. My last event had been in 2019 at the world championships. On top of that, I was still concerned about my lack of competition. I'd been so focused on my kayaking, I thought I might struggle in the outrigger canoe. I was also a little intimidated by the form of the British guys, Stuart Wood in particular. He looked every inch a champion and had been equalling my best times.

While I was confident of my chances in the kayak, there was too much uncertainty for me in the canoe to have any confidence that I'd win a medal, let alone a gold.

When I took to the water, I was seriously nervous, so much so that my hands began to tingle. But I got off to a good start. Stroking hard on my power side, I was ploughing through the water. I was pleasantly surprised to find the wind was helping me stay straight. A cross-breeze coming from left to right meant I didn't have to change the side I was paddling on to keep the canoe in my lane.

Fifty metres from the finish line the boat started to veer. I needed to change my paddling to the other side, but with the line beckoning, I didn't want to. You don't want to be changing sides late as you want to be speeding up at the end and not slowing down. Given the strength of my competition, I wasn't game to correct my boat, so I did my best to straighten it by using my body weight and blade stroke. I was barely inside my lane as I crossed the line, and after I crossed I was out of my lane and hitting a marker. But lane marker crash and all, when I lifted my head I smiled, because I'd won. I was straight through to the final.

The following day, Friday, 3 September, I blitzed my way through the KL2 semi-final with a fully functioning rudder. Facing off against the Cowboy, with the rest of my rivals in the other semi-final, I made a real statement by destroying him. I was no longer concerned about Rufino de Paulo. I wasn't too concerned about the others either, with my time way faster than the one Federico Mancarella had set to win the other semi.

With the final only an hour away, I made sure my rudder was fully locked and tight. Then I hit the water to defend my Paralympic crown. As I made my way to the line, I was the most confident I'd ever been before a race. I'd considered the Cowboy to be my main rival but had just defeated him in the semi-final. As I put the nose of my boat in the bucket, I was in what athletes call 'the zone' – a magical place when you are at the top of your game and have luck on your side. I was bullet-proof.

I looked to my left and saw Markus in the neighbouring lane.

'Good luck, mate,' I said in a gesture of respect.

And then we were away.

I got a good start and knew I was on track by the time I got to the 100-metre mark. I wasn't sure where I was placed but I knew I'd mow down all comers as I began my all-out charge to the line. I went so hard that I was blowing through my teeth and heaving to breathe by the time I approached the finish. I knew I had won as soon as I crossed. Gold.

I had defended my crown and beat Mykola Syniuk by half a boat length. The fast-starting Mancarella finished third, while Markus and the Cowboy both failed to place.

I can't say I really celebrated the win. I couldn't. Not with a race to go, the race I'd been waiting five years for. I collected my gold medal, did my interviews and went home to bed.

***

Saturday, 4 September, was the last race day for canoeing and the day of my VL3 final. My nerves were back. I spent almost an hour alone in the warm-up room, going through my race plan, over and over, playing it out in my head. But after watching the semi-final earlier in the day, I was a lot more confident. Stuart Wood, the British paddler, had won that race, but he looked fatigued at the end. Maybe that's why I was nervous – I knew it was a race I could win. I hadn't given myself a chance before the heat, but now I'd feel I had failed if I did anything other than win.

I did my land warm-up, checked in and took to the water. I practised both my starts and changes. It was then I realised just how much I wanted to win this race. Paddling around, staying warm while I waited to be called to the gate, I began thinking about my journey to get there. About all the effort I'd put in with the outrigger during the lead-up to Rio, only to have it taken away by an administrator's decision. I now had an opportunity to win a gold medal in the boat that had started my dream.

My hands began to tingle as I made my way into my lane. Everything was tingling by the time I got to the gate. Yep. I was still nervous, the tingles a bullet-proof sign.

Ready. Set. Go!

I punched my way out of the gate. A good start. I dug in, stroke after stroke, each pull of the paddle generating more speed. Head down and pulling hard, I had no idea where I was placed but I didn't care. I was executing my race plan to perfection, my first two changes made with precision, so it didn't matter. No one would beat me if I continued to get it right.

When I neared the 100-metre mark, I set myself up for what I hoped would be the final change. I let my boat drift a little, finding the angle I wanted before ripping the paddle across my body. I dug into the water once, twice and then returned the paddle back to my power side. I was completely straight and staring down the dead centre of my lane. That's when I knew I couldn't be stopped. That I was on the verge of claiming back-to-back gold.

I didn't know until I watched the replay, but I won by a huge margin. With every stroke in the run to the line I was extending my lead by more than 30 centimetres. It was the perfect race. I couldn't have performed any better.

I've never been one to celebrate. When I won my first gold medal at Tokyo, I was simply relieved. It had been a case of doing what was expected. But with this one, I was ecstatic. I felt electric. I grabbed a handful of water and threw it into the air.

'Fuck, yeah!' I screamed.

***

It was a strange feeling not to be able to look into the crowd and see my family. To see Rachel. To see no one I knew. The only people in the venue were competitors, officials and the media.

I was ushered away from the water and towards the change rooms and told to change into my team tracksuit for the medal presentation. But even before I took off my wet competition clothes, I reached into my bag and pulled out my mobile phone.

Beep. Beep. Beep. Beep ...

The messages fired in like a machine gun as soon as I turned on the phone. It felt good to know that people had actually watched the race. With no general spectators, there wasn't much atmosphere at the venue, and I'd felt as though I was competing for just myself and the officials.

I only had enough time to read and reply to one message, so I scrolled through until I saw her name. 'I love you,' the message from Rachel said. 'Congratulations. Well done. I am so proud.'

'I love you so much,' I replied. 'I would not have been able to do it without you. This is as much for you as me. I'll call you as soon as I can.'

I was on the podium before I knew it, receiving another gold medal. You're probably expecting to read that I was overcome with emotion and cried tears of joy, but that wasn't the case. Don't get me wrong. I was bloody happy. I felt like I'd just run the perfect race, and the sense of satisfaction and pride I got from that was like never before.

When I got back to my phone, I was completely overwhelmed. There were messages and missed calls from all the most important people in my life. Mum and Dad told me I'd done them proud. My brother and sister had sent heartfelt messages. My mates had sent 'Hell yeahs' and beer emojis.

It was time to celebrate.

When I got back to the village, the party had already started. Competition over, the athletes were on the beers and bourbons. But I had a call to make.

'You were awesome, Curty,' Rachel said. 'Your race was so amazing! You did so well. I'm so proud!' Rachel had been celebrating too.

'Thanks, Rach,' I said. 'I love you and I'm just so pumped I got the double. I wish you were here.'

I teared up at the end of the call. I wanted to be able to share the moment with Rach but I'd have to wait another two weeks to see her. In fact, I wouldn't be able to see *anyone* for two weeks, because as soon as I landed back in Australia, I'd have to quarantine in Sydney. I had one night of freedom left and I intended to make the most of it. So I wiped away the tears and joined the party.

It turned out to be a short-lived celebration. I was two beers in when I almost collapsed. I was completely exhausted. So I farewelled the revellers and took myself to bed.

I sent Rachel another message before I passed out. 'We did it,' I wrote. 'Two from two. Can't wait to get back and start another chapter with you.'

I have no idea what the next chapter will look like, other than it will be written with Rachel by my side. Which is as it should be.

EPILOGUE

YET TO CELEBRATE MY TRIUMPH as I sit alone in a Sydney hotel, now a week into a two-week quarantine, I've had plenty of time to reflect on my journey and my life. And I wouldn't change a thing. Yep, lost legs and all.

It was a question I'd been forced to answer on the eve of the Paralympic Games, nine days after the Taliban reclaimed Afghanistan after a twenty-year war.

'Was losing your legs worth it now you know the war was for nothing?' the reporter asked.

'Let me get back to you,' I replied. I had to carefully consider my response.

'I'll start by saying I'm certainly disappointed with what's happened,' I said when I called the reporter back. 'I'm devastated for the people of Afghanistan. The Taliban are both brutal and inhumane, and my heart breaks for the people subject to their regime. I wish that more could have been done to prevent what's happened, but that doesn't take away from what I and my fellow soldiers did.'

The reporter again asked about my legs. Had my sacrifice been for nought?

'No, my sacrifice was not for nothing. I know that what I did helped. I know that we saved lives. And I know that we helped give them better lives.'

What I didn't tell him was that, in my darkest days, I had wondered if it had been worth it, if I'd lost my legs for nothing. But sitting here now, two gold medals in my bag, the love of my life counting down the days until I get out of quarantine, I can tell you that I wouldn't change a thing.

Regardless of what's happening in Afghanistan now, I'd still take myself off to Defence Recruiting in Brisbane with the idea of becoming an aircraft technician and instead sign up to become something called a combat engineer. I'd still go to places called Kapooka and Kabul. And I would still step on the IED that took my legs.

Had I not, I wouldn't be the person I am today. And I'm proud of who I am and what I've done. I'm proud to be Curtis McGrath: son, husband, former soldier turned Paralympian.

I also know that the IED I stepped on could have been found by a kid. Or maybe gone under the wheels of a school bus.

So yes.

I would do it again. All of it.

ACKNOWLEDGEMENTS

LIKE MY SPORTING ACHIEVEMENTS, this book would not be possible without the support and guidance from a huge team of people.

First and foremost, I thank my wife, Rachel, for always being there for me. Through thick and thin she has stuck by my side in whatever pursuit I set my body and mind to. She has always believed in me and guided me through the challenges of life.

To my parents, Kim and Paul, my siblings, Brent and Sophia, and the rest of my family, thank you for your great love and support and for helping me to bring the memories of my youth and my life to these pages.

Pitch, Livo, Wertsy and Courty are my life savers. From that tragic day on the hill in 2012, I owe you my life and will be eternally grateful for the bravery, sacrifice and support you all gave.

To the many other people who carried me off the battlefield that day and all the way to the welcome-home parade at Enoggera Barracks after months of blood, sweat and steel, you have all contributed to my success and the story within this book.

Thanks to the great friends I've made along the way, who joined me on some epic adventures. Gibbo, Tyson, Mike, Ryan, Loccy, the list is too big to go on, but you know who you are and you have all been a part of my life and this story. To all my mates, who may not be mentioned in this book by name, you have touched my life in some way, and I truly am grateful for having you join me on this journey we call life.

I wouldn't have been able to write even one letter of this book without the help and work of my manager and friend John Dunlop. He's always been there for advice, guidance and wine recommendations, all of which have been instrumental in getting my story onto these pages.

The real star of this book is James Phelps, who had the skill and ability to turn my life into a story that you can read and understand.

Someone who continues to literally keep me on my feet and another good friend is Jens Baufeldt. A man who really does care for everyone he meets, he always goes out of his way to makes sure I have the prosthetics I need to be able to do what I do.

I must acknowledge two men that went from my superior officers to good friends. I thank Matt Galton and Isaac Khan for their unwavering support over the years. You both went above and beyond your duty to make sure my family and I were cared for, even when it came at a cost to your time with your own families – thank you.

Paddling became my life and again there are too many people who have contributed to my success and this story, but I would like to mention a few who sparked my love for this sport. My Wakatipu High School Outdoor Recreation teacher Ken McIntyre and my first coach Andrea Wood: you both saw potential in me and planted the seed, then nurtured it to get me to the start line at the 2016 Rio Paralympic Games. What happened after that is a story that's been told countless times, but this book hopefully captures it in its entirety.

The Tokyo campaign had its fair share of challenges and there again hundreds of people and organisations helped me during that time. Jesse Fleming, Shaun Caven, Kate O'Connell, Paddle Australia and Paralympics Australia to name a few, you all have had an enormous part to play, and I'll always be grateful for the sacrifices you made to get me there and help me fill these pages.

I'm very grateful to everyone who has had a part to play in my story, supported and cheered me on. The veteran community has always been a big part of that support base and making me feel what I am doing is valued and inspiring to the many who may suffer from the effects of their service. It's through their sacrifice we can live in a free and prosperous nation.

On that note, the Australian Army and Defence Force supported me right the way through my career and injury and have got me to point where I am able to journey out into the world on my own. The skills and experiences you gave me help me navigate life and see things from a perspective of hope and opportunity.

Elite athletes are constantly looking for support from the corporate world, to enable us to pursue our dreams. I would like to thank my amazing corporate sponsors, AON and Citibank Australia; and my apparel sponsors, Nelo Kayaks, Jantex Paddles and Oakley. You've made a world of difference and I'm truly humbled by the generosity and support you've given me during my sporting years. I felt more than just an ambassador: I've felt like family.

And lastly, ABC Books/HarperCollins Publishers Australia. Thank you for allowing me to have a platform to share my full story with the world. It has been a pleasure and you've made the process reflective, enjoyable and memorable.

I hope that you, reading my story, can take something from my experiences and story and apply it to your life and experience, in a world that's full of opportunity, adventure and memories.

Thank you for reading.

Curtis McGrath

SPORTING ACHIEVEMENTS AND RECOGNITION

Classifications

VL2: Va'a outrigger canoe, level 2 – prior to restructure of the classification system

VL3: Va'a outrigger canoe, level 3 – using torso and arms to drive the paddle

KL2: Kayak, level 2 – using torso and arms paddle and balance

Paralympics

YEAR	LOCATION	EVENT	RESULT
2016	Rio de Janiero, Brazil	KL2 200m	Gold
2020 (2021)	Tokyo, Japan	KL2 200m VL3 200m	Gold Gold

World Championships

YEAR	LOCATION	EVENT	RESULT
2014	Moscow, Russia	VL2 200m	Gold
2015	Milan, Italy	VL2 200m KL2 200m	Gold Silver
2016	Duisburg, Germany	VL2 200m KL2 200m	Gold Gold
2017	Racice, Czech Republic	VL2 200m KL2 200m	Gold Gold
2018	Montemor-o-Velho, Portugal	KL2 200m VL3 200m	Gold Gold
2019	Szeged, Hungary	KL2 200m VL3 200m	Gold Gold

Invictus Games

YEAR	LOCATION	EVENT	RESULT
2014	London, UK	Swimming Archery	1 Silver 1 Bronze
2016	Orlando, USA	Rowing Indoor rowing Swimming	1 Gold 1 Gold 3 Silver
2017	Toronto, CA	Indoor rowing Wheelchair Rugby	1 Gold 1 Silver

Recognition

2014 Sporting Wheelies and Disabled Association Most Improved Athlete of the Year

2014 Australian Canoeing Paracanoeist of the Year

2014 The Courier-Mail McDonald's Queensland Athlete with a Disability Award

2014 Nominated for Para Performance of the Year – presented by Dairy Australia

2015 Australian Canoeing Paracanoeist of the Year

2016 Flag bearer for the Australian team at the Rio Paralympics Closing Ceremony

2016 Finalist for 'The Don Award', Sport Australia Hall of Fame awards

2016 Australian Canoeing Paracanoeist of the Year

2016 Australian Canoeist of the Year, Olympic/Paralympic Class

2016 Queensland Academy of Sport Peter Lacey Award for Sporting Excellence

2017 Medal of the Order of Australia

2017 Sportsman of the Year at the World Paddle Awards – the first Paracanoeist athlete to win the award

2017 Australian Canoeing Paracanoeist of the Year

2018 Paddle Australia Paracanoeist of the Year

2018 Queensland Sport Athlete with a Disability Award

2019 Paddle Australia Paracanoeist of the Year

2019 Australian Institute of Sport Awards Male Para-athlete of the Year

USEFUL ORGANISATIONS

VETERANS – AUSTRALIA

Mates4Mates

For veterans and their families to find a way forward from service-related injuries
mates4mates.org
Tel. 1300 462 837

Open Arms

Veterans & Families Counselling 24-hour crisis support
www.openarms.gov.au
Tel. 1800 011 046

Department of Veterans' Affairs

Support for those who serve or have served in the defence of our nation, and their families
www.dva.gov.au
Defence All-hours Support: Tel. 1800 628 036
Defence Family Helpline: Tel. 1800 624 608
Free Anonymous Counselling: Tel. 1800 142 072

Beyond Blue

Support. Advice. Action.
www.beyondblue.org.au
Tel. 1300 22 4636

Lifeline Australia

www.lifeline.org.au
24/7 Crisis Support: Tel. 13 11 14
If life is in danger call 000

Returned & Services League (RSL)

www.rslaustralia/veteran-support

VETERANS – AOTEAROA NEW ZEALAND

We Served

Service Directory for NZ Veterans and Service Personnel
www.weserved.nz
Tel. 09 625 8310

NZDF4U

health.nzdf.mil.nz/mind/take-action/0800-faqs
Tel. 0800 693 348

Mental Health Foundation of New Zealand

mentalhealth.org.nz

Lifeline Aotearoa

www.lifeline.org.nz
24/7 Helpline: Tel. 0800 54 33 54 or free text HELP to 4357
Suicide Crisis Helpline: Tel. 0508 828 865

Samaritans Aotearoa New Zealand

www.samaritans.org.nz

Tel: 0800 72 66 66

CANOING AND KAYAKING – AUSTRALIA

Paddle Australia

The peak sporting body for canoeing and kayaking

paddle.org.au

Tel. 02 9763 0670

Email: info@paddle.org.au

CANOING AND KAYAKING – AOTEAROA NEW ZEALAND

Canoe Racing New Zealand

www.canoeracing.org.nz

Tel: 09 476 8670